ADVANCE PRAISE FOR
*UNITED STATES OF DISTRACTION*

"This vibrant and important book shows how propaganda and
lies are flowing through corporate-controlled media, dividing
and ruling. Mickey Huff and Nolan Higdon emphasize what
we can do today to restore the power of facts, truth, and fair,
inclusive journalism as tools for people to keep political and
corporate power subordinate to the engaged citizenry and the
common good. A timely and urgent demand reasserting the
central importance of civic pursuits—not commercialism—in
U.S. media and society."

—**Ralph Nader**

"Higdon and Huff have produced the best short introduction
to the nature of Trump-era journalism and how the 'post-
truth' media world is inimical to a democratic society that I
have seen. The book is provocative and an entertaining read.
Best of all, the analysis in *United States of Distraction* leads
to concrete and do-able recommendations for how we can
rectify this deplorable situation."

—**Robert W. McChesney**, author of *Rich Media, Poor*
*Democracy: Communication Politics in Dubious Times*

"A war of distraction is under way, media is the weapon, and
our minds are the battlefield. Higdon and Huff have written a
brilliant book on how we've gotten to this point, and how to
educate ourselves to fight back and win."

—**Henry A. Giroux**, McMaster University Chair for
Scholarship in the Public Interest and Paolo Freire
Distinguished Scholar in Critical Pedagogy

"The U.S. wouldn't be able to hide its empire in plain sight were it not for the subservient 'free press.' *United States of Distraction* shows, in chilling detail, America's major media dysfunction—how the gutting of the fourth estate paved the road for fascism and what tools are critical to salvage our democracy."

—**Abby Martin**, host of *The Empire Files*

"There are some books that leave us profoundly uncomfortable, unsettled, and even righteously indignant. This is one of them. Nolan Higdon and Mickey Huff provide us with a fearless and dangerous text that refuses the post-truth proliferation of fake news, disinformation, and media that serve the interests of the few. This is a vital wake-up call for how the public can protect itself against manipulation and authoritarianism through education and public interest media."

—**George Yancy**, author of *Backlash: What Happens When We Talk Honestly about Racism in America*

"Here is a book that cuts through the clutter of media nonsense to tell us some powerful truths. How they do it in a way that makes us angry while also inspired, is what makes the book so vibrant, and vital."

—**Robin Andersen**, editor of *The Routledge Companion to Media and Humanitarian Action*

"Through careful analysis of our pervasive pop culture atmosphere and the structures that support it, the authors illustrate with precision our contemporary struggles with truth, accurate information, and critical knowledge. Those who are concerned with the current state of democracy and want insight on how to make change are highly encouraged to read this book. . . . Higdon and Huff believe that the people, armed with accurate information, can make change. With attention to education and critical media literacy, this book will serve as a catalyst for that change and will support those first steps away from the precipice of corporate control."

—**Allison Butler**, Lecturer & Director of Media Literacy Program, Department of Communication, University of Massachusetts, Amherst

"[Mickey Huff and Nolan Higdon] chronicle the culmination of a long history of manufactured consent where American citizens have accepted a 'trickle down' taste of market benefits in exchange for the relentless privatization of news and information. . . . Huff and Higdon open our eyes to an Orwellian landscape where once commercial-free, publicly owned discourses on equality, community, and justice have been substituted by propaganda, and where the responsibility of informed citizenship has been replaced by blind allegiance to a supremely inept leader and his merry band of corrupt plutocrats."

—**Nicholas L. Baham III**, Professor of Ethnic Studies, California State University, East Bay

"*United States of Distraction: Media Manipulation in Post-Truth America* by Mickey Huff and Nolan Higdon challenges our hegemon-media's ideological mind control and the occupation of human thought. Their message is clear: that we are in an era of deliberate propaganda and lies that protect concentrated global capital. Corporate media incite confusion and distraction to ensure ideological domination by the global power elite. Huff and Higdon correctly call for mass critical resistance through truth telling by free minds. Power to the people!"

—**Peter Phillips**, author of *Giants: The Global Power Elite*

"Today, more than ever, news consumers are distracted and misinformed by a media more interested in profit than in real coverage. *United States of Distraction* is a huge wake-up call to anyone concerned that President Trump repeatedly calls coverage he disagrees with 'fake news.' The problem isn't fake news: the problem is that the teaching of both 'critical thinking' and 'media literacy' have been neglected far too long in American schools. Thomas Jefferson said the health of a democracy depends on an informed electorate. If you're not outraged after reading *United States of Distraction*, you're not paying attention."

—**Frank W. Baker**, author, consultant, Media Literacy Clearinghouse

"Historians Mickey Huff and Nolan Higdon bring context to our current Trumpian post-truth moment. They retrace the largely untold history of the roots of neoliberalism and show the devastating effects of a half-century of privatization, deregulation, and the all-out war on the New Deal and Great Society. They not only deconstruct and explain how we got to this moment in history, they prescribe ways we can wrest control from a plutocracy that has co-opted the best elements of American idealism, cynically turning them on their head for the benefit of the few at the expense of the many. This book is a call to action at a moment when not heeding history's warnings, and not dramatically changing course, threaten not only the future of our republic but of global civilization itself."

—**Peter Kuznick**, co-author with Oliver Stone of *The Untold History of the United States*

"*United States of Distraction* is a challenging, inspiring, and indispensable guide to this fateful era of fake news and 'alternative' facts. From the normalization of official lying and disinformation under the Trump administration to the deep historical roots of the corporate ethos that legitimizes restless pursuit of private enrichment at the expense of public goods, Higdon and Huff lucidly analyze the conditions and consequences of our current political crisis. Fortunately, they make equally clear how two fundamental democratic institutions—public education and a truly free press—may still save us, by rejuvenating our civics education, our communities, and our power as citizens."

—**Andy Lee Roth**, co-editor of *Censored 2020: Through the Looking Glass*

"Huff and Higdon's book brilliantly diagnoses the root causes of our current political and cultural malaise—the economic destruction of our free press, the rampant disregard for truth and accuracy in our political discourse, the corporate capture of our education system, and a public culture polluted by hyper-commerical entertainment. But even more importantly, the book explains how critical media literacy and a renewed emphasis on civics education can remedy the problems plaguing our politics and our culture and help us to revitalize and reclaim our democracy. An important and timely read."

—**Steve Macek**, author of *Urban Nightmares: The Media, the Right and the Moral Panic over the City*

# United States of Distraction

Media Manipulation in Post-Truth America
(And What We Can Do About It)

Nolan Higdon and Mickey Huff
Foreword by Ralph Nader

Open Media Series | City Lights Books
San Francisco

Open Media Series Editor: Greg Ruggiero.

Cover design: Victor Mingovits

ISBN: 978-0872867673

Library of Congress Cataloging-in-Publication Data


City Lights Books are published at the City Lights Bookstore
261 Columbus Avenue, San Francisco, CA 94133
www.citylights.com

"Our government is a bird with two right wings. . . .
They're devoted to the perpetuation and spread
of corporate capitalism."

—*Lawrence Ferlinghetti*

*To our students, past and present, with an eye to the future. Thank you for helping us become more compassionate listeners and empathetic counselors, as well as better teachers and sharper critical thinkers. This book is the product of our interactions with fellow students, educators, activists, and journalists, and is drafted in hopes for a better, more informed, civically engaged society.*

# CONTENTS

# FOREWORD
## *By Ralph Nader*

Ever since the few began to control the many, disinformation, fabrications, and distractions have been used to shape consent, impose submission, and maintain domination. Whether by the invoked authority of God, the divine right of kings, the dictatorial embodiment of a fatherland, the "dictatorship of the proletariat," or the tyranny of commercially managed marketplaces, the casualty of such control has always been the ability of ordinary people to give voice to their own realities, needs, demands, and grievances. Given the inherent pragmatism of the human mind, the oppressed have often found it safer to believe rather than think, to obey rather than dissent. Today, such a path is reinforced by a plutocratic political economy that allows corporations to dominate mass media, education, and the production of knowledge and memory.

Human history, however, has not been without its visionaries, seers, and prescient intellectuals, poets, artists, thinkers, and philosopher rebels. Every major religion admonishes its adherents not to allow the merchant class—with its singular focus on aggregating profits at the expense of truth, compassion, and self-restraint—to amass too much power. Such instructions have emanated not from revelation, but from ethics learned via the daily experience of living in community with others committed to the common good.

Unfortunately, it has been the transactional incentives of commerce, not the cooperative bonds of community that dominate the most significant aspects of life in the United States today. The dystopian scenarios portrayed in George Orwell's *1984* and Aldous Huxley's *Brave New World* look like understatements compared to today's plutocratic deployment of communications technologies, many of them developed by taxpayer-funded government programs and grants.

The ultimate success of top-down censorship is self-censorship by the people. The same holds true for mass surveillance. From radio and television, to the internet and smartphones, and all the video platforms and apps in between, commercially controlled media have used seduction and addiction to lure "users" to increasingly stare into screens and "share" personal data and location, thus becoming complicit with authoritarianism and mass surveillance. In the process, the population has become fact-deprived and over-entertained, with lowered expectation levels and reduced attention spans. These technology-driven changes have distracted people from their rights and powers as citizens. As authors Nolan Higdon and Mickey Huff write: "Long before Trump's candidacy, ratings drove programming and news. In the process, celebrity, entertainment, scandal, crime, disaster, and spectacle clearly dominated over the substantive reporting . . . and public interest advocacy capable of questioning and countering abuses of corporate power and government authority." Trump, they note, came right out of this omnipresent "corporate commercialism."

Deadly degradation of media is everywhere. Fueled by Madison Avenue's promotional perfidy, the junk food industry, bypassing parental authority, has lied its way directly into the stomachs of tens of millions of children, creating an obesity epidemic with its attendant diseases. "Alternative facts," anyone?

Forty-five years ago, venerated *CBS News* anchor Walter Cronkite called the three minutes or so devoted to a serious news story merely "a headline service." If anything, the situation has worsened since Cronkite's time. Gone are the "Fairness Doctrine," the "right of reply," and any pretense that the Federal Communications Commission is regulating the broadcasters according to the 1934 Communications Act standard of the "public interest, convenience, and necessity."

The takeover of hundreds of newspapers, local television stations, and radio stations by corporate profiteers is still worsening. These corporations loot vulnerable media operations by cutting out reporters, investigative journalism, whistleblowers, educational content, and local coverage. Magazines are shrinking, going out of business, or just migrating to online-only versions. Social media cannot generate such content in addition to other shortcomings.

Young people today are becoming increasingly *aliterate*. They spend more time staring at screens, but ultimately read less long-form content unless forced to do so for classwork. Fewer people are showing up for town meetings, marches, demonstrations, and rallies, in spite of the ease and immediacy of communication enabled by the internet.

The so-called "Information Age" has become the "Disinformation Era," with the corporate media's exclusion of the civic community being one of its most devastating triumphs. In the 1960s and 1970s, we could not have succeeded in advancing standards for public health and safety, labor, and environmental integrity without the help of mass media reporting on public campaigns and Congressional hearings, or without large audiences tuning in to programs such as the *Phil Donahue Show*, which dedicated airtime to discussing our investigations, reports, and exposés. Now it is not just corporate media, but the Congress itself that is increasingly shutting out citizen groups, accomplished civic leaders, and other valued witnesses whose needs, voices, and demands deserve to be heard and represented. Congress is open for business, but closed to the people—C-SPAN notwithstanding.

Readers of this timely book will note with admiration that its detailed analysis and moral outrage at corporate domination are grounded in irrefutable evidence. The essential question raised by the ongoing "assault on democracy" must still be addressed: How can we *implement* all the constructive proposals for developing information systems that serve the civic values of the people instead of the crass, profit-driven priorities of short-sighted corporations?

Congress can and should acknowledge, address, and implement many of the proposals in this book. There are only 535 elected officials for millions of Americans to instruct. Send them the plans described by Higdon and Huff and demand not just a reply, but that they hold their own town meetings around changing media and education. A petition of 500 citizens, with names, addresses, and occupation clearly marked, can bring a senator or representative to your community. Face to face!

Add to the agenda our proposal to have Congress create a national "audience network"—by returning a few hours of public airwaves to communities, otherwise known as "we the people," for noncommercial programming, on licensed stations every day. Support for developing such a network of radio and TV programming can and should be funded by charging the commercial stations rent for their use of our public airwaves, which, historically, Congress has gifted to commercial corporations free of charge. Congressman Ed Markey held a hearing on the idea of an Audience Network in 1991, but without citizens organized to support the initiative, it went nowhere.

There can be no democracy without democratic media. Look at your *TV Guide* and see how sports, low-grade entertainment, and endless advertising dominate hundreds of outlets. Are there, among the 600+ cable channels, any devoted to workers, consumers, students, taxpayers, or any of the thousands of nonprofit social justice organizations fighting for a better America? Of course not. We have allowed our property and our franchises to be completely seized by the corporatists, with scarcely a whimper. The big foundations do not like funding watchdog groups. But perhaps some enlightened, very wealthy people can be persuaded to do so.

Critical media literacy needs citizen motivation and citizen context. It must relate, at the beginning, to the communities where people live, work, and raise their families. That means that concern over toxic air, dirty water, contaminated food, dangerous disrepair of public services, underfunded schools, inadequate clinics, drug epidemics, and public transportation will generate receptivity to the facts. Fake news, swerves, and propaganda didn't work in Flint, Michigan, when the parents discovered their children were ingesting perilous levels of lead in the drinking water. They were outraged and called loudly for the truth . . . and got it, by organizing and making demands.

Imagine how differently things might have gone if the local community college or high schools taught physics, biology, and chemistry courses as science-for-the-people, and regularly had their students test for heavy metals such as lead, cadmium, and arsenic. Such practices are entirely possible to achieve, but we need to organize them. Doing so could improve public health and safety standards and catch deadly contamination much earlier. Education can and should show students how to get the facts about conditions in their own community. Learning by doing is more memorable than mere instruction.

Finally, nonstop propaganda delivered over the mass media year after year, without equivalent media rebuttals, makes it very difficult to free minds so immersed in disinformation and manipulative fictions—such as the "magic of the marketplace," to use Reagan's fantasy phrase. Our information system needs to be transformed, as Huff and Higdon advocate, to center on the commons, the public interest, and the institutions of democracy currently in place to serve and protect them.

Giving people motivating opportunities to think for themselves on matters of public importance and peril is far superior to pleading, necessary as that is, with networks, the cable industry, and the woeful PBS and NPR. *The United States of Distraction* affords readers plenty of material to begin working together to protect facts, truths, and civic fulfillments from being dislodged or destroyed by the adversaries of a functioning democracy. The time to get started is now. It is easier than we think!

# HOW DID WE GET HERE?

"If you do not change direction, you may end up where you are heading."

—Lao Tzu

"Sorry. It's a terrible thing to say. But bring it on, Donald. Keep going. . . . It may not be good for America, but it's damn good for CBS," exclaimed Les Moonves while he was executive chairman and CEO of CBS, during a Morgan Stanley Technology, Media and Telecom Conference in the summer of 2016. He further noted, "I've never seen anything like this, and this [is] going to be a very good year for us."[1]

Moonves was referring to the boosted ratings and revenues his network reaped from its coverage of Donald Trump's sensationalist 2016 presidential campaign. CBS and other networks were punch-drunk with profits gained by the way the electoral contest had devolved into a circus. At one point, Trump's campaign captured nearly 300 percent more media coverage than Hillary Clinton's campaign, and twenty-three times more coverage than Bernie

Sanders's campaign.[2] Team Trump basked in the equivalent of $2 billion in free media exposure, and the broadcast corporations made money hand over fist.[3] "Man, who would have expected the ride we're all having right now?" asked Moonves, "The money's rolling in, and this is fun."[4]

Whether it's about cosmetics, condoms, or candidates, publicity is the oxygen that fuels successful marketing campaigns.[5] Media corporations have cashed in by covering Trump. Their repetition and amplification of his messages have contributed not only to his family winning the White House, but also to his ongoing campaign for political dominance. How has a former beauty pageant owner and television celebrity with no public-interest experience outmaneuvered critics and rivals who have far more political acumen, understanding, and knowledge? How has the American public allowed itself to be distracted from urgent issues like climate change, economic equality, racial justice, women's issues, LGBTQI rights, fair trade, environmental sustainability, and health care for all?

To begin answering these kinds of questions, we must first understand the role played by systems of government, media, and education to produce knowledge and information for purposes of the public interest, and how those systems have come under the corrupting influence of commercialism and corporate power. For over four decades, these bulwarks of democratic principles and practice have been bruised, battered, defunded, dismantled, diminished, infiltrated, and manipulated by corporate interests. Perpetrated by relentless financial forces exerted from a free-market economy, the glorification of wealth and pursuit of private profit have gradually been elevated over defense of the commons, maintenance of public-interest institutions, nonprofit community and culture, and the processes of social justice and democracy that simply cannot advance without them.

What has remained? A media-refracted society that has become so alienated and distracted that it has allowed Trump's team to take command of the White House, the U.S. military, a nuclear arsenal, and the federal institutions responsible for running the country. For years to come, many will ask, how did they do it? The better question, we argue, is how did we let them do it? Unless and until the corporate economic system served by the Trump regime succeeds in fully deconstructing the administrative state of our democratic republic, our surviving public-interest institutions, no matter how traumatized, should be able to provide sufficient space, protection, and opportunity to advance the independence and agency to sustain and advance non-commercial civilian sovereignty. In the meantime, such institutions remain under serious assault.

Before Trump began marketing himself as a politician, he had already achieved a certain level of superficial tabloid celebrity through glitz and scandal. Trump was able to develop and amplify this celebrity through his employment as the lead character in the television show *The Apprentice*. It was through this platform—and the numerous ways he promoted himself publicly during this time—that Trump used commercial media as a vehicle for marketing his racial bias, suit-and-tie sexism, strong-man posturing, and self-mythology as a successful businessperson. Trump leveraged this celebrity during his candidacy, making a telegenic spectacle of himself and his provocations, brand, and image. The audience-amassing power of this spectacle gave commercial media the free entertainment they needed to reap larger advertising revenues while giving Trump expanded platforms to market himself.

At the same time, Trump strategically partnered with Steve Bannon to attract and harness white anxiety through far-right online platforms such as *Breitbart News*, constant mass rallies, easy-to-understand nationalist slogans of political aggrandizement and social intolerance, and aggressive rhetoric and posturing that appeared to celebrate violence. A host of factors, particularly decades of corporate domination over U.S. economic, political, and social institutions, had sufficiently cultured the population, rendering the values of commercialism increasingly more influential than those of the public interest and the common good. This has resulted in a gradual assault on the resources and solidarities required for what Noam Chomsky has called intellectual self-defense. The steady decline of education and independent media in the face of corporate power has created public vulnerabilities that have led us to the crisis we find ourselves in today.

From a public-interest perspective, commercial domination of media, journalism, and education represents not just an assault on democracy, but a relentless effort to replace the sovereignty of citizenship with the corporate dictates and manufactured consent of consumerism. Schools are clearly not adequately educating young people in media literacy, critical thinking, or the central importance of the public interest and the common good. While the potential for a free press still exists, the momentum created by Ronald Reagan's commercial deconstruction of the "public interest, convenience, and necessity" regulation of the airwaves, the elimination of the Fairness Doctrine, and the abolition of low-power community radio licenses, set the stage for the corporate domination of media seen in the United States today.

Long before Trump's candidacy, ratings drove programming and news. In the process, celebrity, entertainment, scandal, crime, disaster, and spectacle clearly dominated over the substantive reporting, in-depth investigation, and public-interest advocacy capable of questioning and countering abuses of corporate power and government authority. In short, the corporate commercialism that invested in and profited from Trump's tele-celebrity, enabled and fueled his candidacy, and currently feeds the provocative impulses of his presidency. That this is occurring openly is a testimony to the degree of our collective distraction, vulnerability, and complicity with forms of authoritarianism that have been written about at length by Hannah Arendt and anticipated in the contemporary period by a wide range of outspoken thinkers including Noam Chomsky, Angela Y. Davis, and Henry A. Giroux.

The volume of media coverage that favored Trump during his initial presidential run, as well as the overall failure of the press to cover issues of substance, has not gone unnoticed. A 2016 poll found that 75 percent of Americans agreed that Trump was covered too often.[6] In the days that followed the 2016 presidential election, news outlets were criticized for their unequal and trivial reporting, and were even blamed for contributing to the election's outcome.[7] Many major outlets tacitly admitted their failure to report on issues of substance and promised to recommit themselves to investigative journalism. The *New York Times* penned a sheepish letter to readers, the *Washington Post* adopted the tagline "Democracy Dies in Darkness," and CNN aired short clips using a bunch of bananas allegedly hiding an apple as a symbol of their dedication to fact-driven reporting over political narratives, stating, "There's only one way to know what's been covered up. You start digging."[8]

These gestures seemed to offer sober day-after promises from a profession that has historically served as an essential pillar of democracy. So essential that political theorist Edmund Burke proclaimed the press "more important
than they all." Despite their promises to the public, any
changes in corporate journalism after Trump's victory
were either unnoticeable or ineffective in holding Trump
accountable in any meaningful way. However, to simply
blame journalists and media would be to miss the larger
context in which Trump's organization gained control of
the White House and United States military command.

An educated and informed population, one capable of
critical thinking regarding political and historical matters,
would likely have responded differently to Team Trump's
aggression and marketing. Democracy is predicated on
an engaged citizenry not only making informed decisions
in the voting booth, but continually maintaining public
sovereignty by keeping private and state powers in check.
When the press and our schools function properly, the citizenry can effectively participate in the democratic process.
Without an effective public education system and an independent and diverse press, the prerequisite conditions for a
functional democracy do not exist. Educators provide people with tools to be equitable participants in an open and
accountable political culture. Media publish and broadcast
journalists' reports on matters that inform citizens' understanding of key events, policies, and politicians. However,
for nearly half a century these institutions have been under
assault by private interests and a political system skewed to
serve them.

Trump's acquisition of television celebrity and political supremacy was made possible by decades of corporate
domination of U.S. financial, media, and education sys-

tems. In a sense, Trump was made by and for such domination. Since Reagan's neoconservative rollback of public-interest regulations and policies, U.S. economic and political culture has been shaped by deregulation of big business, privatization of public institutions, trickle-up wealth transfer (through tax reductions for the rich and corporate welfare), militarization, divestment from social benefits and safety nets for the needy, blind faith in the primacy of the market, and merit-based systems of measurement. Such pro-corporate policies represent the uncontested common interests served by America's increasingly narrow two-wing electoral spectrum. While Democrats and Republicans openly clash over issues of social justice, women's rights, gun control, diversity, health care, and immigration, certain matters remain quietly uncontested: issues of free markets, globalized trade, militarization, surveillance, corporate power, tax cuts, and bailouts. Simply put, it is a system that serves the rich. Citizen advocate Ralph Nader has described it as a democracy of minimums and a plutocracy of maximums. "In a plutocracy," says Nader, "commercialism dominates far beyond the realm of economics and business; everything is for sale, and money is power. But in an authentic democracy, there must be commercial-free zones where the power of human rights, citizenship, community, equality, and justice are free from the corrupting influence of money."[9] Since Reagan, those zones have been under constant attack.

For nearly the past half century, private interests have systematically targeted, usurped, and commercialized such zones. As business relentlessly invests in political and economic dominance over public interests, "the market" is elevated over social and environmental well-being. In the process, "trickle-down" explanations are used to indoctrinate average Americans with the view that they too are invested, and that they too will profit. Election after election, American voters are told countless times that what's good for the market is good for society, but all they see is a widening gap between haves and have-nots, along with a host of other forms of preventable social injustice.

Over nearly five decades, commercial influence over the production and distribution of information and knowledge has adversely impacted the public-interest value of media and education. Political literacy and civic agency as ethical manifestations of the common good have been deliberately degraded. Donald Trump's arc from television celebrity to commander in chief of the U.S. military, with a direct propaganda feed to 55.5 million voluntary followers, was made possible through this degradation—and a media system openly willing to profit from it, even though it "may not be good for America."

In addition to his plutocratic agenda, Trump's power represents gendered, homophobic, transphobic, and racialized forms of political domination that increasingly project characteristics of authoritarianism and autocracy. Among these characteristics are chronic lying and propagation of disinformation, demonization of criticism and dissent, censorship of language and knowledge, repetition of slogans, hyper-nationalism, valorization of aggression, belittlement, victim blaming, and general intolerance.

The normalization of official lying and disinformation alone should be a matter of alarm for everyone concerned about the integrity of our political system. Acknowledgment of the matter is open and widespread. In December 2017, for example, the *New York Times* published a piece by David Leonhardt and Stuart A. Thompson in which they attempted to catalogue "nearly every outright lie" Trump had told publicly from moment he took the oath of office to the time of writing the article. "There is simply no precedent for an American president to spend so much time telling untruths," wrote Leonhardt and Thompson. "Every president has shaded the truth or told occasional whoppers. No other president—of either party—has behaved as Trump is behaving. He is trying to create an atmosphere in which reality is irrelevant."[10] That atmosphere is clearly malignant to U.S. democracy and the government accountability required to serve and maintain it.

In addition to chronic lying, another Orwellian aspect of Trump's authoritarianism has been the censoring of certain words and phrases in government departments and agencies, particularly in the Department of Health and Human Services. Officials at the Centers for Disease Control and Prevention, for example, were given a list of seven words and phrases that could not be used in budget documents. These were "entitlement," "diversity," "vulnerable," "evidence-based," "science-based," "fetus," and "transgender." Officials were instructed to use the term "Obamacare," and never refer to the Affordable Care Act or ACA, a transparent effort to politically stigmatize the program and those Americans who benefit from it.

Even the State Department was ordered to stop using the term "sex education" and to substitute "sexual risk avoidance." This ban is part of the Trump administration's campaign on Capitol Hill to stress premarital abstinence as the primary form of national health advocacy on the matter. Censorship at the Department of State could ultimately translate into less funding for maternal health and abortions, according to the vice president and director of global health and HIV policy at the Kaiser Family Foundation.[11]

The Health and Human Services (HHS) press briefing

to announce these changes was given anonymously, with the acknowledgment that specific agencies were not being named because language changes were on "close hold."[12] Particularly offensive was the ban on the word "transgender," in view of the high percentage of HIV infections among transgender women, the highest of any gender group. Censorship at the HHS agencies is reprehensible overall, because their programs must be science-based or evidence-based as part of a larger search for truth. As former surgeon general Dr. Vivek Murphy noted, "When science is censored, the truth is censored."[13]

Since Trump took control of the White House, the phrase "climate change" has also been disappearing from government websites. The Environmental Protection Agency, Department of Energy, Department of Health and Human Services, and Department of Transportation have all had websites or press releases purged of references to humanity's role in rising average temperatures.[14]

In addition to censoring administrative language, Trump has repeatedly tried to censor the press. In May 2018, the Environmental Protection Agency attempted to bar reporters from attending a meeting on water contamination. The meeting included more than 200 representatives of regulatory and industry groups. The Associated Press reported that one of its journalists "was grabbed by the shoulders and shoved out of an Environmental Protection Agency building by a security guard."[15][16]

In tones that remind many of World War II–era dictators, Trump has gone beyond censorship and openly raged about media that question and challenge him, aggressively attacking those journalists and free press outlets as "fake news" and "enemies of the people." Trump has threatened to revoke broadcast licenses from media outlets that question or criticize his behavior.[17] Such conduct has raised considerable alarm. "I told the president directly that I thought that his language was not just divisive but increasingly dangerous," said the publisher of the *New York Times*, A.G. Sulzberger, following a White House meeting with President Trump. "I told him that although the phrase *fake news* is untrue and harmful, I am far more concerned about his labeling journalists the *enemy of the people*," Mr. Sulzberger said. "I warned that this inflammatory language is contributing to a rise in threats against journalists and will lead to violence." This is particularly true overseas, Mr. Sulzberger said, where governments are using Mr. Trump's words as a pretext to crack down on journalists. He said he warned the president that his attacks were "putting lives at risk" and "undermining the democratic ideals of our nation."[18] Trump's glorification of an assault on a reporter in Montana at the same time that he tried to minimize the Saudi government's assassination of *Washington Post* reporter Jamal Khashoggi in the Saudi embassy in Turkey, further underscores the seriousness of Sulzberger's concerns.[19]

While Trump's attacks on truth and the press have drawn more public attention to the matter, this has been a bipartisan problem. In April 2019, many Democrats were smiling from ear to vindictive ear as Julian Assange, co-founder and publisher of Wikileaks, was arrested and dragged out of the Ecuadoran embassy in London, where he had been granted refuge since 2012 in his effort to avoid extradition to the United States. In May of 2019, he was sentenced to fifty weeks in a UK jail for violating bail conditions, namely, by seeking refuge to evade the extradition. Many Democrats blamed Assange for their 2016 electoral defeat, after he published leaked emails exposing the party leadership colluding to fix the Democratic Party primary. Interestingly, just a decade earlier, many of these same Democrats were cheering Assange for publishing leaks by whistleblower Chelsea Manning that revealed damning evidence of U.S. war crimes in Iraq during George W. Bush's presidency. These were illustrated most notoriously by the "Collateral Murder" video, which is why the United States now wants to extradite Assange on conspiracy charges. This about-face suggests Democrats' commitment to party over principles. More important, the hyper-partisan war on truth tellers is incompatible with free press principles, no matter who is doing it.

That noted, Trump's ongoing war on truth, language, openness, and the free press is incompatible to an unprecedented degree with the mission of American government to operate openly and accountably as a democracy. Attacking journalists as "enemies of the American people . . . gives aid and comfort to present-day officials and lawmakers who want to avoid being held publicly accountable for their acts,"[20] says Arnold Isaacs, a former editor of the *Baltimore Sun*. Such attacks, coming from an office of such enormous responsibility and power, serve to normalize aggression and intolerance toward those who question and criticize authority; they serve to corrupt the ethical foundation necessary for a republic.

How did we get to this point? Trump did not commercialize society, but his team strategically used commercial mechanisms to manipulate the public and take power. Trump homed in on public vulnerabilities created by decades of pro-corporate influence and policy. Trump, a fourteen-season television game-show character, leveraged his rise on the centrality of America's pervasive entertainment culture, increasingly hyper-partisan narratives, fragmented media landscape, and ineffective education system. He has deftly manipulated the press, exploited potential voters, and lied with nearly complete impunity. It is worth noting that Trump tapped into other cultural vulnerabilities that had existed well before America's corporate age, such as its long history of white supremacy, misogyny, homophobia, xenophobia, and nationalism. However, this book addresses the public vulnerabilities caused by the impact of corporate interests on U.S. educational and mass media systems, and how and why such interests enabled Trump's self-serving messaging to be so effective.

Trump can be seen as the temporary face of an increasingly invasive corporate algorithm, one that views civil liberties, the public interest, the commons, and the democracy-centered institutions mandated to serve them as enemy forces to be administratively "deconstructed." The algorithm unifies by distraction and extraction—distracting the population from the common good and the civic agency required to defend it, while extracting data, resources, and power from the public sector and transferring them to the private sector—a euphemism for the rich. In the process, the United States increasingly drifts toward becoming an authoritarian society in which government represents and protects the interests of the wealthy few. As corporations succeed in replacing the notion of a "citizen" with that of a "consumer," their power concentrates, producing characters like Donald Trump.

As damaging as Trump is to the advance and dignity of women, people of color, Native Americans, the disabled, the LGBTQI community, peace, and social justice, his moment will pass. The algorithm will remain. The structural conditions that created and profit from Trump—the people and corporate entities that continue to invest in him and his re-election—are the forces that will continue to produce new and more virulent forms of authoritarian and fascist threats to the public interest, the common good, and all the institutions and ethical principles associated with them. There is no hiding the fact that Trump is not good for America, but he *is* good for those who profit from the elimination of corporate accountability and restraint.

It would be a mistake to expect Trump's regime to duplicate past authoritarian states, but there are similarities. We are witnessing a kind of corporate plutocracy in which control is primarily achieved not through the cudgel, but through media, spectacle, surveillance, data control, disinformation, propaganda, and consumerism. Gandhi presciently argued that people in the West merely "imagine they have a voice in their own government"; instead, they were "being exploited by the ruling class or caste under the sacred name of democracy."[21] Moreover, a regime in which "the weakest go to the wall" and a "few capitalist owners" thrive, "cannot be sustained except by violence, veiled if not open." This is why, Gandhi predicted, even "the states that are today nominally democratic" are likely to become "frankly totalitarian."[22]

The purpose of this book is to focus on media's role in getting us where we are today, the normalization of media tactics used by those seeking to acquire power through manipulation and deception, and strategies that could be used by the public for intellectual and civic self-defense. Our goal is to counter forms of pro-corporate domination by promoting civic agency, sovereignty, diversity, and dignity through education.

This book operates from an assumption that we cannot fix the problems of today without understanding how we got here. As a result, we take a deep look at the roots of

America's drift into authoritarianism through an analysis of political economy and the changes to journalism, media, and education over the last half century.

We believe education and social solidarity offer the best forms of resistance against threats to the sovereignty of the people, the sustainability of the environment, and the non-commercial democracy required to hold corporations and elected officials subordinate to the common good. However, in order to implement the necessary changes, we must implement new forms of political literacy—identifying power and organizing it in collective forms—in order to break the commercial algorithms of distraction, disinformation, surveillance, and polarization that we have allowed to infiltrate and immobilize civil society. Such a step, should we achieve it, will represent a fundamental shift in consciousness and exercise of public sovereignty, one that democracy and citizenship are capable of delivering through education, organizing, and spontaneous forms of civic rebellion.

ONE

# A CRUMBLING FOURTH ESTATE

"Our republic and its press will rise or fall together. An able, disinterested, public-spirited press, with trained intelligence to know the right and courage to do it, can preserve that public virtue without which popular government is a sham and a mockery. A cynical, mercenary, demagogic press will produce in time a people as base as itself. The power to mold the future of the Republic will be in the hands of the journalism of future generations."

—Joseph Pulitzer

"What could be more fake than CBS, and NBC, and ABC, and CNN? . . . If you look at the level of approval of the media, of general media—if you look at it from the day I started running, to now, I'm so proud I have been able to convince people how fake it is, because it has taken a nosedive."[23] President Donald Trump shared this observation during an interview with Fox News on the eve of his one-year anniversary as president. Trump had reason to celebrate. A year earlier, he had defied most pollsters, astonished pundits, and defeated an assumed political shoo-in, Hillary Clinton. Still, in the midst of his victory he continued to rail against the press, accusing the media of attacking his campaign and presidency.

Trump and his election rival Clinton did not agree on much, but they did share contempt for the press. Clinton, like Trump, claimed that the press had worked to undermine her campaign. In her 2017 book *What Happened*, Clinton argued that none of Donald Trump's scandals generated press coverage comparable to the reportage on her scandals. She joked that "if Trump ripped the shirt off someone at a rally and a button fell off my jacket on the same day," journalists would have reported it as "Trump and Clinton Experience Wardrobe Malfunctions, Campaigns in Turmoil."[24] Although in jest, the comments reveal a deep disdain for the press that Clinton and her surrogates have shared since her husband's presidency, when she referred to negative media coverage as "a vast right-wing conspiracy."[25] We will argue in this chapter that Clinton's antipathy for the press is well placed, but for all the wrong reasons.

Elected leaders have long expressed aversion toward the press. For example, former President Lyndon Johnson once said, "Being president is like being a jackass in a hailstorm. There's nothing to do but stand there and take it."[26] However, the complaints made by Trump and Clinton express something different. They both recognized that in the four decades since Johnson's jackass joke, the press had become less focused on holding politicians publicly accountable and more focused on furthering their own commercial interests.

A free and independent press has long been recognized as an essential element of democracy. In fact, the very first amendment to the U.S. Constitution protects the press's right to operate freely, thus elevating its importance. This protection is meant to enable the press to safely challenge authority, give voice to a diverse range of views, and shed light on the inconvenient truths that powerful people would prefer remain hidden. But such freedoms and protections did not come with a mandate for the press to serve democracy.

Over time, this absence of a public-service mandate has fostered a commercial free-for-all, including corporations hijacking the publicly owned airwaves that were meant to be used specifically to further the "public interest, convenience, and necessity." The small number of corporations that control the media today may argue that they serve the commercial interests of consumers and shareholders, but they have little basis to argue that they serve the non-commercial public interest of citizens. The result is that a key pillar of democracy has been significantly weakened, leaving the American people increasingly deficient in mechanisms for keeping those in power accountable to the public.

## THE FREE PRESS?

To strengthen the relationship between the press and democracy, citizens from the 1930s onward have organized, protested, and lobbied the government to ensure media remain an asset of the public interest. Media that serve the public interest offer fair and accurate reporting, and enable community-level access to local debate and news production. In 1932, during the Great Depression, Franklin Delano Roosevelt was elected president of the United States. Over his unprecedented nearly four terms in office he responded to the public's discontents by working with citizens and policymakers to use government to solve national problems.[27] The result was a much larger and more engaged government. Concerned citizens lobbied Roosevelt to accomplish a diversity of media ownership by ending the monopolizing practices of the day.[28] In response, Congress passed the Communications Act of 1934. This groundbreaking legislation established federal regulation of radio in the public interest; set up the Federal Communications Commission (FCC) to oversee and enforce the new regulations; enacted anti-monopoly provisions regulating the number of stations one business could own; and mandated that broadcast facilities be afforded to the public "at reasonable charges."[29] Media scholar Robert W. McChesney has referred to the Act as "the primary regulatory broadcast and telecast statute in the United States."[30]

Activists sought to bring about diversity not only of ownership, but also of content. For example, protests following World War II led Congress to pass the Fairness Doctrine in 1949.[31] This act of media reform mandated that broadcasters provide equal airtime for differing perspectives.[32] The concept behind the Fairness Doctrine was that a democracy benefits from a multitude of views, when no single view can dominate and differing views of potential benefit can be heard. Its creators believed that it best serves the public to forbid content providers from offering a homogeneity of views in their broadcasts.[33]

Regulations such as the Communications Act of 1934 and the Fairness Doctrine were critical to mitigating the adverse impact that commercially motivated corporations exercised on the public through media. The regulations upheld the primacy of public over private interests, and fostered the possibility of a diverse range of news and views in media. They served as safety valves on America's political system, mitigating the vulnerabilities media owners encourage and exploit when left to their own commercial vices. As we will see, in the late twentieth century these protections were severely weakened and the Fairness Doctrine was eliminated entirely.

## PRIVATIZED DEMOCRACY AND CORPORATE ENCLOSURE OF OUR COMMONS

At the same time that advances were being made in the public interest from the 1930s to the 1960s, pushback was exerted by the private sector, especially pro-business forces such as the U.S. Chamber of Commerce. The corporate sector invested heavily to fight public-interest regulations and social public welfare programs that came out of the New Deal and Great Society programs. Businesses lobbied relentlessly to further their own private interests and sought to undermine whistleblowers and advocates, including the legendary Ralph Nader, who fought to regulate corporations, strengthen consumer protections, and advance public-interest law.

Part of the pushback came from James Buchanan, an economist at the University of Virginia who devised a plan in the 1950s to mitigate the influence of government and allied organizations, such as labor unions, which he and many others saw as threats to individuals' basic liberties.[34] Funded by corporate money, Buchanan began a trend of constructing brain trusts on college campuses to raise money, hire conservative faculty, and produce pro-business content that would shift educational emphasis from liberal notions of the public good to more right-leaning views that regard government as an obstacle to personal freedoms.[35]

At first, Buchanan's ideological positions were a tough sell to a majority of Americans. Buchanan denounced the policies of the New Deal at a time when those policies had lifted many American families out of poverty and into the middle class.[36] As a result, Buchanan realized that his vision would not be adopted on its own merits.[37] To obfuscate the issue, he hid his agenda and ideology behind notions of "liberty" and "choice" while advocating for the economic dismantling of the New Deal by strengthening private property rights (shielding them from the reach of government), and privatizing public property and institutions such as schools, prisons, Western lands, and more, including the airwaves and free press.[38] Buchanan's ideological underpinnings and rhetorical manipulations would inspire far-right thinkers and major donors well into the twenty-first century, including the billionaire brothers Charles and David Koch.[39] In her 2017 book *Democracy in Chains*, historian Nancy MacLean explains that the movement Buchanan inspired aimed "to hollow out Democratic resistance. And by its own lights, the cause is nearing success."[40]

An influential acolyte of Buchanan's philosophy was corporate attorney Lewis F. Powell Jr., who was a board member of eleven major companies. He helped draft a manifesto titled *Confidential Memorandum: Attack on the American Free Enterprise System*. The 1971 document, also known as the Powell Memo, was commissioned by and addressed to then-chairman of the Education Committee of the U.S. Chamber of Commerce Eugene B. Sydnor Jr. (who was also Powell's friend and neighbor). The memo recommended a series of strategies that the larger business community should adopt to promote capitalist ideals and curry favor with public officials, including creating their own think tanks to rival university scholarship, which they claimed was too liberal. Perhaps the most important recommendation of the memo was the call for the launch of a media network to propagate neoconservative political narratives, perspectives, and influence.[41]

Interestingly, two months after the memo appeared, President Richard Nixon appointed Powell to the U.S. Supreme Court, where he would further influence conservative legal interpretations of the Constitution until 1987. Powell's messaging and organizing strategies were advanced, adopted, and implemented by numerous influential conservative ideologues, including the president of Americans for Tax Reform, Grover Norquist, who said of the government, "I don't want to abolish government. I simply want to reduce it to the size where I can drag it into the bathroom and drown it in the bathtub."[42]

The notions put forth in the Powell Memo resonated with American voters who were discontent with the failures of government policies during the 1970s. Corporatists' political narratives are spun from the libertarian notion that markets, free of government intervention or regulation, will lead to endless economic growth that will improve the lives of everyone. As economist David Graeber points out in his book *Debt: The First 5,000 Years*, this utopian vision is grounded in a fabricated historical notion about a pre-market barter society, imagined by Adam Smith, leading to economic prosperity for the masses.[43] Corporatists' narratives assert that big government, regulation, taxation, labor unions, environmental protection, and social safety nets all prevent unfettered economic prosperity from being achieved. As a result, they relentlessly campaign that the powers, policies, and services enforced by government should be reduced, deregulated, or privatized, which means new opportunities for corporations and the wealthy few to further enrich themselves at the public's expense.[44]

Not everyone agrees that corporations have society's

best interests in mind. In his book *The Corporation*, attorney and author Joel Bakan describes these big businesses as entities with a "pathological pursuit of profit and power" that have "risen from relative obscurity to become the world's dominant economic institution."[45] "Corporations govern our lives," Bakan argues, "they determine what we eat, what we watch, what we wear, where we work, and what we do. . . . And, like the church and the monarchy in other times, they posture as infallible and omnipotent."[46] The impact of this dominating influence on government has been pressure to prioritize private interests over all else. In the process, corporations relentlessly seek tax cuts, subsidies, bailouts, and the ability to access and exploit public land and resources—the commons—for commercial purposes of private enrichment.

It was President Ronald Reagan who sold the corporate ethos to the American public in the early 1980s. In his first inaugural address, the former actor and salesman exclaimed, "Government is not the solution to our problem; government is the problem."[47] During the 1970s, Americans witnessed a series of their government's failures, including the Vietnam War, Watergate, oil embargoes (the OPEC crisis), a deindustrializing economy (the collapse of steel production and related major industries), and the Church Committee hearings exposing the extent of U.S. covert counterintelligence operations against American citizens, civil groups, and media.[48] Corporatists seized upon the widespread distrust of government to advance Powell's messaging strategy by arguing that the "liberal media" and government, through their biases and mistakes, were responsible for the crises burdening America.

The pro-corporate propaganda campaign aided in shifting working class voters' support away from government solutions championed by liberal Democrats to neo-conservative economic policies. While Richard Nixon had a Southern Strategy, Reagan won over a demographic that would come to be known as Reagan Democrats—disaffected white voters who were frustrated with their declining status in society and were looking for change, as well as for scapegoats. Reagan delivered, at least rhetorically. However, the legacy of that rhetoric would be decades of conservative government policies that eroded the wealth of a majority of Americans.[49]

The business-dominant economy that gradually emerged invested heavily in the creation of a veritable one-party political system—the pro-corporate party—with two factions, the Republicans and Democrats, funded to uphold corporate interests above all others. In the presidential election of 1992, Democratic candidate Bill Clinton seized upon Reagan's success. He exploited the previous three Democratic Party losses in presidential elections and economic distress of the early 1990s to transform the party.[50] Clinton was an influential part of the Democratic Leadership Council (DLC) that was created in 1985 by Southern politicians who believed that Democrats were losing elections because they were too weak on crime, too soft on communism, and too sympathetic to minorities.[51] They saw the party as foolish for ceding corporate money to the GOP. The Democratic Leadership Council, with the Clintons at the helm, forged a path back to the White House for Democrats. They would largely adopt Buchanan's ideas and Powell's strategies, but code the moves in empty rhetoric that resonated with liberal voters of the time.[52] Bill Clinton's success in the 1992 election cemented the Democratic Party to the vision of the DLC, where it has remained ever since. In fact, the DLC was abolished as a committee because it had succeeded in taking over the party.[53] Overall, both parties' adoption of free market fundamentalism was a testament to the success of Buchanan, Powell, and their adherents in politically formalizing corporate supremacy over social, environmental, economic, and racial justice in the United States.

## CORPORATE CAPTURE OF NEWS MEDIA AND PUBLIC EDUCATION

Consensus among Republicans and Democrats on a pro-corporate political spectrum resulted in many policy changes, including the deregulation of the news media industry. By the 1970s, the press increasingly became the bane of the political class by exposing corruption and outright lies in the Vietnam War, especially the Mỹ Lai massacre and expansion of the U.S. war into Cambodia and Laos. Major media's role in exposing President Nixon's part in the Watergate scandal, based on earlier reporting from alternative media outlets previously ignored, deeply eroded faith in government and considerably elevated the status of the press and investigative journalism. In response, corporations intensified their effort to dominate and control the press. Under Reagan, corporations were also able to successfully lobby for the removal of federal policies protecting children under the age of eight from targeted advertising, even though such policies had been enacted because studies had found that children could not tell the difference between television shows and ads.[54]

A large share of corporate interest in media was based on the practice of limiting ownership and advertising to those businesses that offered the most corporate-friendly messages. In 1974, they succeeded in exempting newspapers from the 1934 Communications Act, opening the way for newspaper monopolies to emerge by removing the limits on ownership.[55] After the Telecommunications Act of 1996 effectively gutted the 1934 Communications Act, diversity of media ownership significantly diminished, with the fifty corporations that owned the bulk of the media during the 1980s being reduced to six by 2012: News Corp, Disney, Viacom, Time Warner, CBS, and Comcast.[56]

In addition to paving the way for media monopolies and oligopolies, corporatists sought to harness news content within a narrow range of purportedly free-market ideologies. Since 1949, the Fairness Doctrine had empowered the FCC to ensure that broadcasters not only had to present important issues to the public, but had to provide multiple perspectives on such issues as well. In 2009, Dan Fletcher wrote a feature about the Fairness Doctrine for *Time* magazine, saying:

> The act is rooted in the media world of 1949, when lawmakers became concerned that by virtue of their near-stranglehold on nationwide TV broadcasting, the three main television networks—NBC, ABC and CBS—could misuse their broadcast licenses to set a biased public agenda. The Fairness Doctrine, which mandated that broadcast networks devote time to contrasting views on issues of public importance, was meant to level the playing field. Congress backed the policy in 1954, and by the 1970s the FCC called the doctrine the "single most important requirement of operation in the public interest— the sine qua non for grant of a renewal of license."[57]

Despite the importance of the Fairness Doctrine, by 1987 corporate lobbyists had grown so powerful that they finally succeeded in pressuring Congress to abolish it. This enabled the unfettered rise of biased and commercial messaging, without any mandate to serve the public interest, over traditional journalistic news content. To maintain their domination over content, they established powerful pro-corporate lobbying organizations such as the National Association of Broadcasters, which continue to successfully exert commercial influence over the FCC and government to this day.

This deregulation bonanza resulted in fewer corporations controlling news media, with no mechanisms to advance diversity, balance, or accuracy in reporting.[58] The industry's focus has been almost entirely on maximizing profit, not on maintaining or improving journalistic standards, strengthening democracy, holding the powerful accountable, or giving voice to concerns, views, and social movements outside the pro-corporate spectrum.

Media corporations have maximized their profits by cutting jobs, especially in overseas bureaus, which has resulted in less diversity and less reporting, especially about foreign affairs. This began at a time when the Cold War was in full swing.[59] The downsizing of reportage, in addition to the influence of the internet, resulted in a fifth of newspaper jobs disappearing between 2001 and 2009.[60] At the same time, Time Warner, Bertelsmann, and News Corp. had a combined wealth of $1.3 trillion in 2009 and $1.4 trillion in 2010.[61] These mega-corporations had even less regulation compelling them to serve non-commercial public-interest goals of providing news and programming that was investigative, fair, and diverse.

Just as the deregulation of traditional media was increasing, internet accessibility complicated Americans' information consumption habits. In 1996, less than 1 percent of the U.S. population had access to the internet.[62] Two decades later, 90 percent of Americans had online access.[63] Widespread access to the internet has transformed American culture and behavior: Standard practice is to shop online rather than in person; write emails rather than contact people via phone; watch programs at any time rather than when they aired; and access news 24 hours a day from multiple outlets on various platforms instead of watching a nightly news broadcast. Many nations in Europe, Asia, and other parts of the world recognized that these dramatic societal changes required a shift in education.[64] They recognized that the internet required people to learn a cluster of skills including keyboarding (typing); navigating connectivity issues; using new applications, hardware, and software; and, perhaps most important, honing critical thinking skills to keep up with evolving technology—specifically, the ability to discern factual information from falsehoods. This last is certainly not the least. Rather than address the root causes of the preventable crisis, the leadership of the U.S. education system focused on conforming to the corporate-backed policies that transformed their information landscape. This only served to deepen a major and growing public vulnerability at the intersection of education and the media.

In the United States, information literacy and media education are practically nonexistent, and appear limited to Drug Abuse Resistance Education (DARE) programs that serve as counter-marketing efforts designed to direct children away from tobacco, alcohol, and narcotics. Just as promised with the media, free market proponents claimed that deregulation and privatization of schools would improve education. They cited a 1983 report from the Reagan White House, *Nation at Risk*, as proof that U.S. schools were in need of a large-scale transformation.[65] The study found that American students' test scores had dropped significantly in a decade's time.[66] Meanwhile, large numbers of students could not "draw inferences from written material," "write a persuasive essay," or "solve a mathematics problem."[67] Finally, it noted that U.S. students were in danger of falling behind other nations in terms of educational ranking.[68] The report recommended that schools increase the number of days students are required to attend; that colleges raise standards; that the government fund more education for people of color in particular; and that content be changed to include areas such as computer science.[69] Even though *Nation at Risk* was challenged by other government studies, Reagan refused to publish those analyses. Subsequent administrations also ignored the differing recommendations, focusing instead on the report's more privatized and corporate-friendly prescriptions that the teaching profession become more "professionally competitive, market-sensitive, and performance-based."[70]

By the 1980s, corporatists were threatened by the near iconic status teachers had achieved.[71] Teachers represented everything that those of Buchanan's and Powell's ilk hoped to destroy: They were unionized, earned a taxpayer-funded salary that approximated a living wage, and worked daily to achieve equity through participatory democracy and responsible economic policy.[72] In order for the public to accept a pro-corporate education agenda, corporatists utilized Powell's messaging tactics to attack and blame teachers for America's failing schools while pushing private businesses as the solution.[73] For example, economics professor and free-market zealot Milton Friedman funded a ten-part PBS series, *Free to Choose*, which sought to indoctrinate viewers that it was in the best interest of students for parents to be able to choose whether their children attended public or private schools.[74]

Friedman's rhetoric was successful in shifting education policy from the public to the private sector, where there were profits to be made and minds to be molded. One episode of *Free to Choose* called for politicians to institute a program that allowed parents to obtain taxpayer-funded vouchers for their child to attend private rather than public schools. Dean Paton of *Yes! Magazine* argued that "to make the case for vouchers, free-market conservatives, corporate strategists, and opportunistic politicians looked for any way to build a myth that public schools were failing, that teachers (and of course their unions) were at fault, and that the cure was vouchers and privatization."[75] The relentless corporate pressure on teachers and the implementation of voucher policies diverted government funds from public education, making schools more dependent upon the private sector. The loss of revenue—some states lost as much as one-third of their budget—resulted in fewer supplies, larger class sizes, overworked teachers, and over-emphasis on standardized testing and rote memorization rather than a more critical pedagogy.[76] In their desperation, many communities turned to market-driven solutions offered by Educational Management Organizations (EMOs) and Edison Schools Inc. to reorganize their schools with a focus on privatization and market efficiency.[77] These early changes began a transformation that blamed teachers for poor educational outcomes and transferred the power and purpose of public schools over to private industries.

The Magna Carta of this educational privatization was the 2002 No Child Left Behind Act (NCLB), passed under President George W. Bush. It should be noted that NCLB was incubated through the 1990s by right-wing, pro-privatization think tanks such as the Hoover Institute at Stanford University, with funding from the conservative John M. Olin Foundation; lobbying by Microsoft's Bill Gates and neoliberal *New York Times* columnist Thomas Friedman; and bipartisan political support, including from Democratic senator Ted Kennedy and Republican congressman John Boehner.[78]

The No Child Left Behind Act relied on standardized test scores to determine which schools deserved funding from the federal government.[79] The tests also sought to determine the effectiveness of teachers. Schools being defunded would be privatized, often under the guise of charters, a process that became known as the Charter School Movement. Studies found that the privatizing of schools and NCLB did not improve educational outcomes but exacerbated inequalities, especially along racial and class lines.[80]

In fact, the data revealed that the policy changes did more to hurt testing outcomes than to improve them.[81] The corporatist policies imposed on public education left schools underfunded and overburdened, with their students often under-educated and overlooked as a result. The increased emphasis on testing led the majority of curricula to focus on what education scholar Neil Postman called "schooling," a form of memorizing and testing rather than "education," which provides the essential critical reasoning skills and diverse perspectives needed to thrive in a democratic republic.[82]

## FOUR PUBLIC VULNERABILITIES

The long-term influence of corporate power on society has exploited public vulnerabilities to the many changes in media, education, and politics. These changes have adversely impacted democratic institutions and people's ability to use them in their own best interest. Increased public receptivity to pervasive commercial entertainment culture, hyper-partisanship, a fragmented news media landscape, and an ineffective education system has created opportunities for exploitation, ones Donald Trump's electoral campaign and presidency have been able to manipulate with great success. Now that this path has been forged and utilized, it is likely others will imitate his strategies in future campaigns.

### *Pervasive commercial entertainment culture*

In addition to their agreement about the failing corporate press, Trump and Clinton appeared simpatico in their beliefs that the news media emphasized the wrong issues during the 2016 presidential election. For example, Clinton complained that the Republican-driven outcry resulting from her managing State Department emails on a private server rather than a government server, departing from federal protocols, was unimportant and covered too often. She claimed the continuous coverage of her private emails "was like quicksand: the more you struggle, the deeper you sink."[83] Meanwhile, Trump thought that Clinton's email scandal, which revealed internal discussions among the Democratic Party leadership, including their effort to marginalize Bernie Sanders's Campaign, was not covered enough.[84]

In fact, both Clinton and Trump were correct. A Tyndall Report study found that the most-watched television news programs, ABC's *World News Tonight*, *CBS Evening News*, and *NBC Nightly News*, dedicated a total of 220 minutes to policy in the 2008 U.S. presidential campaign, 114 minutes in 2012, and finally a mere thirty-two minutes in 2016.[85] While discussing the type of coverage these programs offered, Tyndall noted, "**No trade, no healthcare, no climate change, no drugs, no poverty, no guns, no infrastructure, no deficits.** To the extent that these issues have been mentioned, it has been on the candidates' terms, not on the networks' initiative."[86] By contrast, the Clinton email story received 100 minutes of airtime.[87] While the email leaks received extensive coverage—for some time being referred to as hacks—analysis of actual contents of the emails was minimal. The corporate press turned the emails into a Sherlock Holmes-like conversation about who released them, rather than a meaningful analysis of their significance. News appeared to be produced more to entertain the audience than to offer a critical inquiry into behind-the-scenes political maneuvering and its implications. The episode was all too typical of corporate media coverage that prioritized building larger audiences and increasing advertising revenue, instead of providing the in-depth investigative reporting needed to equip citizens to direct elected officials to address their concerns and act more faithfully in the public interest.

America's pervasive commercial entertainment culture can help explain the dismal press coverage of substantive issues before, during, and after elections. Entertainment spectacles create large audiences for corporate media, which bring increased profits from advertiser revenues. In his 1967 work *The Society of the Spectacle*, French theorist and media scholar Guy Debord wrote that spectacles are an inverted version of society, wherein relations between people are replaced by relations between commodities, and that these relations are mediated by images. "The spectacle is *capital* to such a degree of accumulation," wrote Debord, "that it becomes an image."[88]

Since the 1960s, many other scholars have remarked

on the rise of a culture dominated by spectacle, from the late Neil Postman of New York University to Pulitzer Prize–winning journalist Chris Hedges, both of whom have written about how we are "amusing ourselves to death" in an "empire of illusion." Carl Jensen, founder of the media watchdog organization Project Censored, coined the term "junk food news" to describe how substantive coverage of issues worthy of public concern has steadily been replaced by coverage of the trivial and sensational.

While the significance of these developments and their impact on democratic institutions have long been overlooked or ignored by many, they have not been missed by all. Playwright and critic Gore Vidal once said we live in the *United States of Amnesia*. His point was that history matters, despite our ignorance of it, and that we would be better served if we studied previous eras to understand and contextualize current realities more broadly and deeply. However, the ascendency of commercialized media, entertainment, and celebrity culture has spawned a form of infotainment news that operates with little or no historical contextualization. The adverse impact on the public has been significant, but we can't say we were not warned.

In 1962, historian Daniel J. Boorstin anticipated that the rise of "the image," in combination with U.S. commercial culture, would lead us to increasingly consume news that was based on nothing more than manufactured "pseudo-events." This is the prelude for today's "post-truth" and "fake news" disinformation crises. Boorstin aptly remarked:

> Never have people been more the masters of their environment. Yet never has a people felt more deceived and disappointed. For never has a people expected so much more than the world could of-

fer. We are ruled by extravagant expectations. . . . By harboring, nourishing, and ever enlarging our extravagant expectations we create the demand for the illusions with which we deceive ourselves. And which we pay others to make to deceive us. . . . We have become so accustomed to our illusions that we mistake them for reality. We demand them. And we demand that there be always more of them, bigger and better and more vivid. They are the world of our making: the world of the image.[89]

Further examples of pseudo-events in America, as described by Boorstin, abound. As corporate consolidation continued throughout the 1990s, spectacle became the main form of content disseminated by the six corporations that monopolized U.S. news media.[90] The corporate press hired entertainers and comedians such as Joy Beharto to imitate journalists. The corporate networks also generated news shows that specifically focused on humor over substance, such as Fox News Channel's satirical talk show *Red Eye*.[91] Telegenic personalities soon replaced journalists. Sean Hannity and Bill O'Reilly of Fox have relied on constant provocation, outrage, and denunciation of Democrats to build a nightly program with the semblance of a news broadcast. Their critiques and monologues, regardless of their use of facts, cannot be considered journalism. Their form of programming has increasingly broadcast far-right bias, indoctrination, and propaganda dressed up to look like news.

In addition to fostering divisiveness and disinforming viewers, such operations have served to reinforce the commercial mission of their corporate owners.[92] Just as Powell had prescribed, entertainment, including news, is now packaged to propagate and normalize corporatist policies while marginalizing or ignoring social injustices and the movements that rise to address them.[93] For instance, the corporate press offers constant coverage of companies such as Apple and Amazon, which reap massive profits from the exploitation of labor and customers' privacy, because corporatists value the big tech companies' high returns and entrepreneurial style.[94] Meanwhile, national movements such as Occupy Wall Street and Black Lives Matter have been largely ignored or have received negative coverage, because they challenge and expose practices that contradict corporate interests.[95] This slanted coverage stifles social and political change in general, and results in a majority of Americans being led to form biases against such anti-authoritarian social movements, even if they may support the overall messages and goals of those movements.[96]

Similarly, reporters who do not operate within the ever-narrowing spectrum of acceptable political discourse are often shunned or ejected from the corporate press. For example, CNN has suspended Elise Labott for offering a critical perspective on U.S. policy toward Syria, and fired Marc Lamont Hill for his comments regarding Palestinian-Israeli relations.[97] Such top-down displays of editorial intolerance have a chilling effect: Journalists become too concerned to ask the tough questions of people in powerful positions, report inconvenient facts, or give voice to people whose views do not comport with the reigning pro-corporate, advertiser-friendly view.

In an era where commercialism has achieved both ideological and cultural supremacy, news media increasingly depend upon fame and fortune to draw viewers' attention. Unless a natural disaster or a mass shooting occurs in a given area, the views and opinions of average Americans are usually absent from media. Journalists talk *about* them, but not *with* them. While there are always exceptions, stories of people from low-income neighborhoods and Native American communities are almost nonexistent in the entertainment world. The show *Roseanne* in the 1980s was one of the last sitcoms about working people, until it ended in 1997 and briefly returned in 2018. Currently, shows such as *It's Always Sunny in Philadelphia* are among the few that claim to be about working people, yet the program's main characters are bar owners—and while being a small business owner is hard work, it is also a status few working-class people actually attain.

America's commercial entertainment culture helped manufacture Trump's celebrity in the years prior to the 2016 elections, celebrity that helped Trump win the White House. *Rolling Stone* reporter Matt Taibbi has argued that prior to Trump's run for president, news media had already transformed into a series of institutions that sought spectacle over substance or facts. "I felt sure a collapse of belief in the efficacy of the news media," wrote Taibbi, "if it coincided with widespread (and justified) political discontent could lead in some pretty weird directions. One possible future was one in which politics 'stopped being about ideology and . . . instead turned into a problem of information.'"[98] As a journalist covering Trump's campaign, Taibbi found that reporters' obsession with spectacle and entertainment was so strong that they failed to accurately investigate Trump or hold him accountable to voters in meaningful ways. Donald Trump, says Taibbi, was the one who best understood that presidential campaigns are now just big television shows.[99] By treating Americans like an audience of spectators instead of engaged citizens, Trump has been able to manipulate a profound public vulnerability and deliver entertaining programming day after day. Digital technologies have just reinforced this ability. "Networks had long since abandoned their 'public interest' mandate and were financially dependent on anyone or anything that could revive their flagging ratings," says Taibbi. "They gave Trump as many hours as he could manage and . . . this part of Trump's rise really was the media's fault."[100]

Trump's visual power extended from his television celebrity in much the same way that Reagan's built on his Hollywood celebrity. While Reagan went a more traditional route, gaining political experience by rising through state and party ranks, Trump skipped right to the top, enabled by a captivated fourth estate he repeatedly co-opted and attacked. While the latter is an old Machiavellian tactic, it is arguable that Trump and his handlers were taking it to a new level. The same can be said for the ways they sowed discord that already existed among U.S. historical divides of race, gender, and class.

### Hyper-partisanship

Not only did both Trump and Clinton agree that the press was ineffective at informing voters, they also agreed that the press was too partisan. Partisanship refers to a political bias or preference. Trump had denounced CNN and the "failing *New York Times*" as "fake news" because he claimed that they were partial to the Democratic Party.[101] Clinton wrote that conservative news mogul Rupert Murdoch and former Fox CEO Roger Ailes "probably did more than anyone else to make all this possible. For years, Fox News has been the most powerful and prominent platform for the right-wing war on truth. Ailes, a former adviser to Richard Nixon, built Fox by demonizing and delegitimizing establishment media that tried to adhere to traditional standards of objectivity and accuracy."[102] Again, Trump and Clinton were both targeting a real problem, hyper-partisanship in the press, but focusing only on how it impacted their own ambitions, rather than its adverse effects on American society.

In addition to prioritizing entertainment-centered content, the ratings-driven focus of corporate media has engendered the polarization of differences between the two primary political parties. In this context, hyper-partisanship is not about actual policy differences, but about fostering a militant "us versus them" mentality in regard to competing candidates, issues, and ideas. For example, 48 percent of Alabama voters chose Roy Moore—accused by nine women of sexual misconduct—presumably because the prevailing hyper-partisan culture made the notion of supporting a suspect Republican more tolerable than supporting a Democrat.[103]

Reporter Steve Kornacki argues that by the 1990s, decades of political infighting had led to "tribalism" among party adherents.[104] The result was high-stakes showdowns between the parties, such as government shutdowns that led to an increasingly contentious partisan political culture. In fact, a 2014 Pew Research study, "Political Polarization in the American Public," revealed that "partisan antipathy is deeper and more extensive" than ever before.[105] Their survey of 10,000 people found that since the 1980s, liberals have been moving further left and conservatives further right. They found that "92 percent of Republicans are to the right of the median Democrat, and 94 percent of Democrats are to the left of the median Republican."[106] A 2016 Stanford University study confirmed that the partisan divide deepened quickly in the mid-1990s. Starting in the 1960s, people have generally believed that they may ultimately differ with members of the opposite party on policy, but they believed that they were similar to each other in terms of intellect and selfishness, a Stanford University study found. In the 1960s approximately 20 percent of those polled felt that members of opposing parties were more selfish. However, by 2008, that number more than doubled, with nearly 50 percent of both Democratic and Republican respondents believing that members of the opposite party were more selfish.[107] These outcomes are due in large part to the corporate propagation of increasingly partisan narratives, especially on cable outlets such as Fox News and MSNBC, and online operations such as *Breitbart News* and *Huffington Post*.

Further deregulation has allowed for hyper-partisanship to consume the U.S. news media. Neoconservatives, through the Republican Party, were the first to control a vast portion of an increasingly monopolized media landscape.[108] Starting in the 1970s, a group of billionaires, guided by the Powell Memo and operating under the guise of philanthropy, organized conferences to influence news media with conservative views.[109] The deregulation of media and waning faith in government provided an opportunity for wealthy conservatives to execute their plan through the purchase, creation, and operation of their own media outlets and platforms.[110]

Many of the conservative sympathizers focused on creating a media system to further their own self-interests. These include hedge fund billionaire Robert Mercer and his daughter Rebekah. They not only spent millions on campaigns for neoconservative candidates, they were huge backers of *Breitbart News*, one of the major so-called alt-right websites, managed by self-proclaimed propagandist Steve Bannon, until he became Trump's chief political strategist. (Bannon was later forced out of Trump's orbit, and *Breitbart* as well, and the Mercers looked to invest in other right-wing media outlets).

The neoconservatives have created an investment network that produces media content and studies that propagate their ideology. For example, David and Charles Koch—aka the Koch brothers—are invested in oil and have had seats on numerous boards of directors, including in Boston public broadcasting (WBGH), where they have used their influence to try to censor documentaries critical of their politics and actions. Charles Koch even ran for president in 1980.

Another key figure in this regard has been Richard Mellon Scaife, heir to the Mellon Bank and Gulf Oil fortunes, and a major funder of the right-wing American Enterprise Institute and Hoover Institute, in addition to being the fiscal sponsor of the *American Spectator*, which was paid to dig up dirt on then-president Bill Clinton that helped lead to his impeachment. Numerous other right-wing oligarchs have funded think tanks that produce conservative media content, including Harry and Lynde Bradley, the Midwesterners who were enriched by defense contracts; John M. Olin, in chemical and munitions companies, who funded the Heritage Foundation and other conservative think tanks; the Coors Brewing family which supported the American Legislative Exchange Council and the Heritage Foundation; and the DeVos family of Michigan, who are supporters of Donors Trust, a Koch conduit and a force behind the right-wing Media Research Center, among many similar institutions.[111]

As the public sector becomes more commercialized, business elites who fund and produce right-wing content have made their way from the private sector to the public sector. For example, Betsy DeVos is currently the Trump administration's secretary of the U.S. Department of Education, where she is a champion of privatized charter schools, and her brother, Erik Prince, is the former CEO of Blackwater, now Academi, which offers military contractors and militia—essentially mercenaries—to those who can afford their services.

Pro-corporate, neoconservative ideology has directly impacted U.S. culture through media. This can be seen in such phenomena as the popularity of Rush Limbaugh's national radio show in 1987 (the same year the Fairness Doctrine was revoked), which is credited with ushering in the explosion of neoconservative talk radio in the late 1980s and early 1990s, and the meteoric rise of Limbaugh himself.[112] In 1996 Fox News launched as a conservative news outlet with Roger Ailes, former media consultant to Richard Nixon and Ronald Reagan, running the newsroom. This was the same year that Bill Clinton's pro-corporate Telecommunications Act opened the way for a greater number of media outlets to be owned by fewer and fewer mega-corporations. As a result, by 2010, fully 91 percent of weekly radio programs had neoconservative leanings.[113] The hosts of these programs have cultivated the phrase "liberal media" into an epithet for dismissing coverage that challenges conservative views. Veteran journalist Helen Thomas has argued that in the years following the increased usage of the phrase as a pejorative, major news outlets asked fewer pointed questions, especially of conservative politicians, who could effectively "manage" the press due to the prevalence and repetition of attacks on the so-called "liberal media" coming from the right, especially from far-right radio shows like Limbaugh's.[114] As the fear of being seen to have a "liberal bias" developed, many journalists overcompensated and presented a nearly equal amount of negative coverage for all candidates.[115] The late newspaper columnist Molly Ivins explained why this approach was detrimental to the news industry:

> The very notion that on any given story all you have to do is report what both sides say and you've done a fine job of objective journalism debilitates the press. There is no such thing as objectivity, and the truth, that slippery little bugger, has the oddest habit of being way to hell off on one side or the other: it seldom nestles neatly halfway between any two opposing points of view. The smug complacency of much of the press—I have heard many an editor say, "Well, we're being attacked by both sides so we must be right"—stems from the curious notion that if you get a quote from someone on both sides, preferably in an official position, you've done the job. In the first place, most stories aren't two-sided, they're 17-sided at least. In the second place, it's of no help to either the readers or the truth to quote one side saying, "Cat," and the other side saying "Dog," while the truth is there's an elephant crashing around out there in the bushes. Getting up off your duff and going to find out for yourself is still the most useful thing a reporter can do.[116]

In fact, use of the phrase "liberal bias" as a trope has been increasing for decades. It spiked after September 11, 2001, and reached its highest point on record in 2016.[117] Negative reporting denounces all sides and views rather than offering nuanced defense and explanation of political positions and policies. According to scholars, such negative coverage, predominant since Watergate, inadvertently benefits Republicans, because "the media's persistent criticism of government reinforces the right wing's anti-government message."[118] By the 2018 midterm elections, the GOP, led by Trump, was almost entirely focused on negative campaigning and fearmongering, setting a tone that the news media seemed to follow while cashing in on readers' anxiety regarding another possible "civil war."

In response to their loss in the political communication battle, the Democratic Party (DNC) abandoned New Deal liberalism for corporatist policies and launched its own news outlets. In the 1990s, the Democratic Party became a solidly corporate-backed entity under Bill Clinton as it supported deregulation, privatization, and commercialization. The DNC shifted to policies that aligned with corporate interests, especially those of General Electric, Microsoft, and eventually Amazon, which controlled a Democratic Party version of Fox News with Microsoft-NBC, which became MSNBC, as well as the *Washington Post*.[119] The impact of increased critiques by Democrat-leaning news outlets in an already right-wing-saturated media landscape was intensification of hyper-partisan culture. As news outlets attacked one another and made every statement seem debatable along party lines, faith in the outlets' capacity to provide accurate fact-based reporting declined. In fact, according to one poll, by 2016 just a third of Americans had trust in the major news media.[120] As media became more partisan and less reliable in voters' minds, disinformation, opinions, propaganda, and hard facts became increasingly more difficult to tell apart.

Given the contentious political climate, people increasingly depend upon group affiliation to filter their intake of information and guide their decision-making. A

2018 study found that when people use social media such as Facebook, they judge a statement based on the partisan proclivity of its source, regardless of its validity.[121] The study illuminated how candidates and politicians can garner support for a policy based on party affiliation over and above the logic or facts behind that policy. As a result, a television game-show host—Donald Trump—was able to convert celebrity to political power and manipulate people's understanding of key events and debates through the use of hyper-partisan language, framing, and posturing. Trump's team further fueled this extreme divisiveness by stoking white people's anxieties and fears, marshaling them behind the alt-right slogan "Make America Great Again." Taking advantage of social media and the newly disjointed media landscape has been a core part of Team Trump's propaganda strategy.

### Fragmented media landscape

The rapid development of the internet, along with the proliferation of affordable mobile devices for consumers, has fragmented the traditional media landscape and has transformed how we engage politically and socially with information, news, and one another. In a very compressed window of time, Americans have migrated from print and broadcast media to internet-driven systems. A 2013 poll found that about 75 percent of people ages eighteen to twenty-nine gathered their news exclusively from the internet, the same age group that uses the internet the most, with the trend decreasing, if slightly, with age.[122] In the same poll, people over fifty reported receiving their news at a scheduled time every day, while millennials seem to "graze" for news throughout the day.

Despite this shift, a small number of major corporations dominate the majority of available online news sites, because such sites electronically post and aggregate articles from the six corporations that own 90 percent of media in the United States. While this is an ever-changing list with ongoing mergers and acquisitions, as of 2018 it included AT&T, Disney, Comcast, 21st Century Fox, Viacom, and CBS.[123] Unlike legacy media, today's internet-centered system allows people to search, gather, block, and customize their incoming news feeds, effectively constructing silos that confirm their reality.[124] Search engines and social media increasingly customize the information users view to reinforce rather than challenge their confirmation biases—the tendencies to interpret new information as validation of one's pre-existing beliefs and views.[125]

Scholars have remarked that this degree of confirmation bias has helped usher in a "post-truth" era. The term refers to a time where multiple facts and views coexist, populating a variety of different social and political narratives about what is and isn't happening, real, and important. In such conditions, the power of the scientific model to establish or refute what is real is greatly diminished. In fact, the Oxford Dictionary declared "post-truth" to be the word of the year for 2016.[126] It defined the term thus:

> (*adjective*) relating to or denoting circumstances in which objective facts are less influential in shaping public opinion than appeals to emotion and personal belief.[127]

It wasn't long after Trump's election that his legal counsel Kellyanne Conway began using terms like "alternative facts" to buttress the Trump team's self-created "post-truth" world.[128] In his book *Post-Truth*, Lee McIntyre says

that "post-truth amounts to a form of ideological supremacy, whereby its practitioners are trying to compel someone
to believe in something whether there is good evidence for
it or not."[129] Seen in this context, the fragmentation of the
media landscape and Americans' increasing reliance on social media and non-journalistic sources for information has
reinforced the ability of those in power to use and advance
"post-truth" conditions to serve their interests.

Corporations' algorithmic customization of consumer
preferences has contributed to people receiving information through online silos of confirmation bias, also called
filter bubbles, or echo chambers, by which they are immersed in a curated version of reality. Studies show that users prefer information that confirms rather than challenges
their beliefs.[130] George W. Bush's senior adviser Karl Rove
referred to such user groups as a "reality-based community."[131] If individuals self-identify as MAGA neoconservatives they'll likely go to *InfoWars*, *The Drudge Report*,
*Breitbart*, and Fox News for content that reinforces their
worldview.[132] These platforms often measure success by
how many times they can get users to click a link or share a
post through social media. The relentless quest for bigger
audiences and more online followers has incentivized the
platforms to offer hyper-partisan bias and ad hominem attacks to unprecedented extremes.

The rise and fall of legacy media's previous mono-
lithic influence has strengthened people's ability to curate
and inhabit political and social realities that validate their
emotions, biases, and views, irrespective of facts, evidence,
and arguments to the contrary.[133] These tendencies further
intensify social divisions, leading to contentious disagreements on issues such as race, women's rights, immigration,
climate change, and political candidates and parties. Those

involved in such disagreements seem to rarely interact with each other outside of social media barbs, trolling, and online flaming.

Corporations collect user data to manipulate people and demographic groups through the use of several tools: targeted advertising; bots, software programmed to pose as humans; trolls, provocateurs who seek to cause discord and trigger emotional reactions; and memes, which serve to reinforce users' perceptions with oversimplified imagery and slogans.[134] Shoshana Zuboff calls this "surveillance capitalism," and although Cambridge Analytica is perhaps the most notorious of these corporations, there are more, and they are joined by even larger interests, including the Democratic and Republican Parties. United States, Russia, Iran, North Korea, and China have all utilized user data in attempts to covertly manipulate people's behavior.[135] Theorists and technologists such as Renée DiResta consider these operations a form of "information war."

In the case of President Trump, his messages, tweets, interviews, and rallies have all supported self-serving political and social narratives whether or not such narratives comport with well-established facts, scientific studies, or even the conclusions of U.S. intelligence agencies. Trump's messages, when sent through social media platforms, instantly reach tens of millions of people. They are then re-messaged through supporting platforms such as *Breitbart*, where they reinforce supporters' biases. So, while Trump has fed cable news organizations a steady stream of commercially valuable content, he has also bypassed them and exploited the fragmented information landscape, using social media to reinforce views that further his interests and authority.

Trump's rise and post-truth presidency have been

made possible by the long-term impact of corporate influence on media, democracy, and public consciousness. As the United States became the most media-saturated society in history—increasingly dominated by corporate power, entranced by commercialism and celebrity, and fragmented by the internet and political polarization—institutions of education have struggled to keep up and to help cultivate not only a more critical and media-literate public, but a more civil and civic-minded one as well.

We are sending a generation of Americans into an ever-changing information system without the critical tools with which to navigate it. Not surprisingly, the next vulnerability is the public education system itself, which has been subjected to the same corporate influences described above, resulting in forms of pedagogy reminiscent of Taylorism, the late 19th-century style of quantitative management devised by mechanical engineer Frederick Winslow Taylor, which runs counter to creating a well-informed, critically thinking, civically engaged population.

### Ineffective educational system

The American education system is entrusted with providing people with the tools, experiences, and perspectives required to be equitable and empowered participants in a democratic society. Our education system was developed at a time when an agricultural society was transitioning into an industrial age. Today, we are transitioning from a stationary information society to a mobile one, where we are dependent upon technology and immersed in media. Upgrades in the information infrastructure now have worldwide impact, so much so that they can become subject to serious geopolitical struggle, as in the current case of Western societies' anxiety about Huawei's emerging dominance in wiring the world for 5G information networks, networks that advantage Communist China and its People's Liberation Army.[136] Such anxiety is rooted in the view that "in an age when the most powerful weapons, short of nuclear arms, are cyber-controlled, whichever country dominates 5G will gain an economic, intelligence, and military edge for much of this century."[137] The same holds true for an edge over the systems of information, media, and education that shape public consciousness, knowledge, and memory.

By the late 1990s, researchers were finding that average Americans spent twice as much time watching television as they did talking with family or spending time with their children. Most watched the equivalent of seventy days of television a year; 25 percent fell asleep to it, and 40 percent watched television while eating.[138] By 2015, the media statistics and ratings company Nielsen found that on average, Americans over the age of eighteen consumed some form of media eleven hours a day. This is sobering, considering that the average person is awake sixteen to eighteen hours a day.[139]

The dramatic transition to a media-centered society has not been accompanied by corresponding shifts in education. In 2016, nearly half of U.S. teenagers surveyed revealed that they are online constantly throughout the day.[140] However, they are not being taught how to manage the torrent of images and messages vying for their attention. In fact, according to a major Stanford study from 2016, less than 20 percent of middle school students can distinguish between a news report and a sponsored story. Less than one-third can identify the implicit bias in an article they are reading.[141] Youths' inability to determine fact from fiction is worsened by the online sharing culture that disseminates disinformation and false news stories through social media. In fact, a 2017 *Common Sense* study found that 31 percent of youths ages ten through eighteen admitted to sharing an article online in the previous six months that they later found out to be false.[142] The majority of people in the United States have yet to be educated on how to critically engage and discern the varieties of imagery, information, advertising, opinion, and propaganda that populate the infosphere in which we live.[143]

Most nations in Europe, Asia, and other parts of the world embraced media literacy education to their curriculum four decades ago, but not the United States. The massive transformation of U.S. education that was the No Child Left Behind Act did call for technological literacy by 2007. However, only five states test students on their technological literacy, and only nineteen states have technological literacy requirements in certifying new teachers.[144] One of NCLB's consultants turned critics, the former undersecretary of the Department of Education Diane Ravitch, claims that the No Child Left Behind Act was "hijacked" by partisan politicians and greedy corporations who turned "the standards movement into a testing movement."[145] Ravitch claims that the NCLB's focus on market demands resulted in a "dumbed-down" education for students.[146]

Although the market demands were not conducive to improved education, they were attractive to media corporations. The relatively limited media-oriented curricula that are offered in the United States are dominated by commercial corporations such as Microsoft, Sony, and Apple, whose materials reinforce the supremacy of corporate capitalism and commercial culture.[147] Ravitch argues that "going to school is not the same as going shopping. Parents should not be burdened with locating a suitable school for their child. They should be able to take their child to the neighborhood public school as a matter of course and expect that it has well-educated teachers and a sound educational program."[148] However, in U.S. corporate culture, students are shaped into customers, and teachers into customer service representatives. This has contributed to the current educational crisis we now face.

As a result of these policy shifts, the education system in the United States has shown itself to be ineffective at preparing students to become empowered and engaged citizens capable of advancing a democratic culture that prioritizes the public interest, cultural diversity, social justice, and the common good. In fact, the first generation growing up with the No Child Left Behind Act are the millennials, and fewer than one-third of them believe that living in a democracy is essential to their lives, compared to two-thirds of those born in the 1950s and 1960s, and three-fourths of people born in the 1930s, when fascism was storming the globe. This illustrates a staggering decline in civic literacy and engagement.[149]

Until educational reforms are enacted on a national level, we will continue to send students into a corporate-dominated information system without giving them the critical and creative skills needed to equitably participate, evaluate the bias and authenticity of sources, or protect themselves from surveillance and manipulation.[150] This has resulted in serious public vulnerabilities that have been—and will continue to be—exploited. It was within this commercially driven system of pervasive entertainment, hyper-partisanship, media fragmentation, and an ineffective education system that Trump was able to convince millions of Americans to vote him into office as commander in chief of the United States. "We won with the poorly educated," said Trump at one point. "We love the poorly educated."[151] As the signs of authoritarianism become increasingly evident, it's clear that we need to take action before conditions degenerate further.

# TWO

# BREAKING NEWS, BROKEN NEWS

"We've got our friends at CNN here. Welcome guys. It's great to have you. You guys love breaking news. And you did it. You broke it. Good work."
—Comedian Michelle Wolf, White House Correspondents' Association Dinner, 2018

On March 15, 2016, presidential candidate Senator Bernie Sanders walked onto a stage in Phoenix, Arizona. It had been a rough night. He had lost four of the five Democratic Party primary elections that had been held earlier that day. Despite the setback, Sanders was still firmly in the race, energizing young people and well within a mathematical possibility of victory. As he spoke, Sanders declared that he was running for president in order to address wealth inequality, health care, education, racism, the war on drugs, and much more. Unfortunately, if you were not in that Arizona crowd, chances are you missed what Sanders had to say. The corporate media had sent their camera teams, but aired nothing from the event. While Sanders was speaking, the big news channels were providing a live broadcast of an empty podium in Palm Beach, Florida, the one from which Donald Trump would eventually give a victory speech.[152]

Trump has rarely disappointed the press, and always seems to provide the provocation and controversy needed for attracting attention. His 2016 campaign both offended and energized people, but like the corporate media, it rarely informed them. His combination of celebrity and unpredictable behavior delivered audiences' attention for media corporations to harvest and sell to advertisers. As the big news channels waited for Trump to appear, pundits discussed and predicted what Trump might say when he took the stage. The episode summed up the corporate press coverage in a nutshell—ignoring specific policies of one candidate to engage in trivial conjecture about another: Trump. During the 2016 presidential campaign, the corporate press discussed, analyzed, and explained everything Trump did in lavish detail, while neglecting or selectively covering everyone else. Trump's team knew this and exploited it to the hilt.

During the campaign, the press failed to adequately investigate or explore issues in a substantive manner. Instead, it treated the run for the White House more like a game show. The Shorenstein Center on Media, Politics and Public Policy reported that only 11 percent of media coverage focused on candidates' policy positions, leadership abilities, or personal and professional histories.[153] Trump's campaign strategy and subsequent presidency has depended, in part, upon exploiting the superficiality of commercial media coverage.

Early on, Trump's team and the corporate media seemed to forge an uneasy yet symbiotic dynamic of mutual self-interest and codependency. The media cashed in by spotlighting his provocations and scandalous conduct, and the Trump team attracted more followers and power as a result of the increased coverage and exposure. In fact, research showed that the disparity in coverage between Trump and his opponents was a major factor in his winning the White House.[154]

## STYLE TRUMPING SUBSTANCE

"We [reporters] all sit there because we know the first time we bark is the last time we do the show," explained MSNBC's host of *Meet the Press*, Chuck Todd. "There's something where all of a sudden nobody will come on your show."[155] Todd's candid comment revealed the conflict of interest that renders the corporate press vulnerable to figures like Trump. His response to questions about why he does not ask tough questions to the guests who come on his widely viewed program was that if he did so, the powerful and famous guests would likely stop appearing on his show, and without those guests he'd be out of a job.

The economic model of corporate news media increasingly privileges access to celebrity and power over journalistic ethics or investigative reporting. The Society of Professional Journalists' code of ethics established four principles as "the foundation of ethical journalism and encourages their use in its practice by all people in all media."[156] Reporters should seek truth and report it; minimize harm; act independently; and be accountable and transparent. Many of those working in the corporate press appear to disregard this code, favoring profit-making opportunities that are more likely to abound when these ethical provisions are disregarded.

The business of commercial media is to attract, harvest, and sell people's consciousness to advertisers. Corporations seek to keep people interacting with screens and their personal audio assistants as a way to collect and commodify their attention and data.[157] Those seeking success in the industry need to provide the click-bait of headlines, video, and commentary that will draw that attention. Content about wealthy celebrities tends to grab people's attention more than content about good governance, public policy, social problems, or the common good. As a result, media workers rely on maintaining positive relationships with politicians and celebrities, who then tend to be not only the topics of their stories, but their sources, too.

This cozy, co-dependent relationship between the press and politicos is displayed annually at the White House Correspondents Dinner, an event Ronald Reagan once called the press's "spring prom," where journalists schmooze with the politicians that they are supposed to be keeping in check. The event is rife with ethical conflicts of interest concerning journalistic standards. The *New York Times* forbids its employees from attending; in 2011, the paper's Washington bureau chief explained the prohibition by saying, "It just feels like it sends the wrong signal to our readers and viewers, like we are all in it together and it is all a game."[158] That Donald Trump did not attend the annual dinner is not an indication that he agrees with the *Times*, but rather a display of his administration's militant intolerance of criticism.[159] The event features celebrities and comedians who satirize and mock the president and other politicians to entertain the press, who are supposed to be investigating the political class rather than dining with them.

Even after his failed government shutdown dragged his approval rating down into the 30th percentile in early 2019, focusing on Trump still delivered the goods for commercial media. Where other candidates usually begin a presidential bid with a record of public service and perhaps minor media profile, Trump came with no record of public service but decades of experience as a self-branding tabloid celebrity, similar to Paris Hilton or the Kardashians. He had had onscreen roles in *World Wrestling Entertainment*, *The Little Rascals* movie, and (in a non-sexual cameo) a soft-core pornography video produced by *Playboy*.[160]

Trump spent over a decade as the central character on the television game show *The Apprentice*, where he was cast as a savvy, tough-talking businessman who eliminated contestants by yelling, "You're fired!"[161] The show helped him garner a national media profile and provided free branding for all things Trump. The show uncritically portrayed Trump as a wealthy businessman and successful leader, overlooking his numerous bankruptcies, business failures, and history of corruption.[162]

"The entire premise of *The Apprentice*," wrote Patrick Radden Keefe in *The New Yorker*, was "something of a con."[163] According to two of the show's producers, Steve Braun and Bill Pruitt, "*The Apprentice* portrayed Trump not as a skeezy hustler who huddles with local mobsters but as a plutocrat with impeccable business instincts and unparalleled wealth—a titan who always seemed to be climbing out of helicopters or into limousines."[164] "Most of us knew he was a fake," Braun told *The New Yorker*.[165] "He had just gone through I don't know how many bankruptcies. But we made him out to be the most important person in the world. It was like making the court jester the king."[166] Bill Pruitt, another producer of *The Apprentice*, recalled, "We walked through the offices and saw chipped furniture. We saw a crumbling empire at every turn. Our job was to make it seem otherwise."[167]

After eight years of the relatively well-behaved Barack

Obama, Trump's game-show glitz, even though super-ficial, gave him a commercial advantage over his rivals. Former CBS anchorman Dan Rather rightly warned in the summer of 2016 that the news media were over-covering Trump for all the wrong reasons. "What I worry about," said Rather on CNN's *Reliable Sources*, "is [that], in a way, the media is a political partner, a business partner of Donald Trump. . . . The media wants the ratings," he went on. "Trump delivers the ratings. In a way, they're business partners."[168]

Trump was so good at boosting ratings that the corporate media have increasingly depended on him for their content. During a twenty-four-hour news cycle, a certain story about Trump was broadcast nearly sixty times on Fox, MSNBC, and CNN.[169] A study from the Shorenstein Center on Media, Politics and Public Policy study found that the disparity in coverage was a boost to Trump in the polls because increased news coverage serves to normalize the legitimacy of a candidate and their agenda.[170]

Trump has provided great commercial content for media, and everywhere he goes he seems to draw the spotlight, which he uses to advance his interests at that moment. His bombast, hype, lies, and aggression have continuously dominated news media's daily offerings for years. During the 2016 election, this drew attention away from other candidates and issues of substance. In the process, Trump perpetually avoided explaining how, if at all, he would govern. Instead of investigating the absence of substance regarding his proposed policy plans, the media turned to matters of style. After Trump won the New York State Republican primary, for example, much of the corporate media engaged in days of pundit-led discussions about how Trump suddenly appeared more "presidential."[171]

News analysts filled airtime breaking down Trump's victory speech, discussing his word choice and body language. The *Washington Post* ran an article by Amber Phillips with the headline, "Donald Trump goes for a more presidential tone—for now."[172] "Here's a look at the new Trump," wrote Phillips. "After the race was called, Trump high-fived a supporter, thanked his family, took a shot at the press and then put both hands on the podium and proceeded to give a much more traditional politician-y speech. Jobs in America. A strong military. Get rid of Obamacare. Make America great again. He used a lot of verbs and all but dropped his usual flourish of adjectives."[173] The endless free coverage, even when superficial, only served to reinforce and further his campaign.

The mass amount of Trump coverage was due in part to his ability to provide a kind of entertainment similar to what he offered as a game-show host. Part of the draw has involved Trump's use of insinuation, insults, and belittlement to disparage critics and rivals. For example, he repeatedly called his political rival Senator Ted Cruz "Lyin' Ted," Senator Marco Rubio a "lightweight choker," former Florida governor Jeb Bush "low energy Jeb," and Hillary Clinton "Crooked Hillary."[174] Likewise, he claimed Senator John McCain was a "loser" because he lost the 2008 presidential election, and that he was not a "war hero" because he had been captured while serving in Vietnam.[175] In addition, Trump engaged in "The Wife Feud," in which he threatened to "spill the beans" on Cruz's wife and later tweeted images of his wife next to Cruz's wife, comparing them.[176]

Trump's constant use of ad hominem attacks has attracted supporters who are angry with "the Establishment." Many also find humor in Trump's ridicule, thus reinforcing his top-down culture of intolerance. Trump's name-calling and insults have provided red meat to the corporate media. In most cases, media re-message Trump's attacks and then scramble to get a comment from those he has targeted. Such antics have spread to other candidates as well. Case in point, during the Republican primary, presidential candidate Marco Rubio—whom Trump had been belittling as "Little Marco"—insulted the size of Trump's hands, insinuating that other parts of Trump's body were small, too. Trump took the bait and responded to "Little Marco" at rallies and during debates. "I guarantee you," said Trump, "there's no problem."[177]

His attacks have contributed to a polarized hyper-partisan culture with potentially deadly results. While there is no shortage of mudslinging in the history of U.S. politics, Trump employs disparaging remarks for his opponents as a matter of course. A sampling of these include calling Senator Diane Feinstein (D-CA) "wacko," Representative Maxine Waters "an extraordinarily low IQ person," Senator Sanders "crazy Bernie," Senator Elizabeth Warren "Pocahontas," and former vice president Joe Biden "one percent Biden."[178] He has also made gross verbal attacks on the Democratic Party, calling them an "angry mob," "treasonous," and "un-American."[179] In addition to name-calling, he has promoted aggressive action against his opponents at rallies, with crowd chants such as "lock her up" referring to rival Hillary Clinton, as well as to Senator Diane Feinstein during the Supreme Court confirmation hearings for Bret Kavanaugh.[180]

As entertaining as the corporate press may find Trump's debasing rhetoric, the content does come with consequences. In 2018, these took the form of fourteen bombs sent to Trump critics such as former president Barack Obama, former secretary of state Hillary Clinton, former vice president Joe Biden, Representative Maxine Waters, Senator Cory Booker, Senator Kamala Harris, former CIA director John Brennan, former director of National Intelligence James Clapper, and the offices of CNN.[181]

The explosives had been constructed and mailed by Cesar Sayoc, a registered Republican. Sayoc had been living in a van in Florida, accumulating a list of these and 100 other targets.[182] He found relief in Trump's rhetoric as he faced economic hardship after his career as an exotic dancer came to an end.[183] The fifty-six-year-old known racist had been inspired by Trump's bombastic rhetoric against ideological opponents and "the Establishment." Sayoc's social media posts included images of himself in Trump's "Make America Great Again" hat; derisive remarks about Muslims; unsubstantiated conspiracy theories about Trump's political opponents, the Clintons; and threats to Trump's favorite spittoon, CNN.[184]

As outlandish as Trump's rhetoric has been, media outlets have been responsible not only for refusing to challenge it, but for amplifying it. They've been happy to act as megaphone for his self-promotional bluster, lies, and derision as long as the revenue and audience kept growing. In fact, Trump's sophomoric level of male banter dominated the news at ABC, CNN, CBS, and NBC, received coverage from *Time*, *Variety*, and, of course, was circulated all across the internet. Some of the headlines read "Donald Trump Defends Size of His Penis," "Trump Defends Making His Manhood a Big Issue," and "The History Behind the Donald Trump 'Small Hands' Insult."[185] In the midst of these tabloid-level distractions, the policies and fitness of the candidates, as well as more newsworthy stories, went chronically under-reported and under-discussed.[186]

Furthermore, as the media drew larger audiences by covering Trump's antics, this served to augment rather than undermine the impact of his claims. More important, it kept him in the center of the media spotlight.

Even Trump's intolerance of criticism—particularly from journalists—has garnered coverage and increased his exposure. Trump's verbal attacks on media in general, and on specific networks and journalists in particular, have pressured reporters to discuss the incidents on their shows and to appear as guests on their network's other programs. Trump's dispute with Megyn Kelly, the host of Fox News's *The Kelly File*, epitomized Trump's ability to dominate and manipulate the news cycle. In August 2015, Kelly moderated a Republican primary debate and questioned Trump about misogynistic comments in which he referred to women as "fat pigs," "dogs," "slobs," and "disgusting animals."[187] Rather than answering the question, Trump became combative.

After the debate, reporters sought to get commentary on the exchange between Kelly and Trump. In response, Trump stated that during the debate "[t]here was blood coming out of her eyes, blood coming out of her wherever."[188] The comment drew days of analysis and outrage from commentators. However, the discussion shifted to Kelly's subsequent announcement that she would be taking a vacation.[189] In short, Trump had successfully redirected media attention with his combative posturing, and avoided being held ethically or politically accountable for his misogynistic attacks.

Trump has found a unique ability to control the focus of the media from the palm of his hand. With a direct feed to more than 58 million followers, Twitter has been a core part of Trump's ability to manipulate news and influence the public.[190] Trump uses social media to bypass legacy media, and does so to publish propaganda that targets enemies, rivals, critics, allies, his staff, and foreign leaders.[191] "The FAKE MSM is working so hard trying to get me not to use Social Media," tweeted Trump on June 6, 2017. "They hate that I can get the honest and unfiltered message out."[192]

Historically, political leaders have consolidated their power through whatever means of communication were available at the time. For example, Franklin Roosevelt built his New Deal coalition in part through "fireside chats," radio broadcasts that reached millions of Americans during the Great Depression.[193] Adolf Hitler and the Nazis produced documentary films, such as Leni Riefenstahl's *Triumph of the Will*, to propagate their romanticized view of German history and fascist ideology.[194] Twitter has given Trump the power to broadcast and repeat political messages and propaganda to tens of millions of people, thereby creating and reinforcing his own self-serving narratives. Even though nearly 70 percent of registered voters in a Morning Consult Survey agreed that Trump uses Twitter too often, this has not diminished his impact.[195]

The increasing social migration from legacy media to mobile communications, the instantaneity of digital technology, and the overall level of public pessimism concerning broadcast media in the United States, have all helped Trump to weaponize Twitter as a platform through which he has focused his power to undermine anyone or anything that gets in the way. He has effectively used Twitter to both bypass and manipulate the traditional role of journalism, giving him enormous advantage in message control. As a result, at times the media have become so dependent on Trump's tweets for content that during the brief periods when he goes silent, the absence of presidential tweets itself has become a subject of discussion, proving yet again that he is a master of distraction. As scholar Noam Chomsky astutely summarized:

> In fact, what's going on in the United States . . . is like a two-level wrecking ball. . . . Trump's role is to ensure that the media and public attention are always concentrated on him. . . . He's a con man basically, a showman, and in order to maintain public attention you have to do something crazy, [or] nobody is going to pay attention . . . so every day there is one insane thing after another . . . make some crazy lie . . . meanwhile he's on to something else. And while this show is going in public, in the background, the wrecking crew is working. Paul Ryan, Mitch McConnell, the guys in the cabinet writing executive orders. . . . What they are doing is systematically dismantling every aspect of government that works for the benefit of the population. . . . All efforts are being devoted, kind of almost with fanaticism, to enrich and empower their actual constituency, which is super wealth and corporate power, who are delighted.[196]

## PERFORMANCE ARTIST PRESIDENT

The outcome of the 2016 presidential election was due in large part to Trump's successful exploitation of public vulnerabilities to distraction and manipulation, and his ability to capture the dominant share of media coverage. After winning the White House, Trump did not tone things down. Instead, he remained in an aggressive campaign mode, utilizing the same media tactics, provocations, false assertions, attacks, deflections, and denials.

As president, Trump has continued to do everything possible to maximize media coverage and shape political narratives to his advantage. He has regularly engaged in escalatory name calling, even to the point of threatening a nuclear conflict, as when he called North Korean leader Kim Jong Un "Little Rocket Man" and "a madman,"[197] and said that if the United States were forced "to defend itself or its allies, we will have no choice but to totally destroy North Korea."[198]

Nearly a year after the 2016 election, Trump was still belittling Hillary Clinton, noting, "I was recently asked if Crooked Hillary Clinton is going to run in 2020. My answer was, 'I hope so!'"[199] He then claimed, without evidence, that former FBI director James Comey was a Clinton supporter, who "totally protected" her in the FBI's investigation into her stolen and leaked emails.[200] Similarly, as president, Trump has continued to attack Barack Obama, falsely claiming that Obama and other previous presidents did not call the parents of soldiers killed in battle.[201] Additionally, after Senator John McCain had criticized Trump's "half-baked, spurious nationalism," the president threatened McCain by saying he had better be careful "because at some point I fight back. I'm being very nice. I'm being very, very nice. But at some point I fight back, and it won't be pretty."[202]

As president, Trump has continued to incite feuds that corporate media appear eager to cover. In October 2017, Senator Bob Corker (R-TN) argued that Trump's legacy will be the "debasement of our nation."[203] Trump responded via Twitter that Corker had "begged" Trump to campaign for him, but the senator had dropped out of the race in Tennessee when Trump refused to endorse him, and that since then, Corker had been "only negative on anything Trump."[204] Corker responded, "It's a shame the White House has become an adult day care center. Someone obviously missed their shift this morning."[205]

During that same time, Trump had a war of words with Senator Jeff Flake (R-AZ). On October 24, 2017, CNN and MSNBC covered the quarrels for nearly five and a half hours, while Fox News covered it for just over an hour and a half.[206] Feeling his back against the wall as the result of the Democrats winning control of the House in the 2018 midterm elections, Trump repeatedly threatened to retaliate and be "warlike" if his rivals used their new powers to investigate him.

Trump's jabs at the media have gone from entertainment fodder to a legitimate threat to the First Amendment. Jim Acosta of CNN was among the first journalists to be labeled "fake news" by Trump just prior to his inauguration.[207] Since then, President Trump has attacked all of CNN as "fake news," and even posted a doctored video from a World Wrestling Entertainment event in which Trump is depicted as beating up an individual with a CNN logo over their head.[208] As Matthew Yglesias of *Vox* noted, "broadly speaking, both Trump and CNN enjoy the narrative that Trump is at war with CNN."[209] Indeed, the benefits of the war are little different from public spats between recording artists like Nicki Minaj and Cardi B.[210] For Trump, such feuding generates news when there is none, and serves the propaganda effect of reinforcing his alt-right, anti-establishment persona.

In 2018, CNN found out the hard way that the revenue it garnered from its nonstop Trump coverage came at a high price. After the midterm elections, Trump tried to explain away the more than thirty seats the GOP lost in the House of Representatives.[211] An ensuing episode at a press conference with CNN's Jim Acosta seemed like a good distraction from that humiliating loss. When Acosta began asking Trump about Special Counsel Robert Mueller's investigation into possible election meddling involving his campaign, Trump replied, "That's enough. . . . I tell you what, CNN should be ashamed of itself having you working for them. You are a rude, terrible person. You shouldn't be working for CNN."[212] A few hours after the incident, Acosta tweeted that his White House media pass had been revoked.[213]

Trump did not let the controversy end there. Instead, he continued it by propagating disinformation that many considered to be a diversion from the humiliating GOP electoral loss in the 2018 midterms and the inescapable impact of Mueller's work. Shortly after Acosta was chided by Trump at the press conference, an altered video appeared in which Acosta was allegedly "assaulting" a White House intern. The clip, sourced from Paul Joseph Watson of Alex Jones's *InfoWars*, spread quickly through right-wing websites.[214]

Soon after its release, the actual video of the incident made it clear that the clip published by the White House to justify revoking Acosta's press pass had been doctored.[215] This attack on a major media outlet's First Amendment rights was a historic moment, echoing the hostility of the Nixon years. CNN immediately sued the White House.[216] After considerable pressure, Acosta's credentials were restored, but the White House then released new restrictive rules about the behavior of journalists at press conferences.[217]

Trump's mastery of disinformation, propaganda, and

public manipulation has shown no signs of translating to effective governing. None of his P.T. Barnum–like behavior has helped him to deliver on his marquee promises such as the destruction of the Affordable Care Act or the construction of "a big, beautiful wall" along the U.S.-Mexico border.[218]

Trump has responded to his legislative failures by signing executive orders so as to at least appear to be delivering on some of his campaign promises. Most of his orders have been strictly symbolic.[219] Nonetheless, such gestures have been part of an effective media strategy. Trump often stages press conferences in the Oval Office to publicize the signing of such orders as a way to snub his opponents and energize his supporters. For example, his decertification of the Iran Deal, which he referred to on the campaign trail as "the worst deal ever," did not actually terminate the deal. Instead, it forced Congress to either allow the deal to go into effect or pass sanctions.[220] Similarly, his attempt to use an executive order to gut the Affordable Care Act did not immediately take effect because it faced immediate legal challenges.[221] Since its time in power, Trump's team has worsened the federal government's level of dysfunction, despite its campaign pledges that it would fix a broken system. Trump's once-upon-a-time promise to "drain the swamp" has become a distant memory, a mere pipe dream, especially as a growing number of people from his campaign and inner circle face criminal prosecutions and prison time.

## SLY FOX: BREAKING NEWS OR BROKEN NEWS?

Following Trump's election, much of the corporate media has reinforced the polarization and hyper-partisanship stoked during the campaign. With few exceptions, corporate media have continued to fixate on Trump, repeat his messages, and in some cases, openly serve as instruments of government propaganda, as has been the case with Fox News.[222] While some may criticize CNN for letting Trump's Twitter feed dictate the daily headlines and dominate national discourse, the network's journalistic laziness pales in comparison to the busybody "talent" at Fox News that was outright promoting GOP candidates, shattering any illusion that there was an ethical need for a separation between media, political parties, and the state.

On one occasion, Trump had invited Fox News hosts Sean Hannity and Jeanine Pirro to join him to stump for fellow Republicans at a GOP midterm rally in Cape Girardeau, Missouri. Hours before walking onstage and giving the president a big hug, Hannity had said he would not participate in any political rallies with the president. "To be clear," Hannity tweeted, "I will not be on stage campaigning with the president."[223]

Ironically, the first thing Hannity did after joining Trump onstage was verbally attack members of the press assembled in the back of the hall. Mr. Hannity was clearly unaware that among those he was disparaging as "fake news" were his colleagues from Fox. The incident was such an obvious violation of basic journalistic standards and professional ethics that executives from Fox felt compelled to make a rare public comment. "Fox News does not condone talent participating in campaign events," it said, before referring vaguely to "an unfortunate distraction" that had "been addressed."[224] "I'm not hiding the fact that I want Donald Trump to be the next president of the United States," Hannity had told the *New York Times* in August 2016, adding, "I never claimed to be a journalist."[225]

While it may be true that Hannity's "talent" program is not journalism, it was a lie when executives from the Fox corporation asserted that the business "does not condone" its employees' "participating in campaign events." In fact, evidence shows that that such employees have even received hundreds of thousands of dollars to do just that. "Fox News personalities regularly appear at events for candidates and political parties and sometimes get paid to do them," reported Eric Hannoki in *Salon* in December 2018.[226] "Fox News personalities Lou Dobbs, Sebastian Gorka, Greg Gutfeld, and Pete Hegseth have received money to headline fundraising events. Media Matters recently documented more than $200,000 in speaking fees that Pirro has received from 13 Republican organizations in the past two years."[227]

Corporations producing commercial propaganda operations in the form of "talent" programming disguised as news should be of grave concern to all who believe that the U.S. public should be protected from being manipulated by such forces. Efforts to covertly control the public mind—and thus politics—should be exposed, studied, and abolished. To do anything less would be complicity in what the late political economist Edward Herman and linguist Noam Chomsky have identified as the "manufacture of consent" and the production of "necessary illusions" that propagate "thought control in democratic societies."[228]

It should be of further concern that the 2019 U.S. National Intelligence Strategy declares that "the ability of individuals and groups to have a larger impact than ever before—politically, militarily, economically, and ideologically—is undermining traditional institutions."[229] In light of such declarations, and the history of counterintelligence operations targeting whistleblowers, protesters, community organizers, and movement leaders, it is not unreasonable to expect that ordinary Americans will be subject to more surveillance, disinformation, and propaganda of all types. We need an independent, noncommercial information system—one that includes more education in media and more critical media literacy in classrooms—to counter these forces and help the public have more, not less, impact.

# THREE

# THE TRUTH IS THE GREATEST ENEMY OF THE STATE

"If you tell a lie big enough and keep repeating it, people will eventually come to believe it. The lie can be maintained only for such time as the State can shield the people from the political, economic and/or military consequences of the lie. It thus becomes vitally important for the State to use all of its powers to repress dissent, for the truth is the mortal enemy of the lie, and thus by extension, the truth is the greatest enemy of the State."
—Joseph Goebbels, Reich Minister of Propaganda for Nazi Germany from 1933 to 1945

"Just as I promised the American people from this podium eleven months ago, we enacted the biggest tax cuts and reforms in American history," pronounced Donald Trump at his first State of the Union Address in January 2018. The reaction from those gathered was all too typical of partisan Washington, thunderous applause from members of the president's party and stone-faced silence from those in the opposing party. The partisan display distracted from the content of Trump's false statement. In terms of the biggest tax cuts in U.S. history, Trump's ranked fourth among those since 1940, and seventh of all time.[230]

Trump continued to unload a litany of falsehoods during his address. He claimed that his administration had created 2.4 million new jobs since the 2016 election, when half a million of those were actually created under Obama. Trump then said that wages were "finally" increasing, but they had been on the rise since the 1990s. He denounced automobile companies for not building car plants in the United States "for decades." However, two plants were announced and others had been expanded in the nine years prior to his speech. He then claimed that the Diversity Immigrant Visa Program "hands out green cards without any regard for skill . . . or the safety of the American people," ignoring the fact that the program involved requirements for education and work status as well as a background check. He then claimed that "America has also finally turned the page on decades of unfair trade deals," but the trade deficit had only grown deeper under his presidency. Finally, he claimed that his presidency had restored U.S. "standing abroad." In reality, a Gallup poll that month found that the "approval of U.S. leadership across 134 countries and areas stands at a new low."[231]

Trump's empty boasts were among countless other acts of disinformation he has propagated. By May 2019, a team at the *Washington Post* tallied more than 10,000 false or misleading statements made by President Trump since assuming office.[232] Among the most often repeated claims were that the Mueller investigation was a "hoax" and that Speaker Nancy Pelosi (D-CA) "doesn't mind human trafficking." In fact, the special counsel has revealed significant criminal activity among members of Trump's inner circle and by Russian individuals and entities.[233] There is no basis whatsoever to the claim that Speaker Nancy Pelosi has any tolerance for human trafficking.[234]

Trump's penchant for spreading specious statements was not confined to the United States, but shared abroad. For example, when he met with Canada's Prime Minister Justin Trudeau in 2018, Trump argued with him about the trade statistics between their two nations. At one point, according to Trump, Trudeau claimed, "No, no, we have no trade deficit with you, we have none." Trump immediately shot back, "Wrong, Justin, you do." However, Trump admitted at a fundraising speech in St. Louis that when he made the comment to Trudeau, "I didn't even know [if we had a trade deficit]. . . . I had no idea. I just said, 'You're wrong.'"[235]

Despite the easily disprovable nature of Trump's statements, his supporters continue to believe he has a monopoly on truth. In fact, a 2018 poll found that 91 percent of his followers view Trump as their most accurate source of news and information.[236] The frequency of Trump's lies, and the utter impunity with which he has been able to emit them, have served to normalize the authoritarian climate surrounding his presidency.

In a post-truth era, the quality of statements is measured by how many people believe they are true, not if they are actually true. In many ways, the Trump administration represents a post-truth presidency, in which a constant stream of official disinformation attempts to establish political supremacy over critics, investigators, journalists, and anyone who does not, in the administration's view, behave loyally.

## ALT-RIGHT BUDDIES

Days after his first State of the Union address, Trump could not stop thinking about his performance. He picked up his digital device to engage in his favorite mode of communication: Twitter. His fingers pounded away so he could transmit a critical message: "State of the Union speech. 45.6 million people watched, the highest number in history." In fact, in comparison to Trump, the previous three presidents all had higher ratings for their State of the Union speech.[237] His easily disprovable claim was quickly rebuked and mocked by the press. A CNN headline read, "Donald Trump lied about his State of the Union ratings. Whyyyyyyyy?"[238] A *Huffington Post* headline: "Trump Just Falsely Claimed He Had a Historically Huge Audience. Again."[239]

However, in their comedic corrections the press seemed oblivious to the strategy behind his tweet. From his candidacy into his presidency, Trump's self-promoting propaganda has also served to confirm his supporters' perceptions of him. Contradiction of his messages by common sense or facts has not diluted their impact. For the millions of people who continue to support him, Trump represents an authoritative view of what's wrong and how things need to be fixed. His constructed persona, political narratives, and propaganda have made it appear to them that he has delivered on his promises. The normalization of constant fabrications from the president of the United States continues to be the defining element of our current post-truth political condition.

Trump's messages have sought to confirm the views and biases of his largest base of supporters, the so-called alt-right. The Southern Poverty Law Center defines the alt-right as "a set of far-right ideologies, groups, and individuals whose core belief is that 'white identity' is under attack by multicultural forces using 'political correctness' and 'social justice' to undermine white people and 'their civilization.'"[240] MSNBC host Chris Mathews has referred to the alt-right as "a group of white nationalists." Alexander Zaitchik's 2016 study of the alt-right, *The Gilded Rage: A Wild Ride Through Donald Trump's America*, disagrees with Mathews, arguing that the alt-right consists of generally decent people who have rarely demonstrated a commitment to racism or authoritarianism. However, they have openly displayed sexism toward Hillary Clinton.[241] Mike Wendling's *Alt-Right* was an extensive study of right-wing chat room logs, blogs, videos, websites, and interviews. He concluded that the individuals in the alt-right were products of the internet in both the way they communicate and the news they consume.[242] He further noted that the alt-right has no dominant ideology, but shares an opposition to feminism, radical Islam, and ethnic minorities; anxiety about diversity of race, sexuality, and gender; and in many cases an engagement with Nazi imagery and "humor."[243]

Other researchers have argued that many in the alt-right have experienced real suffering and anxiety that was being ignored by the Democrats. Arlie Hochschild's book *Strangers in Their Own Land* analyzes voters in the districts Trump won during the five years prior to the 2016 election. Hochschild argues that these voters represent "The Great Paradox" of contemporary political ideology. They need government protection more than other citizens, but they vote against the government policies that would help them, including protecting small businesses, preserving family values, and preventing adverse impacts from climate change.[244]

This is not the same as Thomas Frank's iconic *What's*

*the Matter with Kansas*, which focused on anti-elitist right-leaning Americans voting against their own economic self-interests.[245] Prior to Trump's candidacy, "alt-right" culture had been seeping into corporate media through the influence of movements like the Tea Party, web operations such as *Breitbart*, and public figures including Richard Bertrand Spencer, Alex Jones, Ann Coulter, Milo Yiannopoulos, and Tomi Lahren.[246] The internet has enabled alt-right adherents to construct silos of reality where they can communicate and confirm their beliefs while blocking and mocking critics and evidence countering their views.

Yochai Benkler, Robert Faris, and Hal Roberts's 2018 work, *Network Propaganda*, studied the media ecosystem in the United States from 2015 through Trump's first year in office. Their data revealed that right-leaning news consumers tended to believe fake news more than centrist or left-leaning voters. They explained that the right tends to accept falsehood for truth because "on the right is a dynamic that rewards [the stories] that protect the team, reinforce its beliefs, attack opponents, and refute any claims that might have threatened 'our' team from outsiders."[247] Their study suggests that we do not yet live in a fully polarized society:

> Instead, both pre- and post-election, a substantial portion of Republicans and self-identified conservatives occupied a self-reinforcing bubble, while Democrats and independents occupied a media sphere anchored by more traditional media outlets that continue to practice the norms of objective journalism, surrounded by more partisan net native outlets, many of which also adhere to truth-seeking norms rather than purely partisan advantage.[248]

Some of the so-called alt-right's unsubstantiated or outright false claims: Political leftists have falsified crime statistics to hamstring police and incite riots; a genocide of white people is looming; immigration is part of a plan to undermine the stability of white society; "Jews" control the global financial system and media and manipulate them at the expense of Christian institutions; Black Lives Matter is a terrorist organization; men are the most oppressed gender; the Democratic Party runs a massive and secret pedophile ring.[249]

Members of the alt-right not only believe these claims, they often act upon them. For example, on December 4, 2016, Edgar Maddison Welch stocked three guns in his car and drove six hours to Washington, D.C., to shoot up a Comet Ping Pong pizza restaurant there. Maddison committed the act after being influenced by false stories linking Hillary Clinton to an alleged child-sex-trafficking ring run from the restaurant.[250]

Welch was not an outlier. In fact, 46 percent of Trump voters believed that leaked Democratic Party emails specifically confirmed "human trafficking," "Pizza Gate," and "pedophilia." However, none of those terms, nor the purported scandal, was ever mentioned in the emails.[251] During his presidency, a loyal Trump supporter, Cesar Sayoc, mailed pipe bombs to a list of people and organizations known to have public disagreement with Trump: President Barack Obama, former secretary of state Hillary Clinton, former vice president Joe Biden, Representative Maxine Waters, Senator Cory Booker, Senator Kamala Harris, former CIA director John Brennan, former director of National Intelligence James Clapper, and CNN.[252] No one was hurt by the bombs, but all should be concerned about the way the combination of fake news,

Trump supporters' "loyalty," and the president's aggression toward critics can lead to acts of violence.

Trump and his advisers preyed upon the alt-right's antipathy for government, promising to "drain the swamp." The reference was to corrupt individuals and institutions running the U.S. government; the promise was to address them by "deconstructing the administrative state."[253] Through Trump's attacks on Hillary Clinton and Barack Obama, alt-right voters felt they were rejecting the politics they blamed for their current economic situation and the lack of representation from politicians in Washington. These positions and policies, along with pro-Christian posturing, have conjured a lily-white sense of a past that Trump promised to restore in the future, as stated in the campaign slogan "Make America Great Again" (MAGA).[254]

Trump deepened his relationship with the alt-right by taking Stephen K. Bannon—a former "naval officer, Goldman Sachs mergers specialist, entertainment-industry financier, documentary screenwriter and director, [and] *Breitbart News* cyber-agitprop impresario and chief executive"—into his inner circle during the campaign.[255] Before that, Bannon had served at the helm of *Breitbart* following the death of its founder, Andrew Breitbart, in 2012. *Breitbart*'s content was a steady mix of nationalism, xenophobia, Islamophobia, misogyny, racism, and disinformation that demonized Democrats in every way possible. The chief executive of the Anti-Defamation League (ADL) opposed Trump's selection of Steve Bannon as the president's chief strategist precisely because Bannon had once led *Breitbart*, which the ADL considers "the premier website of the Alt Right, a loose-knit group of white nationalists and unabashed anti-Semites and racists."[256]

Among the many baseless claims propagated by *Breit-*

*bart* were that President Barack Obama was a Kenya-born Muslim;[257] Democratic Party aide Huma Abedin sponsored Islamic terrorists; Obama's nominee for secretary of defense, Chuck Hagel (R-NE), received payments for speaking at an event titled after a terrorist organization, "Friends of Hamas"; a Muslim mob inspired a civil war in Germany; and a rash of wildfires in Northern California had been started by an undocumented Latin American immigrant.[258] Advocacy on *Breitbart* has included exhortations that "every tree, every rooftop, every picket fence, every telegraph pole in the South should be festooned with the Confederate battle flag."[259]

In addition to Bannon, Trump aligned himself with dubious figures such as Alex Jones, a self-admitted "performance artist" who posed as a newsperson through the web platform *InfoWars*. Jones's anti-government attacks have included baseless claims that the United States orchestrated the 9/11 attacks, constructed domestic concentration camps for dissidents, controls the weather for nefarious purposes, and manufactures gay frogs.[260] The *InfoWars* host has constantly defended and preached the dogma of President Trump as gospel, even going so far as to say that he would give up his life for him: "Trump is so fire-breathing, so energetic, so cunning, so real, and he's having results so amazing that it just makes me endeared to Trump—I'm ready to die for Trump, at this point. And I'm already ready to die for America, it's the same feeling I have for America, because he is America, you're America."[261]

Trump also found himself in good favor with Fox News host and alt-right darling Lou Dobbs, who claimed that the first hundred days of Trump's presidency were "pretty close to perfect" and that it "may be the most accomplished presidency in modern American history."[262]

Finally, during the 2018 midterm elections, as noted in the previous chapter, Fox News host Sean Hannity violated professional and ethical boundaries by appearing onstage with the president to campaign for Republican candidates and denounce other media outlets as "fake news."[263]

Trump became the kindred spirit of those on the alt-right because he did not discount their unsubstantiated views, as previous Republicans and Democrats had done. Nancy Isenberg's 2016 book *White Trash*, which focused on many of the voters from districts Trump won, found that white Americans in the Midwest and South felt increasingly mocked, marginalized, and ostracized by the dominant culture.[264] As a result, they turned to far-right, "anti-establishment" media figures and online platforms for validation. The Southern Poverty Law Center's Richard Cohen explained that 2016 was a transformative year for the alt-right because its members saw "a kindred spirit in Trump."[265]

Trump has also stoked the alt-right's sense of nationalistic white supremacy by demanding a "travel ban" on people from Muslim-majority countries and by militarizing the U.S.-Mexico border against alleged hordes of dangerous migrant invaders. In fact, Trump used the issue of migrants as a hyper-partisan weapon of fear to boost Republican support during the 2018 midterm elections. He branded the people coming to the border a "caravan of migrants," although they refer to themselves as "Via Crucis Migrantes" or Migrants' Way of the Cross. They are people fleeing violence, political unrest, and poverty. Fox News ignored the social realities these individuals faced and echoed Trump's appeal to fear, describing the migrant group as an "invasion," an "invading horde," and "a full-scale invasion by a hostile force." In the month leading up to the election, migrants were referred to as an "invasion" sixty times on Fox News Channel and seventy-five times on Fox Business Channel.

Trump further stoked xenophobia among the electorate with the repeated claim that the caravan presented a threat to U.S. homeland security. Without evidence, he claimed that if the caravan were to be closely examined, "You're gonna find MS-13, you're gonna find Middle Easterners, you're going to find everything." As if to prove his point, during the build-up to the 2018 midterm elections, Trump deployed 5,200 active-duty troops to the U.S.-Mexico border under a military operation named "Faithful Patriot."[266] Trump's heated rhetoric and actions led to more extreme, armed vigilante behavior: groups of U.S citizens taking it upon themselves to kidnap and illegally detain immigrants at gunpoint on the border. The vigilantes were part of a group that called itself United Constitutional Patriots, and their leader, Larry Mitchell Hopkins, was later arrested and detained on charges of illegal possession of firearms.

Immediately after the midterms, the Pentagon directed U.S. military commanders to stop calling the deployment of active-duty troops to the southern border "Operation Faithful Patriot," a name disparaged by critics as overtly political, while President Trump played up the mission as he stumped for Republican candidates.[267] "We are no longer calling it Operation Faithful Patriot," said Army Lt. Col. Jamie Davis, a Pentagon spokesperson. "We are referring to it as border support. I have nothing further at this time."[268]

## POST-TRUTH NEWS

"You're up there, you've got half the room [Republicans] going totally crazy, wild—they loved everything, they want to do something great for our country," Trump said to a crowd in Ohio a week after his first State of the Union address. "And you have the other side [Democrats], even on positive news—really positive news, like that—they were like death and un-American. Un-American. Somebody said, 'treasonous.' I mean, yeah, I guess, why not? Can we call that treason? Why not? I mean, they certainly didn't seem to love our country very much."[269] Trump's remarks were seen by many as an act of intimidation, and by legal scholars as a categorically inaccurate use of the term "treason."[270] However, Trump was likely not concerned about their reactions; his remarks were meant for far-right supporters who would be energized by the president publicly disparaging his critics.

Saying whatever it takes—including lies—to manipulate the public to support his policies is one of Trump's oldest tricks. For example, in early 2016, Trump buttressed racist and Islamophobic support for his proposed ban on immigrants through fabricated news stories. Among the stories propagated were false claims of a terror attack in Atlanta, Georgia; a "massacre" in Bowling Green, Kentucky; and a refugee coup in Sweden.[271] Similarly, in an effort to defeat the Democratic Party's proposed immigration policy, Trump falsely called the visa lottery "a program that randomly hands out green cards without any regard for skill, merit, or the safety of American people."[272] In fact, as noted earlier, individuals are required to meet standards for education and work history as well as pass a background check before they are legally allowed to immigrate to the United States.

Trump has also heavily relied on falsehoods to denounce fact-based critiques of him and his administration's policies. In January 2017, when Trump's poll numbers were reflected by the small crowd at his inaugural address, White House press secretary Sean Spicer lied about the size of President Trump's inauguration crowd.[273] On January 22, 2017, Trump counselor Kellyanne Conway defended Spicer's crowd-size remarks, arguing that the White House was presenting "alternative facts,"[274] an astounding conceptual creation that caused her interlocutor, Chuck Todd, to gasp, "Wait a minute—alternative facts?!"

There is a hardly a better example of Trump's assault on truth than his defiance of climate change data and experts, and his effort to scrub references to them from government websites, including that of the Environmental Protection Agency.[275] In December 2015, Trump referred to climate change as a "hoax."[276] By then, 97 percent of the world's climate scientists had agreed that the Earth's temperature was increasing and that human activity was the prime cause.[277] In October 2018, Trump said in an interview that he thinks "something's happening. Something's changing and it'll change back again. I don't think it's a hoax; I think there's probably a difference."[278]

That same week, the Nobel Prize-winning Intergovernmental Panel on Climate Change issued a report warning that immediate action was needed to prevent catastrophic consequences worldwide. "The report shows that we only have the slimmest of opportunities remaining to avoid unthinkable damage to the climate system that supports life as we know it," said Amjad Abdulla, the IPCC board member and chief negotiator for the alliance of small island states.[279] "Historians will look back at these findings as one of the defining moments in the course of human affairs," Abdulla said.[280]

Despite the authority of the report, Trump continued to undermine climate studies and asserted in that same interview that scientists have a "very big political agenda" and that no consensus exists on climate change.[281] Despite all of Trump's efforts to sow doubt, 70 percent of citizens believe climate change is real, 49 percent believe it is human-caused, and only 47 percent continue to believe there is no scientific consensus on climate change.[282] Nonetheless, Trump has relied on falsehoods to justify his expansion of the coal industry and his decision to remove the United States from the Paris Accords, an international effort to combat climate change.[283] The continued treatment of climate change data as debatable squanders the precious resource of time, which is absolutely necessary if humans hope to heed warnings that we must change course now, while we still can.

The phrase "fake news" was brought to life in 2016 when Trump pointed to CNN reporter James Acosta and shouted, "You are fake news!"[284] Since then, he has also added ABC, CBS, NBC, the *New York Times*, *The New Yorker*, and the *Washington Post* to his ever-growing list of outlets guilty of being "fake news."[285] The phrase was so ubiquitous that in 2017 it was added to the Merriam-Webster dictionary, and later that year Collins Dictionary recognized the term as "Word of the Year."[286] Trump took credit for creating the phrase, but it has been appearing in the press since at least the 1890s.[287] During one week in January 2018, the phrase's increased influence was demonstrated when the number of Google searches for it spiked to an all-time high.[288] Before Trump popularized it, the term "fake news" was rarely used beyond academic studies about satirical comedy news shows such as *The Daily Show* and *The Colbert Report*.[289]

Fake news can take many forms, including stories that are deliberately falsified or plagiarized. That is precisely what was done by Jayson Blair, who was hired by the *New York Times* in the early 2000s, and Stephen Glass of *The New Republic* in the late 1990s. Both journalists literally manufactured stories that made it to publication, deliberately submitting fake news to well-established journalistic institutions. Blair was additionally found guilty of plagiarism.[290] Other, more innocuous examples of fake content in media have included television news personalities lying about their experiences in attempts to buttress their credentials, such as MSNBC's Brian Williams lying about being in a helicopter firefight in Iraq, watching the Berlin Wall fall in person, and meeting the pope—all false.[291] Similarly, Fox News's Bill O'Reilly has claimed that while reporting for a Dallas television station in 1977, he personally heard the shotgun blast that killed a person associated with Lee Harvey Oswald, and that he rescued a cameraman from an approaching army during the Falklands War in Argentina—despite being far from the Falkland Islands at the time.[292] Williams and O'Reilly likely fabricated the claims about themselves simply to appear more badass.

Historically, much disinformation has reached the population disguised as news as a direct result of government efforts to manipulate the public. For example, the television show *Battle Report Washington* was scripted by the U.S. Defense Department during the 1950s.[293] Similarly, throughout the Cold War the Central Intelligence Agency attempted to influence public opinion by covertly providing content to media such as the *New York Times*, CBS, the *Washington Post* and *Time*.[294] During the 1975–1976 investigation of the CIA by the Senate Intelligence Committee, also known as the Church Committee after its chair, Senator Frank Church of Idaho, the dimensions of the agency's involvement with the press became more apparent. But, according to journalist Carl Bernstein (who was awarded the Pulitzer Prize for public service in 1973), "top officials of the CIA, including former directors William Colby and George [H.W.] Bush, persuaded the committee to restrict its inquiry into the [agency] and to deliberately misrepresent the actual scope of the activities in its final report."[295] As a result, one is left to wonder how much news that appeared to be independently reported was actually planted, and in what form similar operations may still be practiced to this day.

Government bodies, political parties, and campaigns have also planted stories and used disinformation in attempts to manipulate public opinion. The George W. Bush administration paid $240,000 to a journalist to produce favorable stories about its No Child Left Behind initiative.[296] Hillary Clinton's 2016 presidential campaign repeated the unsubstantiated story that angry supporters of Bernie Sanders threw chairs during a Nevada party convention.[297] According to a *New York Times* report by Scott Shane and Alan Blinder, a group of "Democratic tech experts" conducted a clandestine disinformation campaign in the fiercely contested Alabama Senate race in 2017:

> The secret project, carried out on Facebook and Twitter, was likely too small to have a significant effect on the race, in which the Democratic candidate it was designed to help, Doug Jones, edged out the Republican, Roy S. Moore. . . .
>
> One participant in the Alabama project, Jonathon Morgan, is the chief executive of New Knowledge, a small cyber security firm that wrote a scathing account of Russia's social media operations in

the 2016 election that was released this week by the Senate Intelligence Committee.

An internal report on the Alabama effort, obtained by The New York Times, says explicitly that it "experimented with many of the tactics now understood to have influenced the 2016 elections."[298]

The article explains the methodology:

The project's operators created a Facebook page on which they posed as conservative Alabamians, using it to try to divide Republicans and even to endorse a write-in candidate to draw votes from Mr. Moore. It involved a scheme to link the Moore campaign to thousands of Russian accounts that suddenly began following the Republican candidate on Twitter, a development that drew national media attention.

"We orchestrated an elaborate 'false flag' operation that planted the idea that the Moore campaign was amplified on social media by a Russian botnet," the report says.[299]

The execution of such disinformation operations in U.S. domestic political affairs should be of profound concern to everyone who cares about the integrity of our information and electoral systems. Such activities pose a direct attack on civil society by attempting to manipulate people's views and behavior through fraud. Unfortunately, according to one study of 3,015 people conducted by Ipsos Public Affairs for *BuzzFeed News* in 2016, fake news appears to deceive adults approximately 75 percent of the time.[300]

"The 2016 election may mark the point in modern political history when information and disinformation became a dominant electoral currency," said Chris Jackson of Ipsos Public Affairs, which conducted the survey on behalf of BuzzFeed News. "Public opinion, as reflected in this survey, showed that 'fake news' was remembered by a significant portion of the electorate and those stories were seen as credible."

The survey found that those who identify as Republican are more likely to view fake election news stories as very or somewhat accurate. Roughly 84% of the time, Republicans rated fake news headlines as accurate (among those they recognized), compared to a rate of 71% among Democrats.[301]

Individuals' susceptibility to these stories suggests how political polarization and ineffective education have produced a population ripe for manipulation. In addition to using it to directly influence public opinion, President Trump has also weaponized the notion of "fake news" to aggressively disparage journalists and the press. He has referred to journalists as "fiction writers," "bad people," and "downright dishonest."[302]

One of Trump's most often repeated statements has been "Don't believe the main stream (fake news) media."[303] Trump has also repeatedly attacked the *New York Times*, NBC, ABC, and CNN as "the enemy of the American People!"[304] On occasion, Trump has added extra invective, as in his tweet of February 20, 2019 following a detailed report in the *New York Times* titled "Intimidation, Pressure and Humiliation: Inside Trump's Two-Year War on the Investigations Encircling Him."[305] In response, Trump tweeted: "The New York Times reporting is false. They are a true ENEMY OF THE PEOPLE!"[306]

Coming from the president of the United States, such statements only serve to further erode public confidence in journalism and news. Trump's constant insistence that the so-called "mainstream" media are "crooked," "dishonest," or part of a "witch hunt" against him has further driven people to hyper-partisan positions and the online outlets that voice them.[307] "People love it when you attack the press," said Trump in March 2019.[308]

More troubling, Trump's attacks on critics often appear to foster intolerance, incite hate, and celebrate violence. "If you see somebody getting ready to throw a tomato," Trump said of protesters who usually show up at his rallies, "knock the crap out of them, would you? Seriously, OK? Just knock the hell . . . I promise you I will pay for the legal fees. I promise, I promise."[309] On July 2, 2017, Trump tweeted a doctored video that shows him physically attacking a person with the CNN logo superimposed on his head. When the video was shown to then–Homeland Security adviser Tom Bossert on the ABC News program *This Week*, he commented that it was "certainly not" a threat against the media in general or CNN specifically.[310] CNN released a statement criticizing the president for tweeting the doctored video:

> It is a sad day when the President of the United States encourages violence against reporters. Clearly, Sarah Huckabee Sanders lied when she said the President had never done so. Instead of preparing for his overseas trip, his first meeting with Vladimir Putin, dealing with North Korea and working on his health care bill, he is involved in juvenile behav-

ior far below the dignity of his office. We will keep doing our jobs. He should start doing his.[311]

And in the wake of the aggressive shouting at CNN reporter Jim Acosta at a Trump rally in Tampa on July 31, 2018, the president's two eldest sons—Donald Jr. and Eric—disseminated social media posts of the rally crowd heckling Acosta.[312]

The frequency of the Trumps' aggression toward critics and media has served to normalize such conduct, and has tacitly incited his supporters to follow suit. For instance, when police slammed CBS reporter Sopan Deb to the ground and arrested him for doing his job while reporting on a Trump rally, some attendees screamed, "Go back to Iraq," while another asked Deb, an Indian, if he was at the rally to take pictures for ISIS.[313] This was not an isolated incident. After a video surfaced of Trump receiving applause and laughter by rally attendees for openly mocking a disabled reporter, Trump denied that he had ever ridiculed the reporter.[314] Trump supporters clearly mimic his degrading treatment of the press. For example, in 2018, Trump followers surrounded Jim Acosta of CNN during a broadcast, loudly shouting "CNN sucks!"[315] In describing the feeling among journalists, ABC News correspondent Cecilia Vega said, "It really feels like a matter of time, frankly, before someone gets hurt."[316]

Not long into Trump's presidency, people did, in fact, begin getting hurt. As noted previously, during Montana's 2017 special election for the House of Representatives, GOP candidate Greg Gianforte confronted *Guardian* reporter Ben Jacobs. After refusing to address questions at a campaign event, Gianforte verbally abused Jacobs before literally body-slamming him to the ground. Said Jacobs,

"Mr. Gianforte's response was to slam me to the floor and start punching me, [which] thrust me into a national spotlight I did not seek or desire."[317] Despite this assault on a journalist, Gianforte went on to win the election, with many of his supporters cheering his assault on a journalist as if they were part of a professional wresting melodrama rather than a congressional election. Gianforte pleaded guilty to misdemeanor assault charges, apologized, and was sentenced to forty hours of community service and twenty hours of anger management classes.

Numerous free press organizations protested Gianforte's violent behavior. Gabe Rottman of PEN America said, "A member of the House hasn't physically assaulted someone this severely since the Civil War, and we are unaware of any historical precedent for a lawmaker beating up a reporter. . . . Amid a climate of escalating hostility toward the press it is essential for the House to send a clear message to its members and to the nation that hostile treatment of the press will not be tolerated or ignored."[318] Gianforte's conduct was not much different from Trump's. In fact, Trump has repeatedly praised and supported Gianforte, once noting, "Any guy that can do a body slam, he's my kind of—he's my guy."[319]

Trump's elevation of violence and prejudice against journalists has occurred along with a broader and more troubling uptick in attacks against journalists in general. The increase was so significant that it led *Time* magazine to declare fallen journalists "Person of the Year" in 2018.[320] In explaining how *Time* arrived at their decision, the magazine's editor in chief, Edward Felsenthal, wrote that it was a response to extreme forms of "manipulation and abuse of truth" being "the common thread in so many of the year's major headlines, and an insidious and growing threat to freedom."[321] In 2018, the organization Reporters Without Borders ranked the United States among the top five most dangerous places in the world to be a journalist, and on its Press Freedom Index the United States had dropped to 45th out of 180 countries worldwide.

Despite these threats to their profession, and the incendiary rhetoric pouring from the White House bully pulpit, corporate media have largely failed to hold Trump accountable for his misconduct, intolerance, and lies. In fact, some in the corporate press have brought attention to similar-spirited "talent." Some of the alt-right figures who have been given airtime in corporate media include Alex Jones; Ann Coulter, who concluded that Harvey Weinstein was only ousted as a sexual predator because the "ugly girls" who accused him hated the "pretty girls" he sexually harassed and abused; Milo Yiannopoulos, who insinuated he condoned pedophilia; and Tomi Lahren, who claimed that there was no conceivable reason for NFL players to kneel in protest to racism, compared Black Lives Matter to the Ku Klux Klan, and discussed black men as a threat to law enforcement.[322] Incorporating such voices into mainstream commercial programming does not foster debate; it provides validation for social intolerance and bigoted views, including misogyny and white supremacy.

CNN had begun adjusting its choice of personalities and content for Trump supporters even before the primaries had ended. Like Trump, those personalities offered the provocations that delivered increased ratings while at the same time providing opportunity for polarizing views to be normalized. CNN hired former Trump campaign adviser Corey Lewandowski in the summer of 2016.[323] Lewandowski had a sordid past, with no real political experience prior to Trump's 2016 campaign. In 2014, the North

Carolina Board of Elections investigated Lewandowski for reportedly sending "misleading, incorrect and confusing voter registration mailers."[324] While working on Trump's primary campaign, Lewandowski was seen forcibly restraining a journalist.[325] He was reportedly fired from the campaign because racist messages he tweeted threatened the success of Trump in the general election.[326] In his first appearance on CNN, Lewandowski stated that "Trump is the only person who's going to save this country for my children."[327] Lewandowski joined Trump supporter Jeffrey Lord, who was brought into CNN in early 2016. Trump has since called him "a source of truth."[328] The former Reagan White House employee had a history of race baiting, including falsely claiming that USDA official Shirley Sherrod's relative, a person of color, had been "lynched," and repeatedly engaged in overt racism during his broadcasts.[329] Lord falsely and obliviously claimed that the Ku Klux Klan was "a leftist terrorist organization" that sought to "further the progressive agenda."[330] Lord was fired in the summer of 2017 after tweeting the Nazi phrase "*Sieg Heil.*"[331]

CNN's hiring of Lord and Lewandowski was a clear appeal to Trump and his supporters. In fact, CNN's president, Jeff Zucker, essentially admitted that his new pro-Trump panelists were seen not as newsmakers or journalists, but as "characters in a drama."[332] By allowing such characters into their programming, CNN placed commercial interests over those of professional ethics and journalistic integrity. To hire such characters gives credence to the post-truth concept of "alternative facts" and further strengthens Edward Felsenthal's concerns regarding the "manipulation and abuse of truth" being "an insidious and growing threat" to society.

Trump and his political allies have had a unique ability to legitimize their policies and position through the propagation of lies, fantasies, and speculation rebranded as "alternative facts." Case in point, Republican Senator Cory Gardner falsely claimed that when Trump sought to repeal the Affordable Care Act, he then received a deluge of letters, emails, phone calls, and voicemails that were generated by "paid protesters."[333] Analogously, when a 2017 bombing of a Muslim mosque in Bloomington, Minnesota, proved that Muslims can be victims of hate crimes, not solely perpetrators, as the alt-right often claims, Sebastian Gorka, a former *Breitbart* editor and national security adviser for Trump, mused that the bombing may have been "a fake hate crime."[334] Lastly, when the Trump administration's push for direct conflict with Syria was languishing, Sean Spicer pointed to the regime's use of chemical weapons, claiming that Hitler "didn't even sink to using chemical weapons."[335] Instead of acknowledging that Trump lies, CNN's Jeffery Lord once claimed, in a statement evocative of Orwell, that the president wasn't lying; he was speaking another language—"Americanese."[336]

All should be concerned by the culture of deception, aggression, and self-interest that has defined Trump's presidency, and the degree to which corporate media have been willingly complicit in giving a commercial platform to those who seek to normalize such a culture as "Americanese." The assault on the truth has been waged not by Trump alone, but also by commentators, politicians, and other forces that use disinformation to achieve their own goals. Without clear guidelines, truth becomes increasingly viewed as subjective, and the public remains grossly exposed and unprotected. This creates opportunities for propaganda, false advertising, manipulation, and information war. "Truth isn't truth," said Trump's lead lawyer, Rudy Giuliani, evoking Goebbels's view that "the truth is the greatest enemy of the state."[337] Welcome to the United States of Distraction.

FOUR

# WE DISTORT, YOU ABIDE

"Get your facts first, and then you can distort them as much as you please."
—Mark Twain, in an interview with Rudyard Kipling, 1899

"You know I'm automatically attracted to beautiful—I just start kissing them. It's like a magnet. Just kiss. I don't even wait. And when you're a star, they let you do it. You can do anything. Grab them by the pussy. You can do anything." The statement is taken from a 2005 conversation between Donald Trump and *Access Hollywood*'s Billy Bush.[338] An audio recording of Trump's lewd remarks was publicly released for the first time during the final weeks of the 2016 presidential election season. The unmistakable sound of Trump saying he wanted "to fuck" a married woman, among other debasing remarks, seemed like an immediate death sentence to his run for the White House, and to any future in politics.[339]

On October 19, 2016, less than two weeks after the audio leaked to the press, Hillary Clinton and Donald Trump entered their last televised debate before the election. The nation was still months away from the first Women's March and nearly a year away from the eruption of the #MeToo movement. During the debate, Trump tried to quell the claims that he was sexist by stating, "Nobody respects women more than me." Less than three minutes later, as Clinton discussed Social Security and Medicare, Trump interrupted her with the insult that she was "such a nasty woman."[340]

Trump's performance spoke volumes. The meaning of his words, as well as the act of interrupting and speaking over Clinton while she spoke, displayed Trump's sense of male privilege and aggression as clearly as his lewd remarks to Billy Bush. As has become typical, subsequent press coverage followed partisan divides.[341]

On October 21, 2016, two days after the debate, Clinton and Trump were again in the same room for the Alfred E. Smith Memorial Foundation Dinner. The dinner is an annual Catholic fundraiser and has been a popular stop for presidential campaigns since the 1960s. It is customary at the dinner for political opponents to both compliment and joke about each other. This time, however, neither candidate complimented the other. Clinton entered the event under scrutiny after WikiLeaks had released her private emails exposing the Democratic Party's efforts to elevate her campaign against her primary rival, Bernie Sanders, as well as racist language by Clinton campaign chairman John Podesta referring to "needy Latinos."[342]

During her speech, Clinton sidestepped the emails and focused on Trump's sexism: "Donald looks at the Statue of Liberty and sees a 4—maybe a 5 if she loses the torch and tablet and changes her hair." The joke drew laughter. Later in the evening Trump gave his speech which began with laughs and applause. Then, as expected, he broke with tradition stating, "I wasn't really sure if Hillary was going to be here tonight, because, I guess, you didn't send her invitation by email. Or maybe you did, and she just found out about it through the wonder of WikiLeaks. We've learned so much from WikiLeaks. For example, Hillary believes that it is vital to deceive the people by having one public policy and a totally different policy in private."[343] Mild-mannered laughter and applause quickly turned into boos of disgust.

Corporate media covered the event with emphasis on the WikiLeaks revelations and Trump's buffoonish behavior. Concern over Trump's lewd and degrading behavior at the debates had already faded away. In fact, the relevance of the comments only resurfaced much later when several women, including adult film star Stormy Daniels, began voicing allegations of adulterous encounters with Trump, and the various ways he had tried to silence them through lawyers, legal agreements, hush money, and intimidation.[344]

Trump's political ambitions grew after being invited to speak at the Republican Party's 2012 convention. Fear over Trump's inexperience and propensity to make uncouth remarks led the Republicans to hire a media trainer to prep him for his performance. Trump worked with the trainer, but never gave the speech because Hurricane Isaac shut down the convention.[345] However, Trump's decades in the public eye had helped him to fine-tune his knack for self-promotion and marketing. By the time election day approached in 2016, his campaign had become a well-oiled marketing machine, aggressively shaping media narratives with the help of unsavory characters such as Stephen Bannon, Paul Manafort, and self-described "agent provocateur" Roger Stone.[346]

Trump has deftly and routinely overcome negative media coverage that has destroyed previous politicians and campaigns. His constant use of lies ("alternative facts"), counterattacks, sensationalism, and media swerves have helped him do so. A media swerve is a tactic that shifts narrative direction in a particular story to avoid facts or discussion viewed as negative by the party committing the swerve. These mass diversions were employed to manipulate media and distract public attention from facts, ethical considerations, and issues of substance that either were antithetical to Trump's positions or questioned his conduct.

By exploiting vulnerabilities in both traditional and social media, Trump has repeatedly redirected national attention in ways that have allowed him to evade accountability and strengthen his base of supporters. His responses to three major events demonstrate this dynamic: the violent clashes in Charlottesville during the Unite the Right Rally, the 2017 ambush in Niger, and the investigations into Russia's covert operations to influence the U.S. population.

## UNITE THE WHITE

During an August 2017 white supremacist rally in Charlottesville, Virginia, a Nazi sympathizer ran his car into a crowd of peaceful anti-racist protesters, killing one young woman and injuring many people. In response to the rally and hate crime, Trump offered conflicting messages that illuminated both his bigotry and his media skills for avoiding scrutiny about his racism. Shortly after the incident, Trump denounced hatred and violence on "many sides" despite clear video evidence showing that it came from one side—the white nationalists.[347]

Two days later, after critics lambasted the president for conflating Nazis with peaceful protesters, the White House, not Trump, tweeted a denouncement of "white supremacists, KKK, Neo-Nazi and all extremist groups."[348]

On August 14, 2017, while under immense pressure from Republicans, Trump issued a statement saying, "We condemn in the strongest possible terms this egregious display of hatred, bigotry and violence."[349] However, a day later, Trump redirected blame away from the white supremacists in Charlottesville. "You had a group on the other side that came charging in without a permit," he said, "and they were very, very violent."[350]

Many journalists denounced Trump's comments for not directly calling out the violence of white supremacists. Journalist Jeremy Scahill tweeted "Trump, Bannon, Gorka, Miller emboldened these Nazis. Encouraged them. And Trump's 'many sides' bullshit continues that. This is terrorism."[351] Scahill was undoubtedly aware of Trump's popularity with white supremacists, his removal of federal funding for groups that fight racism, and his appointment of known white supremacists to his cabinet, including self-identified white nationalist Richard Spencer's mentee Stephen Miller; former *Breitbart* chief Stephen K. Bannon; and Sebastian Gorka, who once "wore the medal of Vitézi Rend, a Nazi organization."[352]

Trump's campaign had attracted strong support from former grand wizard of the Ku Klux Klan David Duke. During the 2016 campaign, Duke told radio listeners that a vote for Trump's rivals would be "treason to your heritage."[353] Trump had also received the support of the neo-Nazi site *The Daily Caller* and of Richard Spencer.[354] "Each time Trump was asked on Twitter about his white nationalist supporters," wrote Evan Osnos in *The New Yorker* in February 2016, "the candidate, who is ready to respond, day or night, to critics of his debating style or his golf courses, simply ignored the question."[355]

Six months before the racist hate crimes of Charlottesville, the Southern Poverty Law Center had reported that there were more than 900 hate groups operating within the United States.[356] However, the corporate press often treated Trump's racism as a partisan issue rather than a matter of historical fact. Although networks such as CNN had Don Lemon, Jake Tapper, and Van Jones denouncing Trump's connections to white supremacy, Fox News often made false equivalencies between the Black Lives Matter movement and white nationalist groups.[357] Tammy Bruce, a Fox News contributor, claimed on *Fox and Friends* that Trump, like Ronald Reagan before him, had "immediately eviscerated" white supremacist groups.[358] Sean Hannity cherry-picked Trump's denouncement on August 14, 2017, arguing that Trump had made it clear "there's no place in this country for these neo-Nazi, fascist, white supremacists," and that those criticizing him for being racist are making a concerted partisan effort to undermine him and his presidency.[359]

After days of engaging in a war of words over race, Trump deployed a media swerve. As outrage mounted over his false equivalency between the actions of violent white supremacists and those of nonviolent anti-racist demonstrators, Trump began denouncing progressives—who prior to the Unite the Right Rally had convinced the city of Charlottesville to remove Confederate monuments—as "foolish."[360] As the corporate press took the bait and engaged in discussions about the removal of monuments as the origin of the news story, the issue of violence and white supremacy drifted outside the frame.

While the meaning of public historical markers is certainly a national issue, Trump had succeeded in distracting news media coverage from the potential hate crimes and other threats posed by white nationalist groups, many of which were his proud supporters. Furthermore, the national discussion about Confederate monuments, many of which were constructed to iconize white supremacy over Black people, was never adequately addressed by the corporate media.[361] Instead, the media often conflated history and heritage and treated them as partisan issues with conservatives like Tomi Lahren arguing that the removal of Confederate monuments was designed "to erase history and to erase every shred of patriotism."[362]

*Breitbart's* commentary on the matter quoted the Council on American-Islamic Relations (CAIR):

> Removing or relocating from public property all monuments that symbolize white supremacy, hatred, and racism is a crucial and appropriate response to the violence of this weekend," said a statement from CAIR spokesman Zainab Chaudry. "Monuments in public spaces represent what our cities seek to represent as their core beliefs. They shape identity and influence societal values. The enduring values of our cities cannot be rooted in white supremacy. We applaud this move by the Mayor's office that will make it clear that hate has no place in Baltimore."[363]

The *Breitbart* post then reminded its readers that such commentary should be regarded as that of the enemy: "Breitbart News has frequently noted that the CAIR group is so closely entwined with Islamists and with jihadis that court documents and news reports show that at least five of its people—either board members, employees or former employees—have been jailed or repatriated for various financial and terror-related offenses."[364] The alt-right media strategy was to demonize efforts challenging public memorials symbolizing white supremacy.

As the corporate media turned to address issues regarding historical monuments, the original focus of the Charlottesville story dissipated and moved from a discussion of racism, violence, and a complicit president to a debate over history, heritage, and the meaning of the Civil War. Trump's swerve tactic had been successful. In fact, according to Greg Sargent in the *Washington Post*, "President Trump's chief strategist, Stephen K. Bannon, was among the very few top officials around Trump who quietly cheered as he resisted pressure to unequivocally lay the blame for the deadly violence in Charlottesville on Nazis and white supremacists. . . . Bannon confirmed that he views the racial strife and turmoil unleashed by Charlottesville as a political winner for Trump."[365] However, it was not a political winner for Bannon. As criticism continued to mount about Trump's handling of Charolettsville, the White House put the blame on Bannon, and forced him to resign.[366] Thus the episode is yet another testament to Trump's ability not just to redirect the media and evade meaningful accountability, but to do so while energizing his alt-right, white nationalist base.

## NIGER AMBUSH

A few weeks after Charlottesville, U.S. soldiers were ambushed by ISIS fighters in Niger. Four U.S. servicemen were killed and two more injured. The attack was the deadliest in Trump's presidency up to that point. However, for twelve days following the loss, Trump did not make a single statement regarding the incident.[367] To avoid fallout, the U.S. commander in chief relied on silence, partisanship, and another swerve to dodge responsibility.[368]

On October 16, 2017, Trump's first comment on the attacks redirected media attention to previous presidents and the protocol used to make phone calls to Gold Star Families—relatives of U.S. military members who died in combat. Trump, angered by reporters, continued questioning the argument that he had only spoken of the attack to Gold Star Families after being prompted to do so, and then said, "Look at President Obama and other presidents, most of them didn't make calls, a lot of them didn't make calls."[369] When another reporter asked him to clarify the easily disproven statement, Trump responded:

> I was told he didn't, often, and a lot of presidents don't. President Obama, I think, probably did sometimes and maybe sometimes he didn't. I don't know. That's what I was told. All I can do is ask my generals. Other presidents did not call. They'd write letters. And some presidents didn't do anything.[370]

Nonetheless, the comment effectively shifted media inquiries from U.S. military errors that may have contributed to the injuries and fatalities, to the phone calls made, or not made, by previous presidents to Gold Star Families. Trump's swerve led to a war of words with Mrs. Myeshia Johnson, widow of one of the U.S. soldiers killed in the Niger ambush, Sgt. La David Johnson, an Army Special Forces sergeant. Ms. Johnson claimed that when Trump phoned her, his tone and comments were so disturbing that she felt like crying. She found it particularly unsettling that the president had said that her husband "knew what he signed up for," and that Trump couldn't remember her husband's name.[371] Ms. Johnson's account was confirmed by Congresswoman Frederica Wilson (D-FL), who had listened to the phone call.[372]

Trump attacked their portrayal of the conversation and stated that he remembered the call better, because he had "one of the great memories of all time."[373] "I was extremely nice to her," said Trump. "She sounds like a lovely lady. I've never seen her, I've never met her. She sounds like a lovely lady. I was extremely nice to her, I was extremely courteous. As I was to everyone else."[374] The commander in chief also denied not knowing Johnson's name.[375] Trump went further, claiming not only that they misremembered the call, but that they had lied about it. He tweeted, "The Fake News is going crazy with wacky Congresswoman Wilson(D), who was SECRETLY on a very personal call, and gave a total lie on content!"[376]

Fact-checking websites such as *Politifact*, as well as former White House officials from previous administrations, easily exposed Trump's false claims that his predecessors did not call the Gold Star Families.[377] However, *Fox and Friends* denounced the claims of Johnson and Wilson as "spin." This served to portray the account as a matter of opinion rather than a matter of fact.[378] A day later, on Fox's *The Fire*, co-host Kimberly Guilfoyle attacked Wilson's recollection of the phone call as "racist towards General Kelly" and "stepping on the backs of Gold Star families."[379] Others in the press, including former CBS anchorman Dan Rather, lambasted Trump's comments to the widow as "inexplicable, not to mention unforgivable."[380]

The commander in chief's successful avoidance of responsibility was achieved, in part, due to his ability to create diversions and then turn them into fodder for partisan skirmishes. Liberal outlets compared the Niger ambush to the lethal attacks on U.S. soldiers in Benghazi in 2014.

Conservatives had politicized the Benghazi tragedy, propagating disinformation about the Democrats, including that President Obama avoided preventive action, that the United States had the last flying flag in the region, that an ambassador's body was desecrated, and that then-secretary of state Hillary Clinton never asked for additional security.[381]

In a similar show of partisan exploitation, liberals disseminated their own unsubstantiated views following the Niger ambush. Among such claims were that Trump specifically ordered the mission and that his so-called "Muslim travel ban" was responsible.[382] Shortly after the ambush, MSNBC's Rachael Maddow baffled commentators with her opinion:

> If you are looking at the central domestic mystery here, which is why didn't the president even acknowledge those deaths, in the worst combat causalities of his presidency. . . . If you are interested in the central mystery of why the president is so reluctant to talk about that or take questions on that—well it really is true, his administration just took what is widely believed to be absolutely inexplicable action to alienate, anger, and insult the country that has been our most effective military partner against Islamic militants in the part of the world where these attacks just happened.[383]

Maddow was quickly rebuked by scholars such as Andrew Lebovich, a visiting fellow with the European Council on Foreign Relations, who tweeted that "these things are not linked, they have to do with areas on literal opposite ends of the country."[384] Laura Seay of *Slate* argued that Maddow's claim, and those who repeat it, were taking part in "conspiracy mongering."[385] Political accountability for what happened in Niger, and why, was skillfully sidelined by a president adept at creating diversions and by media fueled by hyper-partisan coverage of them.

## THE RUSSIANS ARE COMING . . . OR "THE SINGLE GREATEST WITCH HUNT IN POLITICAL HISTORY"

The long-running federal investigation into Russia's efforts to covertly manipulate the U.S. population during the 2016 presidential election showcased President Trump's weaponization of the term "fake news" to undermine the investigation, its implications, and efforts by the press to cover the unfolding story responsibly. Trump's power was existentially threatened by the investigation and the fact that he staffed his campaign team and parts of his presidential cabinet with individuals known to have lied under oath about their communications with Russia.

In July 2016, the U.S. government began investigating the possibility that Russia had engaged in covert influence operations against the U.S. population during the 2016 presidential election. On January 6, 2017, the U.S. intelligence community released a report titled "Assessing Russian Activities and Intentions in Recent U.S. Elections," a public version of a highly classified report detailing analysis that such operations had been ordered by Russian President Vladimir Putin to "undermine public faith in the U.S. democratic process, denigrate Secretary Clinton, and harm her electability and potential presidency."[386] The report further concluded that the Putin-ordered operations were "multifaceted" and designed with a "clear preference" for Trump, and that they signaled a "new normal" regarding Russian operations against the U.S. population.

By early 2017 there were multiple federal investigations examining the attacks and the propriety of frequent contacts that had occurred between members of the Russian government and Trump's inner circle, including now former attorney general Jeff Sessions; former director of the Defense Intelligence Agency Michael Flynn; former campaign manager Paul Manafort; former Trump lawyer Michael Cohen; and senior advisers to the president Jared Kushner and Donald Trump Jr.[387]

In May 2017, Trump fired FBI director James Comey for what Comey later insinuated was his refusal to pledge loyalty to Trump and to shield him and his cabinet from being investigated.[388] Comey has claimed that during a private White House dinner with the president in January 2017, Trump said, "I need loyalty, I expect loyalty." Comey claims to have replied, "You will always get honesty from me." To which Trump responded, "That's what I want, honest loyalty."[389]

In February 2017, after Michael Flynn had been caught lying about his financial ties to Russia, Trump pressed Comey, saying, "I hope you can let this go."[390] Comey became so uncomfortable by Trump's efforts to pressure him that Comey eventually asked his colleagues to always accompany him during meetings with the president. In February and again in March 2017, Comey claims, President Trump repeatedly asked if he too was under investigation. In April 2017, Comey began refusing to answer the question when Trump asked.[391] In May 2017, Trump made the decision to fire Comey.[392]

A week after Comey's firing, former FBI director Robert S. Mueller was appointed to investigate the possibility that there had been improper contacts between Trump's team and Russia before, during, and after the

2016 election, and if efforts had been made to obstruct justice. At the same time, the FBI was so concerned by the implications of Trump firing Comey that it opened an inquiry into whether Trump was secretly working on behalf of Russia. "Counterintelligence investigators had to consider whether the president's own actions constituted a possible threat to national security," reported the *New York Times* in January 2019.[393] "Agents also sought to determine whether Mr. Trump was knowingly working for Russia or had unwittingly fallen under Moscow's influence."[394] In an interview with CNN's Anderson Cooper on February 20, 2019, former FBI director Andrew G. McCabe said that as of that date, it was still "possible" that President Trump could be a Russian agent.[395] That there ever were reasons to even remotely raise such possible concerns surpassed all historical precedent.

For years, President Trump repeatedly and aggressively attacked the Russia investigation as "ridiculous," "fake news," "a hoax," and the "single greatest witch hunt in political history." The attacks, which numbered nearly 1,200 as of February 2019, were reported by the *New York Times* to be "part of a strategy to beat back the investigations."[396] One of the attempts included a January 2016 tweet in which Trump said, "Intelligence agencies should never have allowed this fake news [Russia Story] to 'leak' into the public. One last shot at me. Are we living in Nazi Germany?"[397]

Trump's attacks prompted those who heard them to make intellectual shortcuts to accept his views of the Mueller investigation rather than perform the complex investigative work required to parse all available claims and evidence. The sheer volume and frequency of the attacks evoked the infamous propaganda strategy of Joseph Goebbels: "If you tell a lie big enough and keep repeating it, people will eventually come to believe it. The lie can be maintained only for such time as the State can shield the people from the political, economic and/or military consequences of the lie."

Many of the ways Trump sought to manipulate public opinion regarding Russia were ginned up in the increasingly partisan corporate press. Since the Mueller Investigation began, right-leaning media operations, such as Fox News and *Breitbart*, largely ignored or minimized Russia's meddling in the election, going so far as to echo Trump's repeated claims that the whole investigation was a "witch hunt." In fact, in December 2018, Sean Hannity of Fox News reduced the multiple investigations into the extent of Russian covert activities in the United States to an obsessive "partisan witch-hunt."[398] However, in light of the multiple guilty pleas and convictions resulting from the Mueller investigation, including high-profile convictions of Trump's former attorney and "fixer" Michael Cohen, it is clear that the Mueller's efforts uncovered serious criminal acts and felonies, potential violations of RICO (the Racketeer Influenced and Corrupt Organizations Act), as well as lurid financial associations involving Russian oligarchs, attempts at poll rigging, and more.[399] Circumstantially, these developments reflect poorly on the Trump administration, but they don't prove initial allegations that Russia's interventions won the election for Trump.

In February 2017, when the FBI's initial investigation was about to be made public, Trump claimed, without evidence, that Obama was "tapping my phones in October" during the "very sacred election process."[400] This claim suggested that Obama and the Democrats, not covert Russian operatives, were meddling in the 2016 presidential election. Trump's attempt to divert culpability to his rivals, including allegations that "Democrats paid for Russians to compile wild allegations about a U.S. presidential candidate" were immediately adopted by Republicans and reinforced relentlessly through alt-right platforms like *Breitbart*.[401]

Among the most surreal episodes occurred when President Trump, standing at Vladimir Putin's side at a press conference in Helsinki in July 2018, publicly declared that he believed Putin over the findings of U.S. intelligence agencies. Julie Hirschfeld Davis described it in the *New York Times*:

> In a remarkable news conference, Mr. Trump did not name a single action for which Mr. Putin should be held accountable. Instead, he saved his sharpest criticism for the United States and the special counsel investigation into the election interference, calling it a "ridiculous" probe and a "witch hunt" that has kept the two countries apart. Mr. Trump even questioned the determinations by his intelligence officials that Russia had meddled in the election. "They said they think it's Russia," Mr. Trump said. "I have President Putin; he just said it's not Russia," the president continued, only moments after Mr. Putin conceded that he had wanted Mr. Trump to win the election because of his promises of warmer relations with Moscow.[402]

Trump's media swerve in Helsinki occurred just days after twelve Russian intelligence operatives were indicted for waging cyber-attacks against the United States that were intended to tip the election in Trump's favor. The indictment accused the twelve Russians of hacking into the computers of the Democratic National Committee and the Clinton presidential campaign, and provided "the most explicit account to date of the Russian government's meddling in American democracy."[403]

Contrary to the findings of multiple U.S. intelligence agencies, Trump's messaging relentlessly attacked anyone supporting the investigation, and aggressively sought to divert public attention to allegations of improprieties committed by investigators and accusers. In January 2018, for example, it was exposed that Lisa Page and Peter Strzok, who briefly worked for Mueller's team, were fired for exchanging anti-Trump texts. Trump's team exploited the news in an effort to suggest bias within the Mueller investigation. In an act reminiscent of the behavior of alt-right figure Alex Jones, Republican officials, including Senator Rob Johnson (R-WI), claimed that Strzok was fired because he was part of a "secret society" that held "off-site meetings" to dismantle the Trump presidency.[404] They relied on leaked text messages from Page and Strzok that included the phrase "secret society." Most commentators who read the messages in context realized that they were in jest, not reference to an actual secret society or the Mueller investigation.[405] Nonetheless, repetition of these and other baseless claims by Trump, high-level officials, and alt-right platforms served to divert public attention and turn it against the investigation, the media that covered it, and Democrats.[406]

In December 2018, the Mueller investigation revealed that Michael Flynn, a one-time Trump confidant who decided to fully cooperate with the Mueller investigation against Trump's wishes, had been so cooperative with the investigation that prosecutors filed a sentencing memorandum requesting that Flynn be spared a prison sentence.[407] Just hours after Mueller released the details of Flynn's cooperation agreement, Trump had to face Obama for the first time since becoming president, at former President George H.W. Bush's funeral.[408] The last time the two had met, ironically, the 44th president had warned Trump not to hire Flynn because of his ties to Russia.[409]

Rather than accept the special counsel's historic finding that members of Trump's cabinet and campaign had known ties to Russia—a nation running covert operations to influence the 2016 election—Trump's supporters sought to ignore, denounce, and distract. A headline on *Breitbart* read: "Michael Flynn Sentencing Document Shows Collusion—Between Media, Deep State, and Obama Admin."[410] The most popular reader comment responding to the article says: "I read the document thoroughly . . . not a nothing burger . . . it's a nothing burger slider. What it proves is that the FBI was spying on Flynn during the transition period. . . . The Obama DOJ spied on the Trump Transition. . . . [T]his is worse than Watergate could have ever been!" More than 275 members of *Breitbart*'s silo clicked in agreement.

Similarly, in 2018 and 2019, when revelations from the Mueller investigation resulted in Trump's former campaign manager Paul Manafort receiving a ninety-month sentence for sharing polling data with Russian operatives and obstructing justice, the hyper-partisan conservative press responded by parroting Trump's witch-hunt narrative.[411] Except for a thirty-second segment that assured viewers that there was "no indication that . . . then-candidate Trump was aware of any interaction," on the day Manafort was sentenced, conservative programs such as *Fox and Friends* continued to ignore the bombshell revelation that Manafort did indeed collude with the Russians.[412] On his radio show, Sean Hannity framed the Manafort verdict as "an unmitigated disaster for Mueller," because Manafort was only found guilty on "10 out of the 18" charges.[413] Newt Gingrich argued that the Manafort charges symbolized the transition of the Mueller investigation from "a witch hunt to an inquisition of Trump and allies."[414] The conservative "news" reaction to Flynn and Manafort illustrated that Trump no longer needed to actively craft a narrative in the face of public criticism; his loyal alt-right followers knew how to distort and divert on their own.

That said, the conservative corporate media were not alone in manipulating narratives to suit political interests. The liberal-leaning corporate press had its own distortions to peddle. While conservative media tended to discount, downplay, or outright ignore potentially damning information regarding Trump and Russia, some in the liberal-leaning press weaved a neo-McCarthyite narrative of speculation and conjecture on the matter. Both poles of the corporate media spectrum used the topic of the Mueller investigation to propagate polarizing, binary, hyperbolic reporting that served as diversion from many other key issues regarding Trump and his administration's policies and actions.

The corporate media's *mea culpa* and promises of more fact-based reporting after the 2016 presidential election never panned out. From the uncritical coverage of shadowy organizations such as PropOrNot; false reports by the *Washington Post* that Russia hacked a power grid in Vermont;[415] and baseless claims that Manafort had met with Julian Assange of WikiLeaks, reported until suddenly dropped by the *Guardian*, *USA Today*, the *Washington*

*Post*, Bloomberg, *Yahoo!News*, *The Hill*, *Rolling Stone*, and CNN;[416] to numerous other purported "smoking gun" stories published in CNN, the *New York Times*, and the *Washington Post*[417] that overstated their cases and were debunked afterwards, certain sectors of the corporate media pushed Russiagate to the point of making a cottage industry of it. As a result, many other substantive issues, including the crises posed by climate change, economic injustice, political corruption, white supremacy, and the destabilization of health care, received less coverage.[418]

In 2017, the right-wing Media Research Center conducted a "study of every broadcast network evening newscast" in the five-week period following the appointment of Special Counsel Robert Mueller. The investigation "found a whopping 353 minutes of airtime devoted to the Russia probe, or 55 percent of all coverage of the Trump presidency during those weeks."[419] Despite the excessive and often speculative coverage that continued from that time until March 2019, when Special Counsel Robert Mueller delivered his long-awaited report to Attorney General William Barr (whose own sordid history covering up government corruption dates back to his days at the CIA under George H.W. Bush regarding the Church Committee and later regarding Iran Contra),[420] pollsters in both 2018[421] and 2019[422] repeatedly found that concerns about Trump and Russia ranked low on voters' list of priorities compared to other issues, regardless of their party affiliation.

*The Rachel Maddow Show*, one of the top-rated programs at MSNBC, tended to cover developments in Mueller's investigation more than all other news stories combined. In fact, between February 20 and March 31, 2017, over 50 percent of Maddow's program, 640 of the nearly 1,200 minutes she was on the air, was devoted to investigating Trump's ties to Russia.[423] *The Intercept* noted that during that same period, other newsworthy stories were ignored or reduced to short segments, such as "Trump's escalating crackdown on undocumented immigrants (1.3 percent of coverage); attempts to repeal Obamacare (3.8 percent); the legal battle over Trump's Muslim ban (5.6 percent), a surge of anti-GOP activism since Trump took office (5.8 percent), and Trump administration scandals and stumbles (11 percent)."[424] *Rolling Stone* journalist Matt Taibbi called the period's obsession with Russia "Putin Derangement Syndrome."[425] For nearly two years, Maddow's ratings soared over those of her competitors at Fox and CNN[426]—until Attorney General Barr's four-page summary of the Mueller Report asserted "no collusion," which exposed the trademark overreach in her reporting around Trump and Russia, immediately costing Maddow nearly a fifth of her audience.[427]

Although collusion between Trump and Russia would be a massively important story, without new details and concrete evidence to report, corporate media filled airtime with speculation. In fact, over the course of the Mueller investigation, *The Rachel Maddow Show* falsely reported that Trump edited a question from a transcript with Russian leader Vladimir Putin[428] and that the Department of Homeland Security found that Russia hacked twenty-one states' election systems in 2016.[429] This kind of inaccurate and partisan-driven reporting ultimately served to reinforce Trump's claims that he was a victim of a witch hunt. Attorney General Barr's four-page summary of Mueller's 400-plus-page report spurred the president to claim "total exoneration" and to resume, like a battle cry, his signature attack on the press as "fake news."

A redacted version of Mueller's report was made public in April 2019. Mueller's investigation did not conclude that evidence it had obtained could prove beyond a reasonable doubt that the Trumps' interactions with the Russian government rose to the level of criminal conduct. Mueller chose not to bring indictments against Trump. At the time of this writing, it remained to be seen whether Congress would pursue charges against Trump based on Mueller's other findings or those derived from a host of other investigations still ongoing at the time of this writing. The never-ending scandals derived from the potential improprieties of the Trumps are not likely to abate, making the release of the Mueller report seem more like halftime than the end of the game. One thing is certain: Trump's reality-show presidency will continue to suck air from everything else, distracting national attention from issues connected to the basic needs of millions of Americans.

It is worth placing the topic of election meddling in a larger historical context here. In his February 17, 2018, news analysis for the *New York Times*, Scott Shane wrote that "Carnegie Mellon scholar Dov H. Levin has scoured the historical record for both overt and covert election influence operations. He found 81 by the United States and 36 by the Soviet Union or Russia between 1946 and 2000, though the Russian count is undoubtedly incomplete."[430] According to retired CIA chief of Russian operations Steven L. Hall, "If you ask an intelligence officer, did the Russians break the rules or do something bizarre, the answer is no, not at all. . . . The United States 'absolutely' has carried out such election influence operations historically, and I hope we keep doing it."[431]

Intelligence scholar Loch K. Johnson, who was a staffer on the Senate Church Committee in the 1970s, said that "Russia's 2016 operation was simply the cyber-age version of standard United States practice for decades, whenever American officials were worried about a foreign vote." Johnson, now at the University of Georgia, Athens, continued, "We've been doing this kind of thing since the C.I.A. was created in 1947. . . . We've used posters, pamphlets, mailers, banners—you name it. We've planted false information in foreign newspapers. We've used what the British call 'King George's cavalry': suitcases of cash."[432] According to Shane's article in the *Times*, U.S. officials have engaged in regime change, the overthrow of democratically elected leaders, political assassinations, and more, and not only during the Cold War but beyond, including President Bill Clinton's administration efforts to influence the 1996 Russian election in favor of Boris Yeltsin.

Covert influence operations—"meddling"—are a reality of international relations, and moral outrage in the United States on the matter is certainly noteworthy (and hypocritical), especially given the historical amnesia by many in the corporate media regarding past U.S. efforts to intervene in elections abroad. Also noteworthy are WikiLeaks' *Vault 7* revelations that the CIA admitted they not only could hack and meddle in other countries' elections and affairs, but, through what they called Marble Framework, could "hamper forensic investigators and anti-virus companies from attributing viruses, trojans and hacking attacks to the CIA," making it look like the attacks came from somewhere else.[433]

While there is clear evidence that Russia engaged in covert influence operations in the 2016 election, there is no known evidence to confirm what, if any, impact such operations had on the outcome. Kevin Roose of the *New York Times* reported that two studies commissioned by the U.S. Senate and revealed in late December 2018 described the covert disinformation campaign Russia was waging in the Unied States across social media. However, those same reports concluded that it was irresponsible to claim that Russia "definitively swung the election," because the "explicitly political content was a small percentage" of the overall content shared on social media. In fact, political content comprised just "11 percent of the total content," and only one-third of user engagement with that content was related to the election. Furthermore, there is no definitive metric to prove whether or not that specifically *Russian* messaging actually influenced people's voting, even though it tried. In their data-rich *Network Propaganda* (cited in Chapter Three), Harvard's Benkler, Faris, and Roberts found that although "the clickbait factories, the Russians, and Cambridge Analytica all took advantage of the intentional design of Facebook's system," the authors did not find significant evidence to confirm that these efforts swayed the outcome of the 2016 U.S. election.

Writing for *The Atlantic*, Russell Berman noted, "The allegations at the center of Robert Mueller's just-completed investigation, electoral collusion between the Trump campaign and the Russian government and obstruction of justice, were rightly considered the biggest presidential scandal in a generation, and perhaps in all of United States history. They were also, for the purposes of congressional oversight, a monumental distraction."[434] Berman went on to list the many things that the media, members of Congress, and the country in general could have been focusing on other than Russia, including violation of the Emoluments Clause of the Constitution, cabinet members' lavish spending and conflicts of interest, security clearance overrides for family and friends, profiting from the inauguration, and violations of international law, to name a few. The list goes on.

On a brighter note, outside the corporate press, there were numerous journalists who had not only responsibly avoided conjecture on the Trumps' ties with Russia but lambasted their colleagues for giving this spectacle the veneer of hard and breaking news, especially in prime time and on front pages. Matt Taibbi argued that the media's coverage of "Russiagate" was "this generation's WMD."[435] Pulitzer winner Chris Hedges called the affair "a shameful period for the press."[436] Glenn Greenwald referred to the corporate media's fixation on the matter as the "saddest media spectacle I've ever seen."[437] In fact, Greenwald claimed that, just as the network had done to Phil Donahue in the months preceding the U.S. invasion of Iraq,[438] MSNBC stopped allowing him to appear on the network, because he would not tout the Trump-Russia collusion narrative.[439]

Three years into Trump's first term, corporate media's coverage of Trump in general, and Russia specifically, revealed that despite their lofty promises of self-reform after the 2016 election, nothing had actually changed. Corporate media remained committed to feeding at Trump's Twitter trough, hoping for some sensational provocations they might use to buttress their ratings. T.A. Frank of *Vanity Fair* mused that positive change for the press was possible: "With any luck, some of the voices who were ignored for much of this stretch will get their due. Journalist Aaron Maté was a polite but dogged skeptic who administered a memorable vivisection."[440] Coverage by the Real News Network was also noteworthy for its journalistic integrity on the subject, as were *The Nation*'s columns by noted

Princeton and New York University Russian studies scholar Stephen F. Cohen.[441]

Substantive self-reform in corporate media seems highly unlikely, because many outlets have yet to address the actual problems that contribute to their inability, or unwillingness, to offer fact-based investigative journalism on a regular basis. Reporting on the Mueller investigation is just another example of what has driven the corporate media for a generation, in a phenomenon that media theorist Richard Grusin calls "premediation." In a piece for *The Atlantic* titled "The Mueller Industrial Complex Collapses," journalist and media studies scholar Ian Bogost explains:

> News analysts, pundits, product designers, influencers, and all the rest now create media in the present whose content anticipates future events or actions. The nonstop coverage of the 2020 Democratic primary offers an effective if humdrum example. That the left perceives the Trump presidency as odious partly explains why his opponents are coming out earlier, but the media landscape also demands and rewards this kind of anticipation. Are Kamala Harris's policies suitable for the Democratic ticket? Is Beto O'Rourke's hacker youth a benefit or a liability? Will Joe Biden run or won't he? These and other stories seem like news about the present, but they are really speculations on information from the future.
>
> The public eats this stuff up. . . . So much media is premediated now, it's almost impossible to find something whose payload isn't partly composed of practice for future events. . . . Most of the time, nobody even notices this phenomenon. Premediation

works because it homes in on natural anxieties or desires amplified by the hyper-mediated ecosystem in which television, smartphones, social media, and all the rest rot and reanimate. . . . In Mueller's case, so many people anticipating the investigation's end also banked on the specific conclusions that might accompany it. . . . The investigation's actual result now also casts a dour shadow over the Mueller-industrial complex's wares and messages. The work came at a great cost: It cannibalized the future for the benefit of the present.[442]

Corporate media also cannibalize the present by selling us the speculative, premediated future, framing coverage and selecting topics based on the interests of the few. While corporate media are fully capable of informing and educating the public, their mission is to generate profit for their owners and shareholders while shaping public opinion in ways that are favorable to those very interests. The programming of both Fox News and MSNBC serves to define the way corporate interests invest in distracting and indoctrinating the public. Until the economic underpinnings of their capitalist practices are meaningfully regulated or eliminated and they are made to serve in the public interest, corporate media will always be a distraction from true and informed civic engagement.

The authenticity of our social order as a democracy depends on the degree of authentic representation provided by our political, media, and education systems. As discussed earlier, over the years these interconnected systems have become increasingly commandeered by the influence of private, rather than public interests. Instead of serving the common good, politicians and media increasingly distract the population from its own collective interests in order to serve theirs. As a result of immersion in systems that represent and reflect wealth and power, people have become so deeply indoctrinated that notions of reclaiming the sovereignty of citizenship from the spectatorship of consumerism become increasingly difficult. While Trump's time on top is limited, he has provided source code for playing our system and exploiting our vulnerabilities to run the "the greatest infomercial in political history."[443] To guard against others doing so in the future, deliberate steps must be taken to think independently of the system. In short, we have to make America think again.

# FIVE

# MAKE AMERICA THINK AGAIN

"In the end, there is no democracy without informed citizens."

—Henry Giroux

"Post-truth is pre-fascism," says Timothy Snyder in his bestselling book *On Tyranny*. Whether or not the people of this country allow authoritarianism, disinformation, and corporate control to be further normalized depends on what we, the American people, do to strengthen ourselves, our public-interest networks, and our democracy. Reclaiming civic sovereignty from corporate influence will require the transformation of key institutions—particularly schools and media—to change with technology in order to ensure that they serve the public rather than exploit it. Given the increasing pervasiveness of communications technology in people's lives, media can be expected to play an ever more critical role in education, community, the production of knowledge, and civic engagement and action.

However, if we permit such technology and media to serve powerful commercial interests above all else, not only will truth, social justice, and democratic society continue to be diminished, but disinformation, injustice, and corruption will increasingly become the norm. For many, Donald Trump's post-truth presidency has offered a glimpse at how quickly and extensively that can occur, and how difficult and divisive a process it is to investigate and correct.

## WHAT CAN BE DONE?

This book has focused on two major institutions required for a free, self-governing society to thrive: public education and a free press. The successful transformation of schools will require a critical media-literacy education that emphasizes the Five C's: Civics education, Critical thinking, Critical awareness of media, Community engagement, and Cultural competency. A successful transformation of contemporary news media will require a shift to BLEWs news that focuses upon: Broader news framing; Local investigative journalism; Educational news media; and Whistleblowers. Taken together, such changes can arm the population with the necessary forms of civic agency and self-defense to continue to maintain public sovereignty in a rapidly changing global information system that is increasingly out of its control. As Yochai Benkler noted in his 2006 book *The Wealth of Networks:*

> We are in the midst of a technological, economic, and organizational transformation that allows us to renegotiate the terms of freedom, justice, and productivity in the information society. How we shall live in this new environment will in some significant measure depend on policy choices that we make over the next decade or so.[444]

It's been well over a decade since Benkler's observations, and well past time to implement his prescriptions. A successful public-interest transformation of schools and news organizations will be neither easy, nor achievable by professionals or insiders alone. Radical reform depends upon an engaged, informed, and organized population. Thus residents, students, parents, and communities must question, investigate, organize—and protest, if necessary—changes in the press and schools. Not to do so would be to permit ever more entrenched forms of authoritarianism, commercialism, and corporate influence to dominate our everyday lives.

## CRITICAL MEDIA LITERACY EDUCATION: THE FIVE C'S

Linguist and scholar Noam Chomsky reminds us that intellectuals are obligated to make changes to improve society, because "intellectuals are typically privileged; privilege yields opportunity, and opportunity confers responsibilities."[445] As Chomsky illustrates, educators need to be agents of change demanding that schools respond to technological evolution. Over the past five decades, the U.S. educational system has become increasingly ineffective at providing students with the skills and content required to strengthen the democratic process. Their ineffectiveness has been due predominantly to pro-corporate influence and reforms that prioritize commercial interests above all else. Media literacy education can help transform U.S. schools and strengthen democracy by emphasizing the Five C's.[446]

An emphasis on Civics and Community can equip students to identify and successfully counter commercialism as a force that seeks to replace citizen power with consumer choice. Similarly, the social disempowerment that results from partisan fragmentation and vulnerability to disinformation and propaganda can diminish with an increased focus on Critical Thinking in education. Lastly, schools can mitigate the impact of a fragmented media landscape by endowing students with increased Critical Media Literacy and Cultural Awareness. The process of transforming education will be long, and requires a patient and committed populace, one that is willing to work over the next generation to overcome the shortcomings of the previous ones. Quick commercial fixes will not solve our problems or decrease our vulnerabilities. In fact, they will only make them worse, leaving students without the skills required to think for themselves and challenge private interests to advance social justice, ecological integrity, and the overall common good.

### Civics Education

If students are to be intellectually, socially, and politically empowered in today's rapidly evolving technology-centered commercial culture, they must be taught civics in a contemporary context. The following point, noted in Chapter One, bears reiteration: A 2016 study found that 72 percent of individuals born in the United States around the 1930s believed democracy was essential to their lives, but only 30 percent of individuals born after 1980 shared that sentiment.[447] The dismal results illuminate schools' inadequacies at teaching young people the value of community, civics, and democracy. This is a result of contemporary schools and universities, in their rhetoric and pedagogy, privileging commercial interests over those of the public interest and commons. These corporate-influenced institutions produce students who are narrowly focused on economic self-interest rather than social justice, ecological sustainability, the public interest, and the common good. In fact, a 2014 study found that millennials, more than previous generations, valued their economic advancement over education.[448] This has been due, in part, to the adverse impact of skyrocketing student debt, which serves to view higher learning as a way to pay off massive loans above all else.[449] Political scientist Daniel Yenkelovich argues that "we will need to upgrade the public's role in our democracy. Americans must become as effective as citizens as they are as consumers."[450]

Educators are uniquely positioned to increase the public's capacity for democratic participation. However, they cannot do it alone. School boards and administrators must require a strong knowledge of civics from students and provide educators with the time, space, and resources to focus on civics. If they do, educators can offer an effective civics-centered pedagogy that combats the commercializing impact of entertainment culture by analyzing the history of organizing, corporate influence, and citizenship with a focus on solutions, sustainability, alternative news narratives, social movements, community, and public protest.[451] To be effective, educators must take a holistic approach to these topics, analyzing problems and solutions with an emphasis on diversity, civil liberties, and collectivism in a global context.[452] They must also rebuild teachers' unions, make them more responsive to the needs of rank-and-file members, and be more interested in critical pedagogy and intersectional curriculum than lobbying and internal politics.

Journalists also possess the ability to increase Americans' capacity for engagement. Journalism provides an essential resource for effective civics education. Given that independent investigative journalism is indispensable to democracy, an effective civics education also analyzes the ways news media and technology, when instruments of commercial private interests, can further their hegemonic capacity over a population, the public interest, and the common good. Scholars agree that a diversity of social, cultural, political, and historical narratives is critical for a robust democracy.[453] The creation of independent media outlets that partner with schools and nonprofits to produce news that strengthens democracy is critical for combating the influence of commercialism on public knowledge and governance. Independent media can and should provide platforms fostering such partnerships. Doing so will help open the way for students to explore information, topics, and perspectives typically not offered by the six major corporations that control 90 percent of the media—particularly nonprofit perspectives such as those of social movements that give voice to correcting inequality, unsustainability, and injustice.[454]

The last component of effective civics pedagogy emphasizes that people understand and appreciate the role that community organizing plays in a democracy-centered society. We must constantly remind ourselves that voting is just one of many ways we can create change. Democracy is a full-time endeavor, not a spectator sport. "Power," Frederick Douglass taught, "cedes nothing without a demand."[455] Change does not occur without sustained protest and organizing. Our education system needs to teach people how to use media as their own voice.[456]

### Critical Thinking

Pedagogy centered on critical thinking can help combat excessive partisanship, social divisiveness, aggression, and alienation. Hyper-partisanship was exploited by Trump both as a candidate and as president. It is so dangerous to a democracy that even George Washington warned about it in his 1796 Farewell Address:

> There is an opinion that parties in free countries are useful checks upon the administration of the government and serve to keep alive the spirit of liberty. This within certain limits is probably true; and in governments of a monarchical cast, patriotism may look with indulgence, if not with favor, upon the spirit of party. But in those of the popular character, in governments purely elective, it is a spirit not to be encouraged. From their natural tendency, it is certain there will always be enough of that spirit for every salutary purpose. And there being constant danger of excess, the effort ought to be by force of public opinion, to mitigate and assuage it. A fire not to be quenched, it demands a uniform vigilance to prevent its bursting into a flame, lest, instead of warming, it should consume. . . . I have already intimated to you the danger of parties in the State, with particular reference to the founding of them on geographical discriminations. Let me now take a more comprehensive view, and warn you in the most solemn manner against the baneful effects of the spirit of party generally.[457]

Partisan narratives can be harmful when they attempt to reduce the world to binaries. A population capable of critical thinking is less susceptible to political bias, disinformation, and propaganda because its members can more readily distinguish such forms of manipulation from real journalism. Critical thinking involves not only being able to identify such attempts at influence and predation, but also being able to assess evidence and arguments, draw conclusions, detect fallacies in the reasoning process, develop creative proposals and solutions, and even work to shift entire paradigms in terms of what may be possible.

An effective critical-thinking pedagogy has many components, but few agree on appropriate testing models.[458] Many of the hallmarks of education in the corporate age come at the expense of teaching critical thinking, such as standardized testing, emphasis on memorization, and limited resources.[459] Educators can effectively teach critical thinking by emphasizing the following: learning over content, identification of fallacies, argumentation and debate, intense writing, engaging with case studies, self-reflection about assumptions, exploration of alternative perspectives, and informed action.[460] Linda S. Behar-Horenstein and Lian Niu, in their critical thinking studies, found that in addition to cognitive elements, "the development of critical thinking skills often involves non-cognitive factors, such as self-esteem, open-mindedness, and personal values."[461]

Given this reality, schools need to provide space, academic freedom, and creative forms of encouragement to maximize the conditions required for critical thinking education to succeed. This will require a change in school requirements that privileges critical thinking and minimizes non-critical thinking modes of schooling, such as standardized testing. Schools must create an egalitarian climate appropriate for all philosophies and views to be considered equally, regardless of whom they may offend, as a complement to providing fact-based analysis. This requires educators to introduce critical perspectives on class, race, cultural privilege, gender discrimination, heteronormativity, capitalism, and more. It must be emphasized that educators are not biased or unethical for offering their own views in the classroom. It is only unethical if students are expected to adopt those views in order to succeed in the course. Educators must provide space for students to engage and analyze these perspectives as a way to become self-reflective regarding their own assumptions and engage in reasoned argumentation and debate.

Critical pedagogy can help diminish the influence of partisanship. First, educators must teach their students to analyze the similarities and differences between the two dominant political parties and various commercial news media outlets. Second, they must teach students to compare and contrast the major political parties and media to independent parties and media. This type of analysis is a critical starting point for being conscious of, rather than subject to, the alienating social polarization that results from extreme partisanship.

Critical thinking equips students with the tools and perspectives to thoroughly and patiently analyze content rather than take intellectual shortcuts. Among the more common intellectual shortcuts is perceiving a claim as a fact because it fits a predetermined partisan conclusion, also known as confirmation bias. In these cases, educators have a responsibility to teach students the skill sets, tools, and perspectives to be critically thinking public citizens who seek evidence to challenge or change their own beliefs. Elected officials and administrators must foster the conditions necessary for educators to transform their classrooms; they must also provide funds for the resources required to combat partisan messaging in a media-saturated society. Doing so will strengthen citizens' ability to better perceive, parse, research, think, and act independently of the influence of disinformation and political bias.

### Critical Awareness of Media

The fragmented media landscape presents some of the most challenging issues for advocates of media literacy and critical thinking. It also presents an area where education can make the largest positive impact. Again, policy makers and school administrators will need to privilege a critical awareness of media over competing requirements such as standardized testing. The internet allows individuals to find and engage like-minded people and develop shared views of evolving situations, regardless of any obvious or readily available facts that may contradict such views. Trump's media tactics have exploited social fragmentation and polarization through disinformation that has legitimized unfounded claims put forth by alienated population sectors. Without a polity that's critically aware of media, any entity—person, group, or corporation—could potentially replicate and go beyond Trump's level of manipulation. An effective critical awareness of media relies on educators to teach students how to analyze the various methodologies used for creating media narratives. Such an awareness also requires educators to provide a nuanced view of digital tools and to encourage students' creativity and cultural diversity.[462]

In the classroom, it is problematic for educators to use and reference news content without explaining how the journalistic process operates, because many students are unaware of the fundamental differences in content quality and veracity between traditional news outlets, blogs, and other platforms. Thus they are not aware of why an article posted by a reputable outlet that employs researchers, journalists, editors, proofreaders, and fact checkers is potentially more reliable as a news source than a blog page or social media post. Schools need to provide students with knowledge of how journalism operates, including its rules, codes of ethics, and editorial processes.

Teaching journalism, critical thinking, and media literacy are all steps toward educating society how to recognize propaganda, disinformation, advertising, and their ever-evolving variations. Doing so provides the necessary intellectual self-defense and elevated immunity from the covert influence that many argue is increasingly common in today's information environment. Such forms of capacity-building are far more efficacious than merely advocating that students rely on "reputable news sources," because they endow students with the ability to recognize bias and guard against persuasion on their own.

A critical awareness of media is also cultivated when educators offer nuanced views of digital tools and content, such as cellphones and social media platforms, in the classroom. When they enter the classroom, most students in the United States today are already familiar with the digital landscape. They are, in large part, already cognizant of some of the positive and negative uses of digital tools, and educators must teach them to be fully aware of the possibilities. While recognizing adverse impacts such as screen addiction, educators must also recognize that technology can be used to foster awareness of public movements, social injustices, and viable solutions that may be unpopular with advertisers and other private interests, including the big tech companies that profit from the sale and use of such digital products.

Scholars contend that a pedagogy that involves student-produced media raises their overall critical awareness and increases their civic agency. Learning to create media means learning to have a voice in the information age. As scholars have noted, digital space for students' creative impulses is essential for promoting positive change among youths.[463] For example, young people have created codes that mimic corporate software, known as "open software." Created in a nonprofit effort among many collaborative parties who may never physically meet one another, such cooperative endeavors generate valuable online resources for use by the public, free of charge.[464] Through the process of creating digital content and tools, students also become more aware of their potential for positive and negative impact. Young people today are a core part of an increasingly networked society, and they have innovatively contributed to—if not driven—many social movements to abolish inequity, violence, and oppression.

### Community Engagement and Cultural Competency

Policy makers and school administrators can break students free from the chains of market demands if they privilege hiring and training educators capable of offering an effective community-engagement and cultural-competency pedagogy in the classroom. This can help overcome the bigotry and siloed realities that also flourish as a result of mobile communications technology. It will also require changes to employment requirements, the creation of teacher-training programs, and curriculum alterations to make space for related content.

A critical concept to teaching community engagement and cultural competency is *empathy*.[465] Psychologist Alfred Adler explains that "empathy is seeing with the eyes of another, listening with the ears of another and feeling with the heart of another."[466] Empathy refers to an individual's ability to put themselves, cognitively, in the position of another person to better understand their perspective.[467] Philosopher and psychologist Alice Miller reminds us of the connection between education and empathy, noting, "We must have empathy, and empathy grows as we learn."[468] In the absence of such emphasis in education today, the population has been increasingly conditioned to believe that expressions of intolerance and aggression, along with insults, name calling, and appeals for popularity, are normal and acceptable aspects of how people communicate online, run for office, govern, and debate.[469] Author and social critic Os Guinness warned that such conduct threatens the very foundations of American democracy, noting:

> Civility must truly be restored. It is not to be confused with niceness and mere etiquette or dismissed as squeamishness about differences. It is a tough, robust, substitutive concept that is a republican virtue, critical to both democracy and civil society, and a manner of conduct that will be decisive for the future of the American Republic.[470]

Civility can be restored through the cultivation of empathy for others. Without empathy, increased social alienation and division is ensured. Empathy bridges divides by elevating the role of listening over attacking, providing space to consider others' stories, experiences, and grievances. Empathy provides a path for appreciating diversity and advancing solidarity across differences of culture, race, gender, age, and location.

Cultural competency education aims to increase empathy, civic agency, and community engagement. The National Education Association defines cultural competency as "having an awareness of one's own cultural identity and views about difference, and the ability to learn and build on the varying cultural and community norms of students and their families."[471] It is an essential life skill for students to understand and appreciate others' social, cultural, and political proclivities. This is especially helpful in understanding bigotry and alienation, as well as mitigating forms of intolerance and authoritarianism on the rise today in the United States and around the world. Empathy across cultures can ameliorate much of the polarization, hatred, and anger fueled by Trump's post-truth impact on the country.

The impact of the fragmented media landscape can be diminished through community engagement praxis. The concept of such praxis, previously termed service learning, derives from the seminal work of John Dewey in 1938, reasoning that students learn more and become more engaged through a pedagogy of embedded experience rather than the traditional classroom.[472] "Education is not preparation for life," wrote Dewey: "Education is life itself."[473] Students should not be taught about a world they are about to enter, but should participate in that world to gain perspective and effective methodologies for survival. As an application of this, service learning courses enable students to attain skills while helping them create meaningful and positive change in their communities.[474]

For example, having students participate in the collection and distribution of food to those with food insecurity could be part of a course focused on organizational communication, management, economics, or sociology. There are various models for service-learning programs that may include person-to-person interactions between students and the community, with the goal of creating awareness projects, compiling studies, or bringing benefits to the community through the restoration and accumulation of needed supplies or resources.[475]

A culturally competent citizen is empathetic and can responsibly engage with others and discuss key topics of the day without being triggered by hyper-partisan cues prevalent in our current information system. Scholars warn that political discussions can be problematic if individuals get bogged down in skirmishes that attempt to determine "who is more authentic, more oppressed, and thus more correct."[476] Teaching empathy allows for more nuanced and evidence-based debate, and encourages those who disagree to do so respectfully, even didactically. Educators must assume that there is little consensus on the value of diversity, equity, and inclusivity in today's commercially dominated society. Educators, therefore, must engage in critical discussion and analysis in order to model and provide evidence as to why these are enriching and indispensable goals at individual, community, and national levels.

## TRANSFORMATION OF THE WAYS WE STAY INFORMED

In addition to education, a transformation of news media is necessary to better arm citizens with the information required to live and function with full civic agency. Citizens cannot be expected to be equitable participants in a democracy unless they are properly informed. They need accurate news stories to help them determine their needs and best interests in a constantly changing world.

As a pillar of democracy, the press should serve public interests over and above private ones. In its current state, however, the press serves the commercial interests of its owners. As citizens, we must demand that policy makers protect journalism as a viable vocation that pays a living wage. Furthermore, we must demand that our tax dollars go toward cultivating new nonprofit press outlets that serve the public interest. In the same way our current budget finances the military and offers tax breaks for commercial corporations, our national budget needs to supply our public sphere and civic infrastructure with a nonprofit media and news system that is free of advertising and commercial motivation.

This transformation may take sustained lobbying and protest to achieve, but U.S. history demonstrates that such transformations are possible. Among the changes that are essential are the following: broadening of news media framing, increasing the roles of local investigative journalism, strengthening educational news programming, and increasing the role of whistleblowers.

### Broadening News Media Framing

In January 2019, award-winning reporter William Arkin of NBC News and MSNBC decided that after thirty years in the business, he had enough. In his public letter of resignation, he explained why in a way only an insider could. He began by stating:

> January 4 is my last day at NBC News and I'd like to say goodbye to my friends, hopefully not for good. This isn't the first time I've left NBC, but this time the parting is more bittersweet, the world and the state of journalism in tandem crisis. My expertise, though seeming to be all the more central to the challenges and dangers we face, also seems to be less valued at the moment. And I find myself completely out of synch with the network, being

neither a day-to-day reporter nor interested in the Trump circus.[477]

Arkin went on to lament not being able to change the system from the inside, despite how hard he tried. He continued, highlighting myopic media framing that mirrored and buttressed state policy, especially on foreign affairs. He noted:

> For me I realized how out of step I was when I looked at Trump's various bumbling intuitions: his desire to improve relations with Russia, to denuclearize North Korea, to get out of the Middle East, to question why we are fighting in Africa, even in his attacks on the intelligence community and the FBI. Of course, he is an ignorant and incompetent impostor. And yet I'm alarmed at how quick NBC is to mechanically argue the contrary, to be in favor of policies that just spell more conflict and more war. Really? We shouldn't get out Syria? We shouldn't go for the bold move of denuclearizing the Korean peninsula? Even on Russia, though we should be concerned about the brittleness of our democracy that it is so vulnerable to manipulation, do we really yearn for the Cold War? And don't even get me started with the FBI: What? We now lionize this historically destructive institution?
>
> Even without Trump, our biggest challenge as we move forward is that we have become exhausted parents of our infant (and infantile) social media children. And because of the "cycle," we at NBC (and all others in the field of journalism) suffer from a really bad case of not being able to ever

take a breath. We are a long way from resolving the rules of the road in this age, whether it be with regard to our personal conduct or anything related to hard news. I also don't think that we are on a straight line towards digital nirvana, that is, that all of this information will democratize and improve society. I sense that there is already smartphone and social media fatigue creeping across the land, and my guess is that nothing we currently see—nothing that is snappy or chatty—will solve our horrific challenges of information overload or the role (and nature) of journalism. And I am sure that once Trump leaves center stage, society will have a gigantic media hangover.[478]

Keeping Arkin's decades of accumulated wisdom in mind, it is in the public interest for news organizations to become less partisan and more diverse in terms of the variety of sources utilized to inform the populations they serve. Rather than constantly presenting politicians as eager to propagate a particular spin or party narrative, news media need to broaden the spectrum of views and voices beyond that of the two-party system to include a wider range of scholars, professionals, experts, journalists, and community voices involved with an issue. For example, in a discussion of climate change, it distracts from the facts to focus on what a politician from either party may espouse. It is more valuable to have climate scientists explain and debate the data and studies.

News organizations need to stop pretending that they are "balanced" because they may present both Republicans and Democrats as guests. The United States is a nation of more than 300 million people, and the two parties represent only a fraction of the population's needs. Partisan debates in contemporary news media traditionally exclude an enormous range of perspectives, including those that voice the concerns and views of low-income families, Native American communities, and individuals and groups whose solutions are critical of corporate power, Wall Street, and capitalism. Such exclusionary practices serve to censor out a wealth of data, knowledge, and scholarly views that may not be favorable to advertisers or the corporate donors that bankroll the two parties' electoral runs. Furthermore, there are numerous national issues that require alliance building, such as dismantling the privileges and structural injustices that led to national movements such as Standing Rock, Black Lives Matter, Occupy, and #MeToo.

Finally, media should prioritize credibility. When a person or institution deliberately lies to the press in an effort to spread disinformation, clear steps should be taken to protect the public from such efforts in the future. This is particularly critical given the degree to which Americans have become inured to chronic presidential lying. In February 2019, the *Washington Post*, which has been cataloguing the number of false statements made by President Trump, announced that he "lied to the American people more than 8,000 times in his first two years" in office, and counting.[479]

As stated earlier, commercial media are in the business of marketing the immediate and sensational, and have no mandate to serve the public interest. While the public can have impact by boycotting businesses deemed to lack credibility, ultimately we need to develop funding and policy to create a nonprofit media system dedicated to serving communities with higher standards of credibility, accountability, and integrity.

### Local and Investigative Journalism

Localism in news is essential for community-level democracy to operate effectively. We all live somewhere, and we need to remain informed about the news, voices, and perspectives in our communities. Journalists are needed at the local level to investigate, report, and raise awareness about the issues, challenges, opportunities, and possible solutions at the local level.

Local news media are experiencing the same threats of extinction as national media. Studies show that more than two-thirds of people in the United States follow local journalism closely.[480] However, due to budget cuts at news agencies, local journalism has been increasingly scaled back in many areas.[481] In fact, the far-right media conglomerate Sinclair Broadcasting has developed a grip on local journalism, buying up 200 television stations across the United States.[482] They have been found to disseminate word-for-word matching scripts that local news anchors are compelled to read as part of their local programming.[483] Reversing this trend will require a series of significant reforms at the very least, but will likely require more radical changes in the long term.

Given the dismal state of the economy for journalists in general, incentives are needed to cultivate independent local news programming and community journalism. Local journalism can be re-created through subsidies from federal and state governments, as well as the involvement of state- and community-level colleges and universities. The federal and state government could offer tax reductions to businesses and individuals who further the ends of local journalism. Policy makers and administrators could divert funds at colleges and universities to develop a more robust journalism program that offers critical local news content.

Students should be taught to engage in deep investigative stories that can transform their communities.

The nonprofit media organization Free Press has developed exemplary programs for strengthening the ways media should serve democracy and social justice in the United States. One such program, New Voices, focused on reinvigorating local journalism around the country. In summer 2018, the program helped secure $5 million to invest in local journalism in the state of New Jersey as a result of something called the Civic Info Bill. While the amount is small in the big picture, it is a huge step toward revitalizing local journalism in one state, and serves as a model for others. With the approval of the state governor, money from the sale of two old public television licenses was used to create the Civic Information Consortium, a nonprofit organization founded to help develop and provide funding for innovative ideas to improve local news and civic information. This is a major breakthrough. As noted by *Neiman Reports*, "Compared to its peers, the United States is notoriously stingy when it comes to government dollars supporting media. Norway spends about $135 per capita each year on its public broadcasters; Germany spends $107, the U.K. $86, France $55, and Canada $22. The U.S. spends about $2.25. (That's about half a Starbucks grande iced caramel macchiato a year.)"[484]

State-level support should be just one of several tiers of support for non-commercial, public-interest media. This is why Free Press founder and media scholar Robert W. McChesney has argued strongly for federally subsidized, but not controlled, media in the United States. Such support could help support the re-emergence of non-commercial community radio stations, local newspapers, and online civic platforms. A decade ago he wrote, with independent journalist John Nichols, about the U.S. founders' belief in a strong and vibrant free press: "The value of federal journalism subsidies as a percentage of gross domestic product in the first half of the 19th century ran, by our calculations, to about $30 billion per year in current dollars. It is this sort of commitment, established by Jefferson and Madison, that we must imagine to address the current crisis."[485]

In February of 2019, the Poynter Institute noted:

> The John S. and James L. Knight Foundation announced a $300 million commitment toward rebuilding local news ecosystems during the next five years, with details on where the first $100 million of that money would go. . . . Knight is concerned about declines in trust for media and other democratic institutions . . . and "[they] think that local news is actually the best place to start rebuilding it."[486]

Organizations and projects slated to receive funding include the American Journalism Project, ProPublica, Frontline, Reporters Committee for Freedom of the Press, News Literacy Project, and the Solutions Journalism Network, among others, all of which sound very promising in efforts to bolster local journalism across the board.[487]

Finally, the long-term goal of efforts to strengthen local journalism should be to develop a system by which journalists can share their local stories with a larger audience—a non-commercial, public interest, local-to-global news media network. Doing so would allow communities to partner with one another and form alliances to better address public health and safety concerns, emerging environmental challenges, social justice issues, and other matters of the public interest. Harvard's NeimanLab asked Victor Pickard, a noted media historian at the University of Pennsylvania's Annenberg School for Communication, to weigh in on its "Predictions for Journalism 2019" series. This is the same series that hinted at the aforementioned focus by the Knight Foundation on local collaboration in the coming year. While Pickard stated that more philanthropic and nonprofit models were good, and outlets such as ProPublica showed great promise, he also argued for more systemic solutions. These included everything from a more robustly funded public media to big tech companies such as Google being "compelled to offset social harms and help create a journalism trust fund." Pickard concluded:

> If we start with the premise that commercial journalism is a dead end for what our democracy requires, it may entirely reorient tired conversations about the future of news. It might free us to think more creatively and more boldly. As the market continues to drive journalism into the ground, here's hoping we can finally accept what stares us in the face and plan a path forward accordingly. We have nothing to lose but our democracy.[488]

### Educational News Media

Emphasis on infotainment and celebrities reflects news media's commercial goal of harvesting the attention of the largest possible audience for sale to advertisers. This goal has led to a serious and sustained dumbing down of news programming. For example, most digital and television news operations, ad agencies, and public relations firms produce content at a middle-school level of understanding, because data show that doing so enables them to acquire the largest possible audience.[489]

Newspapers, past and present, have produced content for high-school-level comprehension.[490] However, the majority of information consumed today is being delivered not through the printed page but via screens. A study found that 67.3 percent of Facebook posts are written at a fifth grader's level or below.[491] Worse, the content provided serves to reinforce rather than offer counter-evidence to users' beliefs. Social media companies' profits derive from advertisers, but that revenue is only realized if users remain on the platform where they can encounter the advertisements.[492] People often stop using their social media when they find information there that they do not like or that challenges their views.[493] As a result, the algorithmic models of social media websites, such as Facebook, actively work to keep people tuned to their screens by reinforcing rather than challenging people's previously held beliefs.[494]

In his book *Anti-Social Media*, Siva Vaidhyanathan argues that Facebook is "the most pervasive and powerful catalyst of information pollution and destructive nonsense." He argues that "we are in the midst of a worldwide, internet-based assault on democracy."[495] Facebook is but one of countless operations, including Reddit, 4chan, and Twitter, that heighten the potential for disinformation to be propagated virally through user sharing. As a result, the public is increasingly exposed to a higher volume of incoming communications that have a decreasing level of credibility, depth, and complexity. As Jonathan Swift noted in 1710:

Falsehood flies, and truth comes limping after it, so
that when men come to be undeceived, it is too late;
the jest is over, and the tale hath had its effect: like
a man, who hath thought of a good repartee when
the discourse is changed, or the company parted; or
like a physician, who hath found out an infallible
medicine, after the patient is dead.[496]

In today's digital media landscape, accessing and
spreading falsehoods takes only a click. We need to slow
down and deliberately think critically about the news and
information we read online, lest we experience the futility
that Swift warned us about so long ago.

This downward trend has been reflected in U.S. political discourse as well. For example, since Abraham Lincoln's
presidency, U.S. presidents have gone from speaking at a
high school level to using roughly a sixth-grade level today.
An analysis of presidential candidates' speeches by researchers in Carnegie Mellon University's Language Technologies Institute (LTI) found that most candidates used words
and grammar typical of students in grades six through eight,
though Donald Trump tended to lag behind the rest.[497]
Of the past fifteen U.S. presidents, President Trump has
demonstrated the lowest level of spoken literacy.

To counter these trends, we clearly need to support
the development of non-commercial educational news
programming that not only explores issues in depth but
also links citizens to resources that allow them to investigate further and connect with community groups and institutions working to address the issues in a public-interest
framework. This is an area where a reform of schools and
media overlaps. By definition, educational news media produce programming with greater detail, context, and depth.

In the past decade, new digital technologies have enabled more grassroots media production in the form of podcasting, video clips, animation shorts, blogs, vlogs, and more. This has lessened some of the constraints of commercial media and has allowed citizen journalists, academics, and others to produce content that is more in-depth and educational, even activist in nature. Some standouts include podcasts such as *MediaRoots* with Abby and Robbie Martin, Eric Draitser's *Counterpunch Radio*, Kevin Gosztola and Rhania Khalek's *Unauthorized Disclosure*, video news productions such as Abby Martin's *The Empire Files*, as well as online news sources including the union reporters at *Truthout*, Mnar Muhawesh's *MintPress News*, Eleanor Goldfield's *Act Out!*, and even what is now referred to as investigative comedy, like Lee Camp's popular *Redacted Tonight* program and stand-up tours, to name just a few. Alternative online news outlets such as the Real News Network out of Baltimore do full video production of investigative reports, in-depth interviews, and coverage of local political events and issues as well as making great strides in connecting local and global issues.

What threads these programs together is that they all report outside the corporate frame of news, and particularly focus on giving people information they do not get from corporate and establishment media—information that can spur dialogue, foster questioning of the status quo, provide key historical and factual context to complicated and controversial issues, and motivate increased civic engagement in society. All of these components should work to create more educational and diverse news media programming.

Another example in public media, *Frontline* on PBS, offers long-format programming to examine a single topic through an analysis of evidence and a diverse array of experts—not a panel of argumentative hyper-partisan talking heads. Educational news media prioritize primary sources, experts, and scholars over political partisans or celebrities. Experts often disagree on assessments, but they can offer a more nuanced understanding of issues' complexities and can help members of the public become more informed and involved as a result.

As the great 20th-century journalist George Seldes once said, "Journalism's job is not impartial 'balanced' reporting. Journalism's job is to tell the people what is really going on." Increasing educational news media can help journalism do exactly that.

### *Whistleblowers*

Whistleblowers are the brave people who risk employment, reputation, friends, freedom, and sometimes their lives, to provide citizens with information that those in power attempt to keep secret. Historically, whistleblower protections date all the way back to the American War for Independence (1778), when the Congress passed a law stating that "it is the duty of all persons in the service of the United States, as well as all other inhabitants thereof, to give the earliest information to Congress or any other proper authority of any misconduct, frauds or misdemeanors committed by any officers or persons in the service of these states, which may come to their knowledge."[498] Explicit protections for whistleblowers were enacted into law in 1989 through the Whistleblower Protection Act, and further expanded in 2012 through President Obama's policy directive "Protecting Whistleblowers with Access to Classified Information." However, despite these apparent protections, in actuality numerous whistleblowers have faced federal threats, or worse, including Barrett

Brown, Thomas Drake, John Kiriakou, Julian Assange, Edward Snowden, Chelsea Manning, and Reality Winner. Under Barack Obama's presidency, more whistleblowers were targeted, persecuted, and prosecuted than in all previous administrations combined. In order to strengthen our democracy, the public, policymakers, and courts must defend the freedom of individuals to blow the whistle.

Whistleblowers provide invaluable information to journalists, educators, and the American public by exposing unethical and corrupt practices that they believe the public has a right to know. For example, Daniel Ellsberg leaked classified documents to the press in order to challenge the U.S. government's public portrayal of its military activities in the Vietnam War.[499] Edward Snowden, a government-contracted employee for the National Security Agency, leaked documents in order to expose the fact that U.S. government was colluding with software companies to secretly collect private information from millions of U.S. citizens' phones and computers.[500]

The corporate press has largely attacked whistleblowers or questioned their motives rather than analyzing the relevance and meaning of the information they have released.[501] For example, in response to Snowden's leak, NBC's popular Sunday morning program *Meet the Press* hosted a panel titled "Why shouldn't you be charged with a crime?"; Michael Grunwald of *Time* tweeted that he "can't wait to write a defense of the drone strike that takes out" Julian Assange of WikiLeaks for helping Snowden; and the editorial board of the *Washington Post* published an op-ed suggesting Snowden surrender himself.

Among the few who supported Snowden were two reporters—Glenn Greenwald and Laura Poitras—who were working for *The Guardian* of London at the time, and whose investigative reporting helped break the story at a time when the U.S. press showed little interest in exposing government lies about surveillance. In 2014, they won the Pulitzer Prize for Public Service for their reporting on the matter, recognition that shows there is hope for a vibrant and free press, one that is willing to publish controversial information to keep the public informed and hold those in power accountable.[502]

Whistleblowers help keep governments and corporations in check. Media outlets—and the population as a whole—need to help cultivate a climate where whistleblowers feel they can safely expose corruption in high places. This will likely require more independent media outlets to provide space and safety for whistleblowers to share data and communicate. While many media outlets accept anonymous news tips, operations such as *The Intercept*, Freedom of the Press Foundation, WikiLeaks, Electronic Frontier Foundation, and Government Accountability Project, as well as filmmakers like Michael Moore, Robert Greenwald, and Oliver Stone, have specifically encouraged and supported whistleblowers and have created platforms for them to send large amounts of data securely.[503] This is a much-needed development in our current culture of media consolidation, censorship, and increased attacks on both whistleblowers and journalists.

## EPILOGUE: INFORMATION WAR

Renée DiResta, research director at the firm New Knowledge, co-authored a major report on disinformation for the Senate Intelligence Committee in late fall of 2018.[504] Several months prior to the release of the report, DiResta independently wrote an influential essay titled "The Digital Maginot Line," examining the implications of living in an era of intense information manipulation. "There is a war happening," wrote DiResta. "We are immersed in an evolving, ongoing conflict: an Information World War in which state actors, terrorists, and ideological extremists leverage the social infrastructure underpinning everyday life to sow discord and erode shared reality."[505]

For DiResta, consciousness itself is the terrain in which disinformation operations are waged. "The human *mind* is the territory," she writes. "If you aren't a combatant, *you* are the territory. And once a combatant wins over a sufficient number of minds, they have the power to influence culture and society, policy and politics."[506] According to DiResta, "influence operations exploit divisions in our society using vulnerabilities in our information ecosystem. We have to move away from treating this as a problem of giving people better facts . . . and move towards thinking about it as an ongoing battle for the integrity of our information infrastructure."[507]

In her essay, she echoes the ethos and instruction of early twentieth-century public relations guru Edward Bernays, nephew of Sigmund Freud, who wrote in his 1928 book, *Propaganda* (in Chapter one, titled "Organizing Chaos"):

> The conscious and intelligent manipulation of the organized habits and opinions of the masses is an important element in democratic society. Those who manipulate this unseen mechanism of society constitute an invisible government which is the true ruling power of our country. We are governed, our minds molded, our tastes formed, our ideas suggested, largely by men we have never heard of. This is a logical result of the way in which our demo-

cratic society is organized. Vast numbers of human beings must cooperate in this manner if they are to live together as a smoothly functioning society. Our invisible governors are, in many cases, unaware of the identity of their fellow members in the inner cabinet. They govern us by their qualities of natural leadership, their ability to supply needed ideas and by their key positions in the social structure. Whatever attitude one chooses toward this condition, it remains a fact that in almost every act of our daily lives, whether in the sphere of politics or business, in our social conduct or our ethical thinking, we are dominated by the relatively small number of persons . . . who understand the mental processes and social patterns of the masses. It is they who pull the wires which control the public mind, who harness old social forces and contrive new ways to bind and guide the world.[508]

Indeed, we are in the midst of a complex set of battles between those who value democratic principles and those who seek to exploit them, on whatever side, and our circumstances have only become more complicated since the time of Bernays, though the battlefield for the public mind remains much the way he outlined it. Seen in the context of information war, inaction is a tacit form of support for the forces seeking to undermine our information systems and manipulate society. Action is needed by everyone who values truth, transparency, and participatory democracy. As historian Howard Zinn argued, "You cannot be neutral on a moving train."[509]

We clearly should not expect any of the many actors—domestic, foreign, corporate—to self-regulate in the public interest. Indications are that the deliberate propagation of disinformation is proliferating, and the American public is being targeted by an increasing number of forces. Simply asking politicians and tech giants like Facebook or Twitter to address and fix the challenges we face is not enough. History has shown that such entities will not respond without significant and sustained public pressure.

Changing the system *is* possible. Doing so will require people to organize, agitate, and insist on policy—and a way of life—that prioritizes the interests of the public over those of corporations. Successful public-interest shifts, particularly in media and education, can provide the population with the tools needed to sustain democratic sovereignty and subordinate corporate interests to the priorities of social justice, environmental sustainability, and the common good.

Without widespread organizing, resistance, and pressure, the information war against public consciousness, truth, and sovereignty will intensify. While characters like Donald Trump and Steve Bannon were able to acquire power, in part, by weaponizing disinformation and exploiting public vulnerabilities, they did not invent the tactics. The very possibility that they could get so far was the result of decades-long corporate influence over the U.S. political economy and democratic culture.

What happens next is up to us, but time is of the essence. We still have the ability to make a difference by acting together, but act we must. In this new millennium, it's long past time for renewed and revelatory directions that favor the public sphere and restoration of the commons, or else we may find ourselves living in the ecologically unsustainable, corporate-dominated, authoritarian surveillance state toward which we've been heading for a long time.

A better future is possible. To help change direction toward a more just and robust civil society, we need to build a non-commercial public media system, and increase media literacy and critical pedagogy in schools. Doing so will help us better arm ourselves with the power that knowledge gives, and enable us to live with greater deliberation, democracy, and dignity.

APPENDIX

# RESOURCES FOR READERS
Encouraging Critical Media Literacy
and Civic Engagement

**FREE ONLINE RESOURCES**
**Action Coalition for Media Education (ACME)** is an independently funded critical media literacy education network that teaches effective approaches to engage, challenge, and create media in ways that empower individuals and communities. Educators can adopt critical media literacy pedagogy in their classrooms with the lesson plans and exercises provided through ACME's website. www.acmesmartmediaeducation.net

**First Draft News** offers a free course on verification curriculum, where students can learn how to verify eyewitness media and detect fabricated websites, visual memes, and manipulated videos. Users can take either the five-unit course, designed primarily for journalists, or the one-hour abridged version, designed for the general public. Both courses are designed so that users can take the course from start to finish or excerpt elements to integrate into classrooms and courses, with clear credit to First Draft and Dr. Claire Wardle. www.firstdraftnews.org

**The Global Critical Media Literacy Project** is a digitally connected network of educators, activists, and students dedicated to cradle-to-grave education in critical media literacy principles and strategies. Their goal is to empower learners of all ages, largely through community engagement, to participate deeply with the world and to take action on issues that matter to them. The project's Educator Resource Guide provides a wealth of content and lesson plans that serve to enhance classrooms with critical media literacy material. In addition, the website publishes student work as a way to demonstrate the powerful outcomes of an effective critical media literacy pedagogy. www.gcml.org

**Project Censored** educates students and the public about the importance of a truly free press for democratic self-government. It exposes and opposes news censorship and promotes independent investigative journalism, media literacy, and critical thinking. The website includes a series of under-reported stories, podcasts, radio programs, and educator content that serves to enhance classroom discussion and strengthen users' understanding of democracy and media. www.projectcensored.org

**Screen Free Week** is an annual international celebration in which families, schools, and communities swap digital entertainment for the joys of life beyond the screen. Instead of watching TV, surfing the web, or playing with apps and video games, they read, play, think, create, get active, and spend more time with family and friends. The organization offers resources and strategies for use of more responsible media resources and/or limiting media consumption. www. screenfree.org

**Verification Handbook** is a groundbreaking new resource for journalists and aid providers authored by leading journalists from the BBC, Storyful, ABC, Digital First Media, and other verification experts. It provides tools, techniques, and step-by-step guidelines for how to deal with user-generated content (UGC) during emergencies. It is free for download from the website. www.verification-handbook.com

## SELECTED TOPICAL READINGS AND RELATED MATERIALS

### Critical Thinking
- Levitin, Daniel J. *Weaponized Lies: How to Think Critically in the Post-Truth Era*. Penguin, 2017.
- Browne, M. Neil, and Keeley, Stuart M. *Asking the Right Questions: A Guide to Critical Thinking*, 12th ed. Pearson, 2018.

### Truth And Intellectualism
- Bartlett, Bruce. *The Truth Matters: A Citizen's Guide to Separating Facts from Lies and Stopping Fake News in Its Tracks*. Ten Speed Press, 2017.
- Frankfurt, Henry G. *On Bullshit*. Princeton University Press, 2005.
- Frankfurt, Henry G. *On Truth*. Random House, 2006.
- Kakutani, Michiko. *The Death of Truth: Notes on Falsehood in the Age of Trump*. Dugan Books, 2018.
- McIntyre, Lee. *Post Truth*. Massachusetts Institute of Technology, 2018.
- Nichols, Tom. *The Death of Expertise: The Campaign Against Established Knowledge and Why It Matters*. Oxford University Press, 2017.
- Stephens-Davidowitz, Seth. *Everybody Lies: Big Data, New Data, and What the Internet Can Tell Us About Who We Really Are*. Harper Collins, 2017.

### Political Economy

- Foer, Franklin. *World Without Mind: The Existential Threat Of Big Tech*. Penguin, 2017.
- Freeland, Chrystia. *Plutocrats: The Rise of the New Global Super-Rich and the Fall of Everyone Else*. Penguin, 2012.
- Graeber, David. *Debt: The First 5,000 Years*. Melville House, 2011.
- Mayer, Jane. *Dark Money: The Hidden History of the Billionaires Behind the Rise of the Radical Right*. Anchor Books, 2017.
- Mazzucato, Mariana. *The Entrepreneurial State: Debunking Public vs. Private Sector Myths*. Vol. 1. Anthem Press, 2015.
- Nader, Ralph. *Breaking Through Power: It's Easier Than We Think*. City Lights Publishers, 2016.
- Parenti, Michael. *Democracy for the Few*, 9th edition. Wadsworth, 2011.
- Phillips, Peter. *Giants: The Global Power Elite*. Seven Stories Press, 2018.
- Piketty, Thomas. *Capital in the 21st Century*. Belknap, 2013.
- **Documentaries**
  - *The Corporation*. Joel Bakan, Zeitgeist Films, 2003.
  - *Requiem for the American Dream*. With Noam Chomsky, Naked City Films and PF Pictures, 2015.

### U.S. Political Culture

- Andersen, Kurt. *Fantasyland: How America Went Haywire: A 500-Year History*. Random House, 2017.
- Kornacki, Steve. *The Red and the Blue: The 1990s and the Birth of Political Tribalism*. Ecco, 2018.
- Vance, J.D. *Hillbilly Elegy*. Harper Collins, 2016.

### American Conservatism

- Maclean, Nancy. *Democracy In Chains: The Deep History of the Radical Right's Stealth Plan for America*. Penguin, 2017.
- Robert O. Self. *All in the Family: The Realignment of American Democracy Since the 1960s*. Hill And Wang, 2013.

### American Liberalism

- Featherstone, Liza, ed. *False Choices: The Faux Feminism of Hillary Rodham Clinton*. Verso Books, 2016.
- Frank, Thomas. *Listen, Liberal: Or, What Ever Happened to the Party of the People?* Macmillan, 2016.
- Hedges, Chris. *Death of the Liberal Class*. Nation Books, 2010.
- Suskind, Ron. *Confidence Men: Wall Street, Washington, and the Education of a President*. Harper, 2011.

### Media History/Theory, Propaganda, and Censorship

- Bagdikian, Benjamin. *The New Media Monopoly*. Beacon Press, 2004.
- Benkler, Yochai, Robert Faris, and Hal Roberts. *Network Propaganda: Manipulation, Disinformation, and Radicalization in American Politics*. Oxford University Press, 2018.
- Bernays, Edward. *Propaganda*. Introduction by Mark Crispin Miller. Ig Publishing, 2004 (1928).
- Boorstin, Daniel J. *The Image: A Guide to Pseudo-Events in America*. Penguin, 1962.
- Dines, G., Humez, J.M., Yousman, B., & Yousman Bindig, L., eds. *Gender, Race and Class in Media: A Critical Reader*. Sage Publications, 2018.
- Frechette, Julie, and Rob Williams, eds. *Media Edu-*

*cation for a Digital Generation*. Routledge, 2016.

- Fuchs, Christian. *Social Media, A Critical Introduction*. Sagecrest, 2017.

- Hedges, Chris. *Empire of Illusion: The End of Literacy and the Triumph of Spectacle*. Nation Books, 2009.

- Herman, Edward, and Noam Chomsky. *Manufacturing Consent: The Political Economy of the Mass Media*. Pantheon Books, 1988.

- Huff, Mickey, and Andy Lee Roth. *Censored 2019: Fighting the Fake News Invasion*. Seven Stories Press, 2018.

- Levitsky, Steven, and Daniel Ziblatt. *How Democracies Die*. Harvard, 2018.

- McChesney, Robert W. *Digital Disconnect: How Capitalism is Turning the Internet Against Democracy*. The New Press, 2013.

- McChesney, Robert W. *The Problem of the Media: U.S. Communication Politics in the 21st Century*. Monthly Review Press, 2004.

- Michael, David. *Doubt Is Their Product: How Industry's Assault on Science Threatens Your Health*. Oxford University Press, 2008.

- Pickard, Victor. *America's Battle for Media Democracy: The Triumph of Corporate Libertarianism and the Future of Media Reform*. Cambridge University Press. 2015.

- Postman, Neil. *Amusing Ourselves to Death: Public Discourse in the Age of Show Business*. Penguin, 1985.

- Roth, Andy Lee, and Mickey Huff. *Censored 2018: Press Freedoms in a 'Post-Truth' World*. Seven Stories Press, 2017.

- Stanley, Jason. *How Propaganda Works*. Princeton University Press, 2015.

- Tufekci, Zeynep. *Twitter and Tear Gas: The Power and Fragility of Networked Protest.* Yale University Press, 2017.
- Wendling, Mike. *Alt-Right: From 4chan to the White House.* Pluto Press, 2018.
- Wu, Tim. *The Attention Merchants: The Epic Scramble to Get Inside Our Heads.* Vintage, 2017.
- **Documentaries**
  - *The Century of the Self.* Adam Curtis. BBC, 2002.
  - *Boogie Man: The Lee Atwater Story*, Interpositive Media, 2008.
  - *Project Censored the Movie: Ending the Reign of Junk Food News*, Hole in the Media Productions and Project Censored, 2013.
  - *Merchants of Doubt.* Sony Pictures Classics, 2014.
  - *Get Me Roger Stone*, Netflix, 2017.
  - *The Facebook Dilemma.* Frontline, 2018.

### *Authoritarianism*

- Fuchs, Christian. *Digital Demagogue: Authoritarian Capitalism in the Age of Trump and Twitter.* Pluto Press, 2018.
- Giroux, Henry. *American Nightmare: Facing the Challenges of Fascism.* City Lights, 2018.
- Paxton, Robert O. *The Anatomy of Fascism.* Vintage, 2007.
- Snyder, Timothy. *On Tyranny: Twenty Lessons from the Twentieth Century.* Tim Dugin Books, 2017.
- Stanley, Jason. *How Fascism Works: The Politics of Us and Them.* Random House, 2018.
- Wolin, Sheldon S. *Democracy Incorporated: Managed Democracy and the Specter of Inverted Totalitarianism*, New Edition. Princeton University Press, 2017.

## MEDIA WATCHDOG GROUPS

**Fairness And Accuracy in Reporting (FAIR)** is a national media watch group offering well-documented criticism of media bias and censorship. It works to invigorate the First Amendment by advocating for greater diversity in the press and by scrutinizing media practices that marginalize public-interest, minority, and dissenting viewpoints. It maintains a regular dialogue with reporters at news outlets across the country, providing constructive critiques when called for and applauding exceptional, hard-hitting journalism. www.fair.org

**Politifact** publishes fact-based assessments of public statements and claims in order to provide citizens with the information needed to govern themselves in a democracy. Politifact's principles are independence, transparency, fairness, thorough reporting, and clear writing. www.politifact.com

## COMMUNITY ENGAGEMENT AND PUBLIC INTEREST INSTITUTIONS

**American Museum of Tort Law** was founded by Ralph Nader "to educate, inform and inspire Americans about two things: trial by jury; and the benefits of tort law. Tort law is the law of wrongful injuries, including motor vehicle crashes, defective products, medical malpractice, and environmental disasters, among many others." www.tortmuseum.org

**Public Interest Research Groups (U.S. PIRGs)**, influenced and proposed by Ralph Nader in the early 1970s, are noted advocates for the pubic interest. PIRGs have delivered results-oriented citizen activism, stood up to powerful special interests, and used "the time-tested tools of investigative research, media exposés, grassroots organizing, advocacy, and litigation" to win real results on issues that matter. www.uspirg.org

**PeoplesHub** was started by Sarah van Gelder, founding editor of *YES! Magazine*. The nonprofit PeoplesHub "offers live, interactive trainings and workshops to build community power and make your grassroots work more effective." Its belief is that "real change can only happen when everyday people come together in their communities—especially in the most marginalized areas throughout the country. The deep change we need will come from the grassroots and spread, community to community, town to city, and city to town." www.peopleshub.org

**Credder** is the world's first "crowd-contested media" interactive online platform to rate the accuracy and quality of news sources and journalists based on critical media literacy. Founded by Chase Palmieri, Credder, formerly called Tribeworthy, builds on the popular and now nearly ubiquitous digital models of Yelp! and Rotten Tomatoes (for evaluating restaurants and movies, respectively) to rate the efficacy of news sources online. www.credder.com

ACKNOWLEDGMENTS

In many ways, this book resulted from years of research, discussion, and friendship that began when Nolan Higdon enrolled as a student in Mickey Huff's U.S. History course at Diablo Valley College over fifteen years ago. Since then the authors have formed a bond of friendship, as well as a professional relationship, that has resulted in numerous publications, public talks, and social gatherings. In those years we never lost focus on our desire to strengthen the democratic process by educating ourselves and the citizenry. We believe that education is the best boat to save society from drowning. Nonetheless, our theories, research, and motivation would not have resulted in this book without the support of so many wonderful people and institutions.

We especially thank our amazing editor, Greg Ruggiero, publicist Chris Carosi, City Lights publisher Elaine Katzenberger, along with Stacey Lewis, Linda Ronan, Elizabeth Bell, and the rest of the City Lights family; they offered critical feedback and wonderful support that enabled the completion of this project. It is a privilege to work with an editor as keen and sharp as Greg, and an honor to be invited to write a book for the historic City Lights Publishers. And a special happy 100th birthday to the inspiring founder of City Lights, Beat poet and artist Lawrence Ferlinghetti, who once wrote, "Our government is a bird with two right wings. . . . They're devoted to the perpetuation and spread of corporate capitalism." This book follows his analytical flight path and offers a prescription for a better world.

It is impossible to imagine that this manuscript could have been completed without the understanding and intellectual involvement of our partners, Meg Huff and Kacey

Van der Vorst, as well as our families. Their support through the long phone calls and late-night research, writing, and editing sessions were indispensable in our completing the manuscript.

Much gratitude is owed to our colleagues on the Media Freedom Foundation Board and Project Censored team, who always provided critical perspectives to enrich our work, including Susan Rahman, Nicholas Baham III, Mary Cardaras, T.M. Scruggs, Elaine Wellin, Ben Boyington, Christopher Oscar, Doug Hecker, Bri Silva, Allison Butler, and Kenn Burrows, with very special thanks to Andy Lee Roth and Peter Phillips.

We also thank the great staff members at our public affairs program on Pacifica Radio, *The Project Censored Show*, now in its ninth year, for their candor and questions concerning the topics covered in this manuscript: Chase Palmieri, Anthony Fest, and Dennis Murphy. We also thank the staff producing our new podcast, *Along the Line*: Nicholas Baham III, Desiree McSwain, Aimee Casey, Janice Domingo, and Jorge Ayala.

As part of our work at the Media Freedom Foundation and Project Censored we have collaborated and crossed paths with many brilliant thought-provoking individuals who left an indelible mark on this book, including Ian Davis, Robin Anderson, Abby Martin, Mnar Muhawesh, Kevin Gosztola, P. Louis Street, Anthony DiMaggio, Henry Giroux, Eleanor Goldfield, David Lindorff, Albert Ponce, Adam Bessie, Emil Marmol, Rob Williams, Steve Macek, Dorothy Kidd, and Michael Niman. In addition, we work with numerous organizations who support our collective work: Union for Democratic Communication; Action Coalition for Media Education; Project Censored; Pacifica Radio; the National Coalition Against Censorship;

Banned Books Week; and the Mount Diablo Peace and Justice Center. We also thank the indefatigable and prodigious author, attorney, and activist Ralph Nader for taking the time to pen a stellar foreword for this volume. We are grateful to have such an ally in our joint efforts.

As college educators we constantly come into contact with the future. Our students ask questions and offer perspectives that help us think more deeply about many of the important issues covered in this book. Their feedback strengthened our work on this project. Great thanks are in order to all of our students around the San Francisco Bay Area. We would like to specifically thank those who served as research assistants on this book, because their patience, commentary, and perspective were invaluable to this project: Matthew Aldea, Ryan Wilson, Katherine Epps, Monika Richards, and Chelsea Corby. The authors also thank Aaron Wood, Lucas Martin, Allison Pelland, Shanice Thomas, Shante Thomas, David Dube, and Elsa Denis for their work reviewing and proofing the manuscript.

Last, but certainly not least, we thank you, the reader, for caring to support independent publishers and daring to defy the Amazon-Google culture currently working to destroy local community bookstores and independent media outlets in the name of convenience, profit, and homogeneity. We can, must, and will work to create a different world. We hope this book is a modest contribution to that end, not only as a defense against the dark arts of propaganda and media manipulation, but as a quest for information veracity and integrity, and a call to collective action.

With gratitude, and hopes for a better educated and more informed world,
Nolan Higdon and Mickey Huff
Northern California, May 2019

1. Nick Visser, "CBS Chief Les Moonves Says Trump's 'Damn Good' for Business," *Huffington Post*, March 1, 2016, www.huffingtonpost.com/entry/les-moonves-donald-trump_us_56d52ce8e4b03260bf780275.

2. Zach Cartwright, "Amy Goodman Blasts CNN for Airing Trump's Empty Stage Instead of Sanders' Speech," *U.S. Uncut*, March 20, 2016, www.usuncut.com/politics/amy-goodman-calls-media-blacking-bernies-speech/; Will Bunch, "More Americans Support Bernie Than The Donald—but He Gets 1/23 the TV Coverage," *Philadelphia Daily News*, December 10, 2015, www.philly.com/philly/blogs/attytood/More-Americans-support-Bernie-than-The-Donald----but-he-gets-123-the-TV-coverage.html?arc404=true.

3. Michael Calderone, "Donald Trump Has Received Nearly $2 Billion in Free Media Attention," *Huffington Post*, March 15, 2016, www.huffingtonpost.com/entry/donald-trump-2-billion-free-media_us_56e83410e4b065e2e3d75935.

4. Paul Bond, "Leslie Moonves on Donald Trump: 'It May Not Be Good for America, but It's Damn Good for CBS,'" *The Hollywood Reporter*, February 29, 2016, www.hollywoodreporter.com/news/leslie-moonves-donald-trump-may-87146.

5. Sarah Oates, "Trump, Media, and the 'oxygen of publicity,'" *Us Election Analysis 2016*, www.electionanalysis2016.us/us-election-analysis-2016/section-1-media/trump-media-and-the-oxygen-of-publicity/; Nick Gass, "Study: Trump Boosted, Clinton Hurt by Primary Media Coverage," *Politico*, June 14, 2016, www.politico.com/story/2016/06/media-study-trump-helped-clinton-hurt-224300.

6. Dylan Bryers, "Donald Trump Has Had Too Much Media Coverage, 75 percent of Americans Say," *CNNMoney*, March 31, 2016, www.money.cnn.com/2016/03/31/media/trump-media-pew-survey.

7. Philip Bump, "Assessing a Clinton argument that the media helped to elect Trump," *Washington Post*, September 12, 2017, www.washingtonpost.com/news/politics/wp/2017/09/12/assessing-a-clinton-argument-that-the-media-helped-to-elect-trump/?utm_term=.e71c3abb2f9d.

8. Keith J. Kelly, "New York Times Edits Its Election Apology Letter," *New York Post*, November 15, 2016, www.nypost.

com/2016/11/15/new-york-times-edits-its-election-apology-letter/;
Clark Mindock, "CNN hits back at Trump's 'fake news' attacks
by explaining what an apple is," *The Independent*, October 23,
2017, www.independent.co.uk/news/world/americas/us-politics/
cnn-trump-fake-news-apple-advert-video-a8015616.html; Paul
Farhi, "The Washington Post's new slogan turns out to be an old
saying," *Washington Post*, February 24, 2017, www.washingtonpost.
com/lifestyle/style/the-washington-posts-new-slogan-turns-out-
to-be-an-old-saying/2017/02/23/cb199cda-fa02-11e6-be05-
1a3817ac21a5_story.html?utm_term=.1939a67c6ad6.

9. Ralph Nader, *Breaking Through Power: It's Easier Than You Think*,
City Lights Books, Open Media Series, 2016, p. 13.

10. David Leonhardt and Stuart A. Thompson, "Trump's Lies,"
*New York Times*, November 11, 2017, updated December 17, 2017,
www.nyti.ms/2sZqacl.

11. Lena H. Sun and Juliet Eilperin, "Words banned at HHS
agencies include 'diversity' and 'vulnerable,'" *Washington Post*,
December 16, 2017, www.washingtonpost.com/national/
health-science/words-banned-at-multiple-hhs-agencies-
include-diversity-and-vulnerable/2017/12/16/9fa09250-e29d-
11e7-8679-a9728984779c_story.html?noredirect=on&utm_
term=.524e4433ccd5.

12. Ibid., Sun and Eilperin, "Words banned at HHS agencies
include 'diversity' and 'vulnerable,'" *Washington Post*, December 17,
2017, p. 16.

13. Sheila Kaplan and Donald G. McNeil Jr., "Uproar Grows Over
a Reported Word Ban at the Centers for Disease Control, *New
York Times*, December 19, 2017, p. 15.

14. Julia Belluz and Umair Irfan, "The disturbing new language
of science under Trump, explained," Vox, January 30, 2018, www.
vox.com/2017/12/20/16793010/cdc-word-ban-trump-censorship-
language.

15. Associated Press (David Bauder), "EPA Blocks Some Media
from Pruitt Summit," *Bloomberg*, May 22, 2018, www.bloomberg.
com/news/articles/2018-05-22/epa-blocks-some-news-outlets-
from-water-contaminants-summit.

16. Paul Farhi, "EPA denies access to summit for reporters from 3
news groups," *Washington Post*, May 23, 2018, p. 9.

17. Noah Bierman and Jim Puzzanghera, "President Trump
threatens NBC's broadcast licenses following critical stories,"
*Los Angeles Times*, October 11, 2017, www.latimes.com/politics/
washington/la-na-pol-essential-washington-updates-president-
trump-goes-after-nbc-s-1507732128-htmlstory.html.

18. Mark Landler, "New York Times Publisher and Trump Clash Over President's Threats Against Journalism," *New York Times*, July 29, 2018, www.nytimes.com/2018/07/29/us/politics/trump-new-york-times-sulzberger.html.

19. David Leonhardt, "The President Praises Assault," *New York Times*, October 19, 2018, https://www.nytimes.com/2018/10/19/opinion/trump-greg-gianforte-assault.html.

20. Arnold Isaacs, "Learning the Power of Lies: Facts vs. Falsehoods in the Age of Trump," *TomDispatch*, www.tomdispatch.com/post/176470/tomgram%3A_arnold_isaacs%2C_moments_of_truth/#more.

21. Pankaj Mishra, "Gandhi for the Post-Truth Age," *The New Yorker*, October 22, 2018, www.newyorker.com/magazine/2018/10/22/gandhi-for-the-post-truth-age

22. Ibid.

23. Ian Schwartz, "Full Lou Dobbs Interview: Trump Asks What Could Be More Fake Than CBS, NBC, ABC and CNN?" *Real Clear Politics*, October 25, 2017, www.realclearpolitics.com/video/2017/10/25/full_lou_dobbs_interview_trump_asks_what_could_be_more_fake_than_cbs_nbc_abc_and_cnn.html.

24. Hillary Rodham Clinton, *What Happened* (New York: Simon and Schuster, 2017).

25. Stephanie Condon, "Hillary Clinton: The 'vast, right-wing conspiracy' is 'even better funded' now," *CBS News* February 3, 2016, www.cbsnews.com/news/hillary-clinton-the-vast-right-wing-conspiracy-is-even-better-funded-now.

26. John Dickerson, "Jackass in a Hailstorm," *CBS News*, July 23, 2015, www.cbsnews.com/news/a-jackass-in-a-hailstorm.

27. Lizabeth Cohen, *Making a New Deal: Industrial Workers in Chicago, 1919–1939* (New York: Cambridge University Press, 1991).

28. Robert W. McChesney, *Telecommunications, Mass Media, and Democracy* (Oxford University Press, 1995); Jaroslav Pelikan, "General Introduction," *The Press*, edited by Geneva Overholser and Kathleen Hall Jamieson (New York: Oxford University Press, 2005).

29. "Communications Act of 1934," www.it.ojp.gov/PrivacyLiberty/authorities/statutes/1288.

30. McChesney, *Telecommunications, Mass Media, and Democracy*, p. 188.

31. Victor Pickard, *America's Battle for Media Democracy: The Triumph of Corporate Libertarianism and the Future of Media Reform* (New York: Cambridge University Press, 2015).

32. FCC Rept. 1246, "In the Matter of Editorializing by Broadcast Licensees" (1949).

33. Victor Pickard, *America's Battle for Media Democracy*, op. cit.

34. Nancy MacLean, *Democracy in Chains: The Deep History of the Radical Right's Stealth Plan for America* (New York: Penguin Books, 2017).

35. Ibid.

36. Eric Rauchway, *The Great Depression and the New Deal: A Very Short Introduction* (Oxford, UK: Oxford University Press, 2008).

37. Nancy MacLean, *Democracy in Chains: The Deep History of the Radical Right's Stealth Plan for America* (New York: Penguin Books, 2017).

38. Ibid.

39. Ibid.

40. Ibid.

41. Lewis Powell, "The Powell Memo (also known as the Powell Manifesto)," first published August 23, 1971, reproduced and analyzed at *Reclaiming Democracy*, www.reclaimdemocracy.org/powell_memo_lewis/.

42. Robert G. Kaiser and Ira Chinoy, "Scaife: Funding Father of the Right," *Washington Post*, May 2, 1999, www.washingtonpost.com/wp-srv/politics/special/clinton/stories/scaifemain050299.htm; Ronald Reagan, "Inaugural Address," January 20, 1981, archived at the American Presidency Project, www.presidency.ucsb.edu/ws/?pid=43130; Mara Liasson, "Conservative Advocate," *Morning Edition*, *NPR*, May 25, 2001, www.npr.org/templates/story/story.php?storyId=1123439.

43. David Graeber, *Debt: The First 5000 Years* (Brooklyn, NY: Melville Publishing, 2011, 2012, 2014).

44. Manfred B. Steger, and Ravi K. Roy, *Neoliberalism: A Very Short Introduction*, Vol. 222 (Oxford, UK: Oxford University Press, 2010).

45. Joel Bakan, *The Corporation: The Pathological Pursuit of Profit and Power* (New York: Free Press, 2005).

46. Ibid.

47. Ronald Reagan, "First Inaugural Address," January 20, 1981.

48. Jefferson Cowie, *Stayin' Alive: The 1970s and the Last Days of the Working Class* (New York: The New Press, 2010); Bruce Schulman, *The Seventies: The Great Shift in American Culture, Society, and Politics* (New York: The New Press, 2001); Judith Stein, *Pivotal Decade: How the United States Traded Factories for Finance in the Seventies* (New Haven, CT: Yale University Press, 2010).

49. Joseph E. Stiglitz, *The Price of Inequality: How Today's Divided*

*Society Endangers Our Future* (New York: WW Norton & Company, 2012).

50. Thomas Frank, *Listen Liberal: Or What Ever Happened to the Party of the People?* (New York: Metropolitan Books, 2016).

51. Ibid.

52. Ibid. Frank, *Listen Liberal*; and Lance Selfa, *The Democrats: A Critical History* (Chicago: Haymarket Books, 2008, 2012).

53. Ibid. Frank, *Listen Liberal*.

54. William Kleinknecht, *The Man Who Sold the World: Ronald Regan and the Betrayal of Main Street America* (New York: Nation Books, 2009), p. xiii; BJ Bushman BJ, "Comfortably Numb: Desensitizing Effects of Violent Media on Helping Others," *Psychological Science*, 2009 21(3): pp. 273–277; Federal Trade Commission, www.ftc.gov/.

55. Dan Fletcher, "A Brief History of the Fairness Doctrine," *Time*, February 20, 2009, www.time.com/time/nation/article/0,8599,1880786,00.html#ixzz2aTB9x7MV.

56. Ben H. Bagdikian, *The Media Monopoly* (Boston: Beacon Press, 1983); Ashley Lutz, "These 6 Corporations Control 90% of the Media in America," *Business Insider*, June 14, 2012, www.businessinsider.com/these-6-corporations-control-90-of-the-media-in-america-2012-6#ixzz2lCpSO188.

57. Op. cit. Fletcher, "A Brief History of the Fairness Doctrine."

58. Op. cit. Bagdikian, *The Media Monopoly*; and op. cit. Lutz, "These 6 Corporations Control 90% of the Media in America."

59. Gillian Doyle, *Understanding Media Economics* (UK: SAGE Publications, 2013); Robert McChesney and John Nichols, *The Death and Life of American Journalism: The Media Revolution That Will Begin the World Again* (New York: Nation Books, 2011).

60. Jennifer Saba, "Specifics on Newspapers from 'State of News Media' Report," *Editor and Publisher*, March 16, 2009, www.editorandpublisher.com/PrintArticle/Specifics-on-Newspapers-from-State-of-News-Media-Report.

61. Scott Warren Fitzgerald, *Corporations and Cultural Industries: Time Warner, Bertelsmann, and News Corporation* (Lanham, MD: Lexington Books, 2011).

62. U.S. Census Bureau, "1996 Census"; Farhad Manjoo, "Jurassic Web," *Slate*, February 24, 2009, www.slate.com/technology/2009/02/the-unrecognizable-internet-of-1996.html.

63. Staff, "Internet/Broadband Fact Sheet," *Pew*, February 5, 2018, www.pewinternet.org/fact-sheet/internet-broadband/.

64. Nolan Ray Higdon, "Effective critical media literacy pedagogy

in higher education: turning social justice theory into practice," Doctoral Dissertation, San Francisco State University, 2017.

65. American President Ronald Reagan's National Commission on Excellence in Education, "A Nation at Risk," U.S. Government, April 1983, www2.ed.gov/pubs/NatAtRisk/recomm.html.

66. Ibid.

67. Ibid.

68. Ibid.

69. Ibid.

70. "Education at Risk," *Edutopia*, March 9, 2007, www.edutopia. org/landmark-education-report-nation-risk.

71. Dean Paton, "The Myth Behind Public School Failure," February 21, 2014, *Yes! Magazine*, www.yesmagazine.org/issues/ education-uprising/the-myth-behind-public-school-failure.

72. Ibid.

73. Ibid. Paton; and Linda Darling-Hammond, *The Flat World and Education: How America's Commitment to Equity Will Determine Our Future* (New York: Columbia University Press, 2013).

74. Ibid. Paton.

75. Ibid. Paton; Darlington-Hammond, op. cit.

76. Gloria Penner, Megan Burke, and Natalie Walsh, "Prop 13's Impact On Schools," *KPBS*, March 26, 2010, www.kpbs.org/ news/2010/mar/26/prop-13s-impact-schools/; Dave Jamieson, "How Tax Cuts Paved the Way for America's Growing Teacher Revolt," *Huffington Post*, March 13, 2018, www.huffingtonpost. com/entry/tax-cuts-teacher-strikes-west-virginia-oklahoma_ us_5aa7de92e4b087e5aaee2357.

77. Lewis D. Solomon, "Edison Schools and the Privatization of K-12 Public Education: A Legal and Policy Analysis," *Fordham Urban Law Journal* 30, no. 4 (2002).

78. Diane Ravitch, *The Death and Life of the Great American School System: How Testing and Choice Are Undermining Education* (New York: Basic Books, 2016), pp. 12–13; James E. Schul, "Unintended Consequences: Fundamental Flaws That Plague the No Child Left Behind Act," Ohio Northern University, 2011, www.nau.edu/uploadedFiles/Academic/COE/About/Projects/ UnintendedConsequences.pdf; Andrew Rudalevige, "The Politics of No Child Left Behind, *Education Next* 3, no. 4 (Fall 2003): www. educationnext.org/the-politics-of-no-child-left-behind/.

79. Heather E. Price, "Does No Child Left Behind Really Capture School Quality? Evidence from an urban school district," *Educational Policy* 24, no. 5 (2010): pp. 779–814.

80. Carol Lloyd, "Are Charter Schools Better?" *Great Schools*, May

14, 2015, www.greatschools.org/gk/articles/charter-schools-better-than-traditional/); Staff, "The economic impact of the achievement gap in America's schools," *McKinsey & Company*, 2009.

81. James Antle III, "Leaving No Child Left Behind: The Grassroots Revolt Against Bush's Centralizing Education-Reform Plan," *American Conservative*, August 1, 2005, www.theamericanconservative.com/articles/leaving-no-child-left-behind/; Linda Darling-Hammond, *The Flat World and Education: How America's Commitment to Equity Will Determine Our Future* (New York: Columbia University Press, 2013).

82. Neil Postman, *The End of Education: Redefining the Value of School* (Visalia, CA: Vintage, 1995), p. 17.

83. Hillary Rodham Clinton, *What Happened* (New York: Simon and Schuster, 2017).

84. "Trump's Twitter Archive," August 4, 2017, www.trumptwitterarchive.com/archive/fake%20news%20%7C%7C%20fakenews%20%7C%7C%20fake%20media/ttff/1-19-2017_

85. Eric Boehlert, "Study Confirms Network Evening Newscasts Have Abandoned Policy Coverage For 2016 Campaign," *Media Matters*, October 26, 2016, www.mediamatters.org/blog/2016/10/26/study-confirms-network-evening-newscasts-have-abandoned-policy-coverage-2016-campaign/214120; Staff, "Year in Review: 2016," *Tyndall Report*, tyndallreport.com/comment/20/5778/.

86. Ibid.

87. Margaret Sullivan, "Hillary Clinton thinks the news media was unfair to her. She's right," *Washington Post*, October 8, 2017, www.washingtonpost.com/lifestyle/style/hillary-clinton-thinks-the-news-media-was-unfair-to-her-shes-right/2017/10/08/da9807ba-a9d3-11e7-b3aa-c0e2e1d41e38_story.html?utm_term=.2cbf9def22b3.

88. Guy Debord, *The Society of the Spectacle* (New York: Zone Books, 1967).

89. Daniel J. Boorstin, *The Image: A Guide to Pseudo-Events in America*" (New York: Vintage Books, 1962), pp. 3–6.

90. Ashley Lutz, "These 6 Corporations Control 90% of the Media in America," *Business Insider*, June 14, 2012, www.businessinsider.com/these-6-corporations-control-90-of-the-media-in-america-2012-6#ixzz2lCpSO188.

91. Tim Stanley, "Jon Stewart, a comic genius who became just as partisan as his target," *The Telegraph*, August 7, 2015, www.telegraph.co.uk/culture/tvandradio/11788512/Jon-Stewart-a-comic-genius-who-became-just-as-partisan-as-his-targets.htm.

92. Lee Artz, *Global Entertainment Media: A Critical Introduction*

(Hoboken, NJ: John Wiley & Sons, 2015); Julie Frechette, "Cyber-Democracy or Cyber-Hegemony? Exploring the Political and Economic Structures of the Internet as an Alternative Source of Information." *Trends* 53, no. 4 (2005): p. 555.

93. Ibid. Frechette; and Noam Chomsky, *Necessary Illusions: Thought Control in Democratic Societies* (Boston: South End Press, 1989).

94. Franklin Foer, *World Without Mind: The Extensional Threat of Big Tech* (New York: Penguin Press, 2017); Staff, "When Technology Makes Headlines," *Pew Research Center*, September 27, 2010, www.journalism.org/2010/09/27/when-technology-makes-headlines/.

95. Patrick Morrison, "Media Monopoly Revisited: The 20 Corporations That Dominate Our Information and Ideas," *Fairness and Accuracy in Reporting* (2011, October 1), www.fair.org/extra-online-articles/media-monopoly-revisited; Megan Tady, "The 'Media Circus' of Occupy Wall Street Coverage," *Free Press*, 2011, www.freepress.net/blog/11/10/21/media-circus-occupy-wall-street-coverage; Mickey Huff and Andy Lee Roth, *Censored 2016: Media Freedom on the Line* (New York: Seven Stories Press, 2015).

96. Lydia Saad, "Support for 'Occupy' Unchanged, but More Criticize Approach," *Gallup*, November 21, 2011, news.gallup.com/poll/150896/support-occupy-unchanged-criticize-approach.aspx; Jonathan Easley, "Poll: 57 percent have negative view of Black Lives Matter movement," *The Hill*, August 2, 2017, thehill.com/homenews/campaign/344985-poll-57-percent-have-negative-view-of-black-lives-matter-movement.

97. Glenn Greenwald, "CNN Punished Its Own Journalist for Fulfilling a Core Duty of Journalism," *Common Dreams*, November 20, 2015, www.commondreams.org/views/2015/11/20/cnn-punished-its-own-journalist-fulfilling-core-duty-journalism; Staff, "CNN fires contributor Marc Lamont Hill for criticising Israel," *Al Jazeera*, November 30, 2018, www.aljazeera.com/news/2018/11/cnn-fires-contributor-marc-lamont-hill-criticising-israel-181130061452765.html.

98. Matt Taibbi, *Insane Clown President: Dispatches from the 2016 Circus* (New York: Random House, 2017).

99. Ibid.

100. Ibid. p. xxviii.

101. Staff, "All the President's tweets," *CNN*, January, 7, 2018, www.cnn.com/interactive/2017/politics/trump-tweets/.

102. Hillary Rodham Clinton, *What Happened* (New York: Simon and Schuster, 2017).

103. Staff, "Support from women hands Democrats victory in

Alabama: Exit polls," *ABC News*, December 12, 2017, abcnews. go.com/Politics/alabama-voters-split-allegations-moore-exit-polls/ story?id=51739957.

104. Steve Kornacki, *The Red and the Blue: The 1990s and the Birth of Political Tribalism* (New York: Ecco, 2018).

105. Staff, "Political Polarization in the American Public: How Increasing Ideological Uniformity and Partisan Antipathy Affect Politics, Compromise and Everyday Life," *People Press*, June 12, 2014, www.people-press.org/2014/06/12/political-polarization-in-the-american-public/.

106. Ibid.

107. Matthew Gentzkow, "Polarization in 2016," *Stanford University*, 2016, www.web.stanford.edu/~gentzkow/research/PolarizationIn2016.pdf.

108. Bryan Hardin Thrift, *Conservative Bias: How Jesse Helms Pioneered the Rise of Right-wing Media and Realigned the Republican Party* (Gainesville, FL: University Press of Florida, 2014); David Brock, *The Republican Noise Machine: Right-Wing Media and How It Corrupts Democracy* (New York: Crown Publishers, 2005).

109. Jane Mayer, *Dark Money: The Hidden History of the Billionaires Behind the Rise of the Radical Right* (New York: Doubleday, 2016).

110. Ibid.

111. Ibid. For more searchable databases on conservative political funding, see Center for Media Democracy's *Sourcewatch*, www. sourcewatch.org/index.php/Richard_and_Helen_DeVos_ Foundation; and www.conservativetransparency.org.

112. Dylan Matthews, "Everything you need to know about the Fairness Doctrine in one post," *Washington Post*, August 23, 2011, www.washingtonpost.com/blogs/ezra-klein/post/everything-you-need-to-know-about-the-fairness-doctrine-in-onepost/2011/08/23/gIQAN8CXZJ_blog.html?utm_term=.a628ea1c9b1l.

113. Bill Press, *Toxic Talk: How the Radical Right Has Poisoned America's Airwaves* (New York: Thomas Dunn Books, 2010).

114. Helen Thomas, *Watchdogs of Democracy* (New York: Scribner, 2006).

115. Brett Edkins, "Study: Trump Benefited from 'Overwhelmingly Negative' Tone of Election News Coverage," *Forbes*, December 13, 2017, www.forbes.com/sites/brettedkins/2016/12/13/trump-benefited-from-overwhelmingly-negative-tone-of-election-news-coverage-study-finds/#622329fd3202.

116. Molly Ivins, "Introduction," in Jeff Cohen and Norman Solomon, *Adventures in Medialand: Behind the News, Beyond the*

*Pundits* (Monroe, Maine: Common Courage Press, 1993), pp. ix–x.
117. Op. cit. Edkins, "Study: Trump Benefited From
'Overwhelmingly Negative' Tone Of Election News Coverage."
118. Ibid. Edkins.
119. Yvonne Jewkes, *Captive Audience: Media, Masculinity, and Power in Prisons* (New York: Routledge, 2013); David Weigel, "Jeff Bezos, Inscrutable Libertarian Democrat," *Slate*, August 5, 2013, www.slate.com/blogs/weigel/2013/08/05/ jeff_bezos_inscrutable_libertarian_democrat.html; Daniel Marans, "Sanders Calls Out MSNBC's Corporate Ownership — In Interview On MSNBC," *Huffington Post*, May 7, 2016, www. huffingtonpost.com/entry/bernie-sanders-asks-who-owns-msnbc_ us_572e3d0fe4b0bc9cb0471df1; Tim Wu, *The Attention Merchants: The Epic Scramble to Get Inside Our Heads* (New York: Vintage, 2016).
120. Ariel Edwards-Levy, "Mistrust Plagues Both White House and Media: Poll Shows Just 1 in 10 Americans Surveyed Say They Trust Both," *Huffington Post*, May 16, 2017, www.huffingtonpost. com/entry/white-house-media-poll_us_591aec90e4b05dd15f0b299 5?ncid=inblnkushpmg00000009.
121. Michael J. Coren, "A Facebook experiment with California liberals and Alabama conservatives suggests beliefs, not facts, are what really divide us," *QZ*, January 25, 2018, www. qz.com/1187566/spaceship-media-will-pair-5000-women-on- facebook-to-repair-the-rift-in-us-politics/.
122. Nolan Higdon, "The Millennial Media Revolution Part IV: The Response Tells You If It's Working," *Project Censored* (2014), www.projectcensored.org/millennial-media-revolution-part-iv- response-tells-working/; "Share of adults in the United States who use the internet in 2018, by age group," *Statistica*, 2018, www. statista.com/statistics/266587/percentage-of-internet-users-by-age- groups-in-the-us/.
123. William F. Baker, "Google's Monopoly on the News: Left Undiscussed in the FTC's Investigation Is the Search Giant's Ability to Limit What We All Read," *The Nation*, 2013, www. thenation.com/article/172378/googles-monopoly-news; Ben H. Bagdikian, *The New Media Monopoly: A Completely Revised and Updated Edition with Seven New Chapters* (Boston: Beacon Press, 2014); Robert W. McChesney, *Rich Media, Poor Democracy: Communication Politics in Dubious Times* (Champaign, IL: University of Illinois Press, 1999). Nicholas Rapp and Aric Jenkins, "Chart: These 6 Companies Control Much of U.S. Media," *Fortune*, July

24, 2018, www.fortune.com/longform/media-company-ownership-consolidation/.

124. Chris Anderson, *The Long Tail* (Amsterdam: Wereldbibliotheek: 2013); Rebecca J. Rosen, "Truth, Lies, and the Internet," *The Atlantic*, December 29, 2011, www.theatlantic.com/technology/archive/2011/12/truth-lies-and-the-internet/250569/; Fatima Wahab, "How to Customize the News Feed in Microsoft Edge Browser in Windows 10," *The Addictive Tips*, July 13, 2015, www.addictivetips.com/windows-tips/how-to-customize-the-news-feed-in-microsoft-edge-browser-in-windows-10/; Victor Luckerson, "Here's How Facebook's News Feed Actually Works," *Time*, July 9, 2015, time.com/collection-post/3950525/facebook-news-feed-algorithm/.

125. Eli Praiser. *The Filter Bubble: What the Internet Is Hiding from You* (New York: Penguin Press, 2011); Olaf Blecker and Bianca Bosker, "The Binge Breaker: Tristan Harris believes Silicon Valley is addicting us to our phones. He's determined to make it stop," *The Atlantic*, November 2016, www.theatlantic.com/magazine/archive/2016/11/the-binge-breaker/501122; Tristan Harris, "How Technology Is Hijacking Your Mind—from a Magician and Google Design Ethicist," *Thrive Global*, May 18, 2016, www.journal.thriveglobal.com/how-technology-hijacks-peoples-minds-from-a-magician-and-google-s-design-ethicist-56d62ef5edf3; Joseph Turow, *Breaking up America: Advertisers and the New Media World* (Chicago: University of Chicago Press, 2007); Joseph Turow, *Niche Envy: Marketing Discrimination in the Digital Age* (Cambridge, MA: Massachusetts Institute of Technology Press, 2008).

126. Katy Steinmetz, "Oxford's Word of the Year for 2016 Is 'Post-Truth,'" *Time*, November 15, 2016, www.time.com/4572592/oxford-word-of-the-year-2016-post-truth/.

127. Oxford Dictionaries, "The Word of the Year for 2016 is . . . ," www.en.oxforddictionaries.com/word-of-the-year/word-of-the-year-2016

128. Op. cit., Steinmetz, "Oxford's Word of the Year for 2016.'"

129. Lee McIntyre, *Post-Truth* (Cambridge, MA: MIT Press, 2018).

130. David M.J. Lazer, Matthew A. Baum, Yochai Benkler, Adam J. Berinsky, Kelly M. Greenhill, Filippo Mcnczer, Miriam J. Metzger et al. "The science of fake news," *Science* 359, no. 6380 (2018): pp. 1094-1096.

131. Kurt Anderson, *Fantasyland: How America Went Haywire: A 500-Year History* (New York: Random House, 2017).

132. Tuncay Kardaş, "Trump and the Rise of the Media-Industrial

Complex in American Politics," *Insight Turkey* 19, no. 3 (2017): p. 93.

133. K. Elsner, "China Uses an Army of Sockpuppets to Control Public Opinion – and the US Will Too," *The Liberty Voice*, November 27, 2013, guardianlv.com/2013/11/china-uses-an-army-of-sockpuppets-to-control-public-opinion-and-the-us-will-too/; Leo Benedict, "Invasion of the troll armies: from Russian Trump supporters to Turkish state stooges," *The Guardian*, November 6, 2016, www.theguardian.com/media/2016/nov/06/troll-armies-social-media-trump-russian

134. Chengcheng Shao, Giovanni Luca Ciampaglia, Onur Varol, Alessandro Flammini, and Filippo Menczer, "The spread of misinformation by social bots." *arXiv preprint arXiv:1707.07592* (2017).

135. Heather Kelly, "Facebook says Cambridge Analytica may have had data on 87 million people," *CNN*, April 4, 2018, www.money. cnn.com/2018/04/04/technology/facebook-cambridge-analytica-data-87-million/index.html; Nick Schifrin, "Inside Russia's propaganda machine," *PBS*, July 11, 2017, www.pbs.org/newshour/show/inside-russias-propaganda-machine; Matthew Yglesias and Andrew Prokop, "The Steele dossier, explained," *Vox*, February 2, 2018, www.vox.com/2018/1/5/16845704/steele-dossier-russia-trump.

136. David E. Sanger, Julian E. Barnes, Raymond Zhong, and Marc Santera, "U.S. Scrambles to Restrict Beijing's Control Over 'Central Nervous System' for Internet," *New York Times*, January, 27, 2019, www.nytimes.com/2019/01/26/us/politics/huawei-china-us-5g-technology.html.

137. Ibid.

138. Art Silverblatt, *Media Literacy: Keys to Interpreting Media Messages*, 3rd edition (Santa Barbara, CA: Praeger, 2007).

139. Molly Brown, Nielsen reports that the average American adult spends 11 hours per day on gadgets, *Geek Wire* (2015), www.geekwire.com/2015/nielsen-reports-that-the-average-american-adult-spends-11-hours-per-day-on-gadgets.

140. Monica Anderson and Jingjing Jiang, "Teens, social media and technology 2018," *Pew Research Center*, May 31, 2018, www.pewinternet.org/2018/05/31/teens-social-media-technology-2018/.

141. Brooke Donald, "Stanford researchers find students have trouble judging the credibility of information online," Stanford History Education Group, November 22, 2016, www.ed.stanford.edu/news/stanford-researchers-find-students-have-trouble-judging-credibility-information-online; Sue Shellenbarger, "Most

Students Don't Know When News Is Fake, Stanford Study Finds," *Huffington Post* (2016), www.wsj.com/articles/most-students-dont-know-when-news-is-fake-stanford-study-finds-1479752576.

142. Staff, "News and America's Kids," *Common Sense*, March 8, 2017, www.commonsensemedia.org/research/news-and-americas-kids-infographic.

143. Joseph Kahne, Jessica T. Feezell, and Nam-Jin Lee, "Digital Media Literacy Education and Online Civic and Political Participation," *Youth & Participatory Politics* 6 (2012): pp. 1-24.

144. Vanessa Elaine Domine, *Rethinking Technology in Schools Primer* (Bern, Switzerland: Peter Lang, 2009); Molly Brown, "Nielsen Reports That the Average American Adult Spends 11 Hours Per Day on Gadgets," *Geek Wire* (2015), www.geekwire.com/2015/nielsen-reports-that-the-average-american-adult-spends-11-hours-per-day-on-gadgets/.

145. Ravitch, *The Death and Life of the Great American School System* (New York: Basic Books, 2016), p. 17.

146. Ibid., p. 92.

147. Apple, *Apple in Education* Apple (2014); Catherine Gewertz, "Teachers Say They Are Unprepared for Common Core," *Education Week* 32 (2013): pp. 1-12; Douglas Kellner and Jeff Share, "Critical Media Literacy, Democracy, and the Reconstruction of Education," in D. Macedo and S. R. Steinberg, eds., *Media Literacy: A Reader* (New York: Peter Lang, 2007), pp. 3-23.

148. Op. cit. Ravitch, *Death and Life of the Great American School System*, p. 234.

149. Stefan Foa Roberto and Yascha Mounk, "The Danger of Deconsolidation: The Democratic Disconnect," *Journal of Democracy* 27 (July 2016), pp. 5–17.

150. Douglas Kellner and Jeff Share, "Critical media literacy, democracy, and the reconstruction of education," in D. Macedo & S.R. Steinberg, eds., *Media Literacy: A Reader* (New York: Peter Lang, 2007), pp.3–23; Cameron White and Trenia Walker, *Tooning In: Essays on Popular Culture and Education* (Lanham, MD: Rowman & Littlefield, 2007).

151. Chris Riotta, "Majority of Republicans Say Colleges Are Bad for America," *Newsweek*, July 10, 2017, www.newsweek.com/republicans-believe-college-education-bad-america-donald-trump-media-fake-news-634474; Josh Hafner, "Donald Trump loves the 'poorly educated' — and they love him," *Politico*, February 24, 2016, www.usatoday.com/story/news/politics/onpolitics/2016/02/24/donald-trump-nevada-poorly-educated/80860078/

152. Jon Queally, "Blackout Tuesday: The Bernie Sanders Speech

Corporate Media Chose Not to Air," *Common Dreams*, March 16, 2016, www.commondreams.org/news/2016/03/16/blackout-tuesday-bernie-sanders-speech-corporate-media-chose-not-air; Zach Cartwright, "Amy Goodman Blasts CNN for Airing Trump's Empty Stage Instead of Sanders' Speech," *U.S. Uncut*, March 20, 2016, www.usuncut.com/politics/amy-goodman-calls-media-blacking-bernies-speech/.

153. Sarah Childress, "Study: Election Coverage Skewed by 'Journalistic Bias,'" *PBS Frontline*, July 12, 2016, www.pbs.org/wgbh/frontline/article/study-election-coverage-skewed-by-journalistic-bias/.

154. Ibid.

155. Jason Easley, "Chuck Todd Defends Not Challenging Republican Lies on Meet the Press," *Politicus USA*, December 28, 2014, www.politicususa.com/2014/12/28/chuck-todd-defends-challenging-republican-lies-meet-press.html.

156. Society of Professional Journalists, "SPJ Code of Ethics," September 6, 2014, www.spj.org/ethicscode.asp.

157. Tim Wu, *The Attention Merchants: The Epic Scramble to Get Inside Our Heads* (New York: Vintage, 2016); Olaf Blecker and Bianca Bosker, "The Binge Breaker: Tristan Harris believes Silicon Valley is addicting us to our phones. He's determined to make it stop," *The Atlantic*, November 2016, www.theatlantic.com/magazine/archive/2016/11/the-binge-breaker/501122/.

158. Ian Crouch, "Why Donald Trump Is Skipping the White House Correspondents' Dinner," *The New Yorker*, April 28, 2017, www.newyorker.com/culture/cultural-comment/why-donald-trump-is-skipping-the-white-house-correspondents-dinner.

159. Mark Leibovich, *This Town: Two Parties and a Funeral-Plus, Plenty of Valet Parking!-in America's Gilded Capital* (New York: Blue Rider Press, 2013, 2014); and Crouch, Ibid.

160. Tim Walker, "Donald Trump once appeared in a softcore porn movie," *Independent* (UK), October 1, 2016, www.independent.co.uk/news/world/americas/us-politics/donald-trump-porn-softcore-playboy-movie-a7340376.html; Dan Gartland, "It's Been 10 Years Since the Leader of the Free World Shaved Vince McMahon's Head," *Sports Illustrated*, March 30, 2017, www.si.com/extra-mustard/2017/03/30/donald-trump-vince-mcmahon-wrestlemania-hair-match.

161. Staff, "Omarosa: 'The Apprentice' TV Show's Most Popular Contestant Has the Nation Talking and Watching," *Business Library*, April 12, 2004, www.archive.is/20120708100604/www.

findarticles.com/p/articles/mi_m1355/is_15_105/ai_n6006380/#sel
ection-405.0-405.9.
162. Lauren Carroll and Clayton Youngman, "Fact-checking
Claims About Donald Trump's Four Bankruptcies," *Politifact*,
September 21, 2015, www.politifact.com/truth-o-meter/
statements/2015/sep/21/carly-fiorina/trumps-four-bankruptcies/;
Annette Hill, *Reality TV* (New York: Routledge: 2014).
163. Patrick Radden Keefe, "How Mark Burnett Resurrected
Donald Trump as an Icon of American Success," *The New Yorker*,
January 7, 2019, www.newyorker.com/contributors/patrick-radden-
keefe.
164. Ibid.
165. Ibid.
166. Ibid.
167. Ibid.
168. Marina Fang, "Dan Rather Worries That the Media Has
Become 'A Business Partner of Donald Trump,'" *Huffington
Post*, June 26, 2016, www.huffingtonpost.com/entry/dan-
rather-donald-trump_us_576ff802e4b017b379f63ec8?section=.
169. Michael Calderone, "Donald Trump Shouldn't Have Bothered
Buying Airtime. Cable News Ran His Ad 60 Times for Free,"
*Huffington Post*, January 5, 2016, www.huffingtonpost.com/entry/
donald-trump-cable-news-airtime_us_568c0d96e4b014efe0dbe5a4.
170. Nick Gass, "Study: Trump Boosted, Clinton Hurt by Primary
Media Coverage," *Politico*, June 14, 2016, www.politico.com/
story/2016/06/media-study-trump-helped-clinton-hurt-224300
171. Deirdre Fulton, "Voting Problems Plague High-Stakes
Primary Day in New York," *Common Dreams*, April 19, 2016, www.
commondreams.org/news/2016/04/19/voting-problems-plague-
high-stakes-primary-day-new-york.
172. Amber Phillips, "Donald Trump goes for a more presidential
tone — for now," *Washington Post*, April 20, 2016, www.
washingtonpost.com/news/the-fix/wp/2016/04/20/donald-
trump-goes-for-a-more-presidential-tone-for-now/?utm_
term=.1bc8967b7227.
173. Ibid.
174. Jenna Johnson, "Donald Trump Creates a New Nickname
for Marco Rubio: 'Lightweight Choker,'" *Washington Post*,
November 10, 2015, www.washingtonpost.com/news/post-politics/
wp/2015/11/10/donald-trump-creates-a-new-nickname-for-
marco-rubio-lightweight-choker/; Brooke Singman, "Trump
Dares 'Crooked' Hillary to Run Again After She Blames Loss

on Comey 'Shiv,'" *Fox News*, October 16, 2017, www.foxnews.com/politics/2017/10/16/trump-dares-crooked-hillary-to-run-again-after-blames-loss-on-comey-shiv.html; Christopher Cadelago, "Nickname and shame: Trump taunts his 2020 Democratic rivals," *Politico*, October 2, 2018, www.politico.com/story/2018/10/02/2020-democrats-trump-nicknames-856800.

175. John Hubbell, "Sorry, Trump: The Story of John McCain the War Hero," *Newsweek*, July 20, 2015, www.newsweek.com/sorry-trump-story-john-mccain-war-hero-355617.

176. Mika Brzezinski, "Mika to Cruz, Trump: Move On from Wife Feud," video clip from *Morning Joe*, MSNBC, March 24, 2016, www.msnbc.com/morning-joe/watch/mika-to-cruz-trump-move-on-from-wife-feud-651367491745; "Cruz Calls Trump a 'Sniveling Coward' over Wife Tweet," *Fox News*, March 24, 2016, www.foxnews.com/politics/2016/03/24/cruz-calls-trump-sniveling-coward-over-wife-tweet.html; Patrick Healy, "Donald Trump and Ted Cruz Continue Clash over Spouses," *New York Times*, March 27, 2016, www.nytimes.com/politics/first-draft/2016/03/27/donald-trump-and-ted-cruz-continue-clash-over-spouses/; Theodore Schleifer and Julia Manchester, "Donald Trump Makes Wild Threat to 'Spill the Beans' on Ted Cruz's Wife," CNN, March 24, 2016, www.cnn.com/2016/03/22/politics/ted-cruz-melania-trump-twitter-donald-trump-heidi; Paul Waldman, "Ted Cruz and Donald Trump are Fighting over Their Wives. This Was Inevitable," *Washington Post*, March 25, 2016, www.washingtonpost.com/blogs/plum-line/wp/2016/03/25/ted-cruz-and-donald-trump-are-fighting-over-their-wives-this-was-inevitable/.

177. Gregory Krieg, "Donald Trump Defends Size of His Penis," CNN, March 4, 2016, www.cnn.com/2016/03/03/politics/donald-trump-small-hands-marco-rubio/.

178. William Cummings, "Sen. Dianne Feinstein becomes new target of Trump supporters' 'lock her up' chant," *USA Today*, October 10, 2018, www.usatoday.com/story/news/politics/onpolitics/2018/10/10/dianne-feinstein-lock-her-up-chant-donald-trump-rally/1587135002/; John Wagner and Avi Selk, "Be careful what you wish for Max!" *Washington Post*, June 25, 2018, www.washingtonpost.com/news/the-fix/wp/2018/06/25/democratic-congresswoman-calls-for-hasrrassment-of-trump-officials/?utm_term=.b07084213b76; Christopher Cadelago, "Nickname and shame: Trump taunts his 2020 Democratic rivals," *Politico*, October 2, 2018, www.politico.com/story/2018/10/02/2020-democrats-trump-nicknames-856800.

179. Jonathan Chait, "Calling Democrats the 'Angry Mob' Is Trump's Biggest Lie Yet," *New York Magazine*, October 13, 2018, nymag.com/intelligencer/2018/10/calling-democrats-the-angry-mob-is-trumps-biggest-lie-yet.html; Staff, Video: "Trump: Democrats 'treasonous, un-American,'" *BBC*, February 5, 2018, www.bbc.com/news/av/world-us-canada-42954829/trump-calls-democrats-treasonous-and-un-american.

180. William Cummings, "Sen. Dianne Feinstein becomes new target of Trump supporters' 'lock her up' chant," *USA Today*, October 10, 2018, www.usatoday.com/story/news/politics/onpolitics/2018/10/10/dianne-feinstein-lock-her-up-chant-donald-trump-rally/1587135002/.

181. Vanessa Romo and Joel Rose, "Judge Orders Pipe Bomb Suspect Cesar Sayoc Held Without Bail," *National Public Radio*, November 6, 2018, www.npr.org/2018/11/06/664796199/judge-orders-pipe-bomb-suspect-cesar-sayoc-held-without-bail; Emily Sullivan, "Mail Bomb Suspect Reportedly Had List of More Than 100 Potential Targets," *National Public Radio*, October 30, 2018, www.npr.org/2018/10/30/662000228/mail-bomb-suspect-reportedly-had-list-of-more-than-100-potential-targets.

182. Ibid.

183. Pete Williams, Rich Schapiro, Adiel Kaplan and Corky Siemaszko, "Pipe bomb suspect Cesar Sayoc is a registered Republican and a Trump fan with a criminal record," *NBC*, October 26, 2018, www.nbcnews.com/news/us-news/mail-bomb-suspect-cesar-sayoc-custody-allegedly-sending-pipe-bombs-n924856.

184. Jon Swaine and Erin Durkin, "Florida man charged with sending 13 pipe bombs to Trump critics," *The Guardian*, October 26, 2018, www.theguardian.com/us-news/2018/oct/26/suspicious-package-pipe-bombs-latest-found-cory-booker-florida.

185. Emily Shapiro, "The History behind the Donald Trump 'Small Hands' Insult," *ABC News*, March 4, 2016, www.abcnews.go.com/Politics/history-donald-trump-small-hands-insult/story?id=37395515; Jen Christensen, "Trump and the Small Hands Equals Small Manhood Myth, or Reality?" *CNN*, March 8, 2016, www.cnn.com/2016/03/08/health/trump-small-hands-penis/; F. Brinley Bruton, "Donald Trump Makes His Penis a Campaign Issue During Debate," *NBC News*, March 4, 2016, www.nbcnews.com/politics/2016-election/donald-trump-makes-his-penis-campaign-issue-during-debate-n531666; "Social Media Explodes after Donald Trump Talks about His Penis Size During

GOP Debate," *CBS*, March 3, 2016, www.newyork.cbslocal.
com/2016/03/03/donald-trump-penis-size/; Gregory Krieg,
"Donald Trump Defends Size of His Penis," *CNN*, March 4, 2016,
2016, www.cnn.com/2016/03/03/politics/donald-trump-small-
hands-marco-rubio/; Philip Rucker and Robert Costa, "Donald
Trump: 'My Hands Are Normal Hands,'" *Washington Post*,
March 21, 2016, www.washingtonpost.com/news/post-politics/
wp/2016/03/21/donald-trump-my-hands-are-normal-hands/;
"Donald Trump Discusses Penis Size at GOP Debate (Watch),"
*Variety*, March 3, 2016, www.variety.com/2016/biz/news/donald-
trump-penis-gop-debate-rubio-video-1201722389; Daniel White,
"Watch Trump Talk about His Private Parts at the Debate," *Time*,
March 3, 2016, www.time.com/4247366/republican-debate-donald-
trump-small-hands-penis/.
186. Nick Corasaniti, "Fox News Slams Donald Trump for 'Sick
Obsession' with Megyn Kelly," New York Times, March 18, 2016,
www.nytimes.com/politics/first-draft/2016/03/18/fox-news-slams-
donald-trump-for-sick-obsession-with-megyn-kelly/.
187. Ibid.
188. Evelyn Rupert, "Trump Offers Belated Defense of Megyn
Kelly 'Blood' Comment," *The Hill*, May 6, 2016, thehill.com/blogs/
blog-briefing-room/news/279097-trump-offers-belated-defense-of-
megyn-kelly-blood-comment.
189. Megyn Kelly, "R & R for Megyn Kelly," *The Kelly File*, Fox,
video and transcript, filmed August 12, 2015, published August 13,
2015, www.nation.foxnews.com/2015/08/13/r-r-megyn-kelly.
190. As of February 7, 2019, Twitter listed 58.1 million followers
for the account of Donald J. Trump, @realDonaldTrump, the
45th President of the United States of America: twitter.com/
realDonaldTrump.
191. David Kravets, "The Twitter Presidency Is Getting Old,
According to a New Voter Survey," *ARS Technica*, June 7, 2017,
arstechnica.com/tech-policy/2017/06/growing-tired-of-trumps-
tweets-new-poll-says-most-americans-are/.
192. Tweet from President Donald J. Trump's verified account,
@realDonaldTrump, 4:58 a.m., June 6, 2017, twitter.com/
realDonaldTrump/status/872059997429022722.
193. Doris Kearns Goodwin, *No Ordinary Time: Franklin & Eleanor
Roosevelt: The Home Front in World War II* (New York: Simon and
Schuster, 2013).
194. *Nazi Propaganda: The Power and the Limitation*, David Welch,
ed. (New York: Routledge, 2014).

195. David Kravets, "The Twitter Presidency Is Getting Old," www.arstechnica.com/tech-policy/2017/06/growing-tired-of-trumps-tweets-new-poll-says-most-americans-are/

196. "Noam Chomsky: Donald Trump Is a Distraction," Anonymous, March 3, 2018, video interview with Noam Chomsky viewed at www.youtube.com/watch?v=uQvig0KvUaE.

197. Matthew Stevens, "Trump and Kim Jong-un, and the Names They've Called Each Other," New York Times, March 9, 2018, www.nytimes.com/2018/03/09/world/asia/trump-kim-jong-un.html; and Evan Osnos, "Trump's Irrational Hatred of the Iran Deal: Even fierce critics of Tehran called the agreement vital to international security," The New Yorker, October 23, 2017, www.newyorker.com/magazine/2017/10/23/trumps-irrational-hatred-of-the-iran-deal.

198. Aaron Burke, "Why Trump's threat to 'totally destroy' North Korea is extraordinary," Chicago Tribune, September 19, 2018, www.chicagotribune.com/news/nationworld/ct-trump-destroy-north-korea-speech-20170919-story.html.

199. Christal Hayes, "Trump Wants to Run in 2020 Election Against the Woman He Already Beat: Hillary Clinton," Newsweek, October 16, 2017, www.newsweek.com/trump-wants-run-2020-election-against-woman-he-already-beat-hillary-clinton-685743?amp=1.

200. Brooke Singman, "Trump Says Comey 'Totally Protected' Clinton, Swipes at DOJ as New Documents Confirm Claims," Fox News, October 18, 2017 www.foxnews.com/politics/2017/10/18/trump-says-comey-totally-protected-clinton-swipes-at-doj-as-new-documents-confirm-claims.html.

201. Amanda Terkel, "Trump Says His Predecessors Didn't Call the Families of Fallen Service Members. That's Not True," Huffington Post, October 16, 2017, www.huffingtonpost.com/entry/trump-call-service-members-families_us_59e4f6ace4b0ca9f4839b525?0ob.

202. Arthur Delaney, "Trump Threatens to Stop Being 'Nice' to John McCain," Huffington Post, October 17, 2017, www.huffingtonpost.com/entry/trump-mccain-speech_us_59e635b9e4b00905bdace11b

203. Hayley Miller, "Bob Corker: Donald Trump's Legacy Will Be the 'Debasement of Our Nation,'" Huffington Post, October 24, 2017, www.huffingtonpost.com/entry/bob-corker-donald-trump_us_59ef3032e4b03535fa93ce16.

204. Ibid.

205. Maegan Vazquez, "Trump-Corker feud explodes ahead

of critical Hill visit," *CNN*, October 24, 2017, www.cnn.
com/2017/10/24/politics/corker-trump-photo-op-tax-plan/index.
html.

206. Lis Power & Craig Harrington, "Cable News Obsesses
Over Flake and Corker's Meaningless Grandstanding, but Barely
Acknowledges Their Pro-Trump Votes," *Media Matters*, October
25, 2017, www.mediamatters.org/blog/2017/10/25/cable-news-
obsesses-over-flake-and-corkers-meaningless-grandstanding-
barely-acknowledges-their-pro/218330

207. Amber Jamieson, "'You are fake news': Trump attacks CNN
and BuzzFeed at press conference," *Guardian*, Jan. 11, 2017, last
modified Feb. 9, 2018. www.theguardian.com/us-news/2017/
jan/11/trump-attacks-cnn-buzzfeed-at-press-conference.

208. Matthew Yglesias, "Jim Acosta vs. the Trump White House,
explained," *Vox*, November 14, 2018, www.vox.com/policy-and-
politics/2018/11/14/18091838/jim-acosta-cnn-sues-trump.

209. Ibid.

210. Bryan Rolli, "Why Nicki Minaj's New Music Benefits Cardi
B (And Vice Versa)," *Forbes*, April 12, 2018, www.forbes.com/sites/
bryanrolli/2018/04/12/nicki-minaj-new-music-benefits-cardi-b-
vice-versa/#2b8326f33912.

211. Louis Jacobson, "Were GOP's House losses dramatically
smaller than historical pattern?" *Politifact*, November 8th, 2018.
www.politifact.com/truth-o-meter/statements/2018/nov/08/
donald-trump/were-gops-house-losses-dramatically-smaller-histor/

212. Matthew Yglesias, "Jim Acosta vs. the Trump White House,
explained," *Vox*, November 14, 2018, www.vox.com/policy-and-
politics/2018/11/14/18091838/jim-acosta-cnn-sues-trump.

213. Colin Horgan, "The Acosta Video Debate Is the Future of
Fake News: Video manipulation technology is making it harder
than ever to believe what you see," *Medium*, November 8, 2018,
medium.com/s/story/the-acosta-video-debate-is-the-future-of-
fake-news-bd8202902deb.

214. Ibid.

215. Ibid.

216. Brian Stelter, "CNN sues President Trump and top White
House aides for barring Jim Acosta," *CNN*, November 13, 2018,
www.cnn.com/2018/11/13/media/cnn-sues-trump/index.html.

217. Michael M. Gryn, "CNN's Jim Acosta Has Press Pass
Restored by White House," *New York Times*, November 19, 2018,
www.nytimes.com/2018/11/19/business/media/jim-acosta-press-
pass-cnn.html

218. Chris Hedges, "Trump, the Quintessential American," *Truthdig*, December 17, 2018, www.truthdig.com/articles/trump-the-quintessential-american/.

219. Michael Grunwald, "Trump's Executive Orders Are Mostly Theater: The President Knows How to Stage a Photo Op, but So Far His Signature Hasn't Changed Much," *Politico*, April 28, 2017, www.politico.com/magazine/story/2017/04/28/trumps-executive-orders-are-mostly-theater-215081.

220. Patrick Lawrence, "Donald Trump Has Had a Lot of Help in Sabotaging the Iran Deal: Washington Is Just Not Equipped to Negotiate Its Way Into the 21st Century," *The Nation*, October 16, 2017, www.thenation.com/article/donald-trump-has-had-a-lot-of-help-in-sabotaging-the-iran-deal/; Evan Osnos, "Trump's Irrational Hatred of the Iran Deal," *The New Yorker*, October 23, 2017, www.newyorker.com/magazine/2017/10/23/trumps-irrational-hatred-of-the-iran-deal.

221. Dylan Scott, "Trump's Executive Order to Undermine Obamacare," *Vox*, Oct 12, 2017, www.vox.com/policy-and-politics/2017/10/12/16458184/trump-obamacare-executive-order-association-health-plans-short-term-insurance.

222. Staff, "New York Times Publisher Vows to 'Rededicate' Paper to Reporting Honestly," *Fox News*, November 12, 2016. www.foxnews.com/politics/2016/11/12/new-york-times-publisher-vows-to-rededicate-itself-to-reporting-honestly.html6.

223. Oliver Darcy, "Sean Hannity said he wouldn't campaign on stage at Trump's rally. Hours later, he did exactly that," *CNN Business*, November 6, 2018, www.cnn.com/2018/11/06/media/trump-rally-missouri-hannity/index.html.

224. Jim Rutenberg, "Sean Hannity Erased a Line by Taking the Stage With Trump," *New York Times*, November 6, 2018, www.nytimes.com/2018/11/06/business/media/sean-hannity-trump-fox-news.html.

225. Jim Rutenberg, "Sean Hannity Turns Adviser in the Service of Donald Trump," *New York Times*, August 21, 2016, www.nytimes.com/2016/08/22/business/media/sean-hannity-turns-adviser-in-the-service-of-donald-trump.html.

226. Eric Hannoki, "Jeanine Pirro was paid to speak at GOP event with Kevin McCarthy — who thanked her the next day," *Salon*, December 17, 2018, www.salon.com/2018/12/15/jeanine-pirro-was-paid-to-speak-at-gop-event-with-kevin-mccarthy-who-thanked-her-the-next-day_partner/.

227. Ibid.

228. Noam Chomsky, *Necessary Illusions: Thought Control in Democratic Societies* (Boston: South End Press, 1989).

229. National Intelligence Strategy of the United States 2019, www.dni.gov/files/ODNI/documents/National_Intelligence_Strategy_2019.pdf

230. Allison Graves, Jon Greenberg, Louis Jacobson, John Kruzel, Katie Sanders, Amy Sherman, Manuela Tobias, and Miriam Valverde, "Fact-checking Donald Trump's 2018 State of the Union speech," *Politifact*, January 30, 2018, www.politifact.com/truth-o-meter/article/2018/jan/30/fact-checking-donald-trumps-2018-state-union-speec/.

231. Eugene Kiely, Brooks Jackson, Lori Robertson, Robert Farley, D'Angelo Gore, Vanessa Schipani, and Saranac Hale Spencer, "Trump's State of the Union: The president exaggerates his accomplishments in his address to Congress," *FactChecking*, January 31, 2018, www.factcheck.org/2018/01/factchecking-trumps-state-union.

232. Glenn Kessler, Salvador Rizzo, and Meg Kelly, "President Trump has made more than 10,000 false or misleading claims, *Washington Post*, April 29, 2019, www.washingtonpost.com/politics/2019/04/29/president-trump-has-made-more-than-false-or-misleading-claims/?utm_term=.856ebcacc61a; for previous ongoing tallies, see "In 745 days, President Trump has made 8,459 false or misleading claims," *Washington Post*, February 3, 2019, www.washingtonpost.com/graphics/politics/trump-claims-database/?utm_term=.411bcfb4d239.

233. Ibid.

234. Ibid.

235. Tamara Keith, "Trump Admits to Making Up Trade Deficit in Talks with Canadian Prime Minister," *NPR*, March 15, 2018, www.npr.org/2018/03/15/593844812/trump-admits-to-making-up-trade-deficit-in-talks-with-canadian-prime-minister.

236. Jack Holmes, "To Supporters, Trump Isn't Just Right—He Controls the Truth," *Esquire*, July 31, 2018, www.esquire.com/news-politics/a22600827/donald-trump-supporters-believe-the-media.

237. Adam K. Raymond, "Of Course Trump Is Lying About His State of the Union Ratings," *New York Magazine*, February 1, 2018, nymag.com/daily/intelligencer/2018/02/trump-is-lying-about-his-state-of-the-union-ratings.html.

238. "Donald Trump lied about his State of the Union ratings. Whyyyyyyyy?" Analysis by Chris Cillizza, CNN Editor-at-

large, updated 9:34 a.m. ET, February 2, 2018, www.cnn.
com/2018/02/01/politics/donald-trump-sotu-ratings/index.html.
239. Lee Moran, "Trump Just Falsely Claimed He Had a
Historically Huge Audience. Again," *Huffington Post*, February
1, 2018, www.huffingtonpost.com/entry/trump-state-of-the-
union-viewers-lie_us_5a730284e4b0bf6e6e221d6c.
240. Staff, "Alt-Right," *Southern Poverty Law Center*, www.splcenter.
org/fighting-hate/extremist-files/ideology/alt-right.
241. Alexander Zaitchick, *The Gilded Rage: A Wild Ride Through
Donald Trump's America* (New York: Skyhorse, 2016).
242. Mike Wendling, *Alt-Right From 4chan to the White House*
(London: Pluto Books, 2018).
243. Ibid.
244. Arlie Russell Hochschild, *Strangers in Their Own Land: Anger
and Mourning on the American Right* (New York: New Press, 2016).
245. Thomas Frank, *What's the Matter with Kansas? How
Conservatives Won the Heart of America* (New York: Metropolitan
Books, 2007).
246. Nolan Higdon, "Disinfo Wars: Alex Jones' War on Your
Mind," *Project Censored*, September 26, 2013, www.projectcensored.
org/disinfo-wars-alex-jones-war-mind/; Staff, "Alex Jones: 'I'm
Ready to Die for Trump,'" *Media Matters*, February 6, 2017,
www.mediamatters.org/video/2017/02/06/alex-jones-i-m-ready-
die-trump/215248; Corky Siemaszko, "InfoWars' Alex Jones Is a
'Performance Artist,' His Lawyer Says in Divorce Hearing," *NBC
News*, April 17, 2017, www.nbcnews.com/news/us-news/not-fake-
news-infowars-alex-jones-performance-artist-n747491.
247. Yochai Benkler, Robert Faris, and Hal Roberts, *Network
Propaganda: Manipulation, Disinformation, and Radicalization in
American Politics* (New York: Oxford University Press, 2018), p. 93.
248. Ibid. pp. 97–98.
249. Spencer Hsu, "'Pizzagate' gunman sentenced to four years
in prison, as prosecutors urged judge to deter vigilante justice,"
*Washington Post*, June 22, 2017, www.washingtonpost.com/local/
public-safety/pizzagate-gunman-sentenced-to-four-years-in-prison-
as-prosecutors-urged-judge-to-deter-vigilante-justice/2017/06/22/
a10db598-550b-11e7-ba90-f5875b7d1876_story.html?utm_
term=.89781d5f5b49; John Nolte, "'Ferguson Effect': America's
New Crime Wave Is All Part of the Plan," *Breitbart*, May 30,
2015, www.breitbart.com/big-government/2015/05/30/ferguson-
effect-americas-new-crime-wave-is-all-part-of-the-plan/; Jonathon
Morgan, "The Charts Show How Racist and Radical the Alt-Right

Has Gotten This Year," *Washington Post*, September 26, 2016, www.washingtonpost.com/?utm_term=.6403d7426322; Paul Elam, "Classics: the myth of women's oppression," *A Voice for Men*, August 4, 2015, www.avoiceformen.com/feminism/the-myth-of-womens-oppression/; Luke O'Brien, "My Journey to the Center of the Highline," *Huffington Post*, November 3, 2016, huffingtonpost.com/articles/en/alt-right/.

250. Ibid. Spencer Hsu, "'Pizzagate' gunman sentenced to four years in prison."

251. Kathy Frankovic, "Belief in conspiracies largely depends on political identity," *YouGov*, December 27, 2016, www.today.yougov.com/news/2016/12/27/belief-conspiracies-largely-depends-political-iden/.

252. Vanessa Romo and Joel Rose, "Judge Orders Pipe Bomb Suspect Cesar Sayoc Held Without Bail," *National Public Radio*, November 6, 2018, www.npr.org/2018/11/06/664796199/judge-orders-pipe-bomb-suspect-cesar-sayoc-held-without-bail; Emily Sullivan, "Mail Bomb Suspect Reportedly Had List of More Than 100 Potential Targets," *National Public Radio*, October 30, 2018, www.npr.org/2018/10/30/662000228/mail-bomb-suspect-reportedly-had-list-of-more-than-100-potential-target6.

253. Cecil Stoughton, "The Normalization of Conspiracy Culture: People who share dangerous ideas don't necessarily believe them," *The Atlantic*, June 17, 2017 www.theatlantic.com/technology/archive/2017/06/the-normalization-of-conspiracy-culture/530688/; David Folkenflik, "Radio Conspiracy Theorist Claims Ear of Trump, Pushes 'Pizzagate' Fictions," *National Public Radio*, December 6, 2016, www.npr.org/2016/12/06/504590375/radio-conspiracy-theorist-claims-ear-of-trump-pushes-pizzagate-fictions; Aaron Bandler, "Alex Jones, the Guy Trump Called Post-Election, Says Hillary Personally Murdered Children," *Daily Wire*, December 7, 2016, www.dailywire.com/news/11418/alex-jones-guy-trump-called-post-election-says-aaron-bandler; Sarah Posner, "How Donald Trump's New Campaign Chief Created an Online Haven for White Nationalists," *Mother Jones*, August 22, 2016, www.motherjones.com/politics/2016/08/stephen-bannon-donald-trump-alt-right-breitbart-news.

254. Ibid.

255. Christopher Caldwell, "What Does Steve Bannon Want?" *New York Times*, February 25, 2017, www.nyti.ms/2mpDili.

256. Julie Zauzmer and Colby Itkowitz, "Anti-Defamation League decries Stephen Bannon, while many other Jewish groups stay silent," *Washington Post*, November 15, 2016, www.washingtonpost.

com/news/acts-of-faith/wp/2016/11/15/anti-defamation-league-
decries-stephen-bannon-while-other-jewish-groups-stay-
silent/?utm_term=.652eba4cb18c.
257. Joseph Goldstein, "Alt-Right Gathering Exults in Trump
Election With Nazi-Era Salute," *New York Times*, November 21,
2016, www.nytimes.com/2016/11/21/us/alt-right-salutes-donald-
trump.html; Peter Baker, Maggie Haberman, "A Conspiracy
Theory's Journey From Talk Radio to Trump's Twitter," *New York
Times*, www.nytimes.com/2017/03/05/us/politics/trump-twitter-
talk-radio-conspiracy-theory.html; Lori Robertson, "Trump's
ISIS Conspiracy Theory," *FactCheck.org*, Annenberg Public Policy
Center of the University of Pennsylvania, June 16, 2016, www.
factcheck.org/2016/06/trumps-isis-conspiracy-theory/.
258. David Weigel, "'Friends of Hamas': The Scary-Sounding
Pro-Hagel Group That Doesn't Actually Exist," *Slate*, February 14,
2013, www.slate.com/blogs/weigel/2013/02/14/_friends_of_hamas_
the_scary_sounding_pro_hagel_group_that_doesn_t_actually.
html; Agence France-Presse in Berlin, "German police quash
Breitbart story of mob setting fire to Dortmund church," *The
Guardian*, ISSN 0261-3077, www.theguardian.com/world/2017/
jan/07/german-police-quash-breitbart-story-of-mob-setting-fire-
to-dortmund-church; Brianna Sacks, Talal Ansari, "Breitbart Made
Up False Story That Immigrant Started Deadly Sonoma Wildfires,
Sheriff's Office Says," *BuzzFeed*, www.buzzfeed.com/briannasacks/
no-an-undocumented-immigrant-did-not-start-the-deadly?utm_
term=.lpbyb6Oej#.rgmV5wyD2; Daniel Victor and Liam Stack,
"Stephen Bannon and Breitbart News, in Their Words," *New York
Times*, November 14, 2016, www.nytimes.com/2016/11/15/us/
politics/stephen-bannon-breitbart-words.html?mtrref=undefined&
gwh=67891184CB5B8760A126F2542A30FB1A&gwt=pay.
259. Joseph Goldstein, "Alt-Right Gathering Exults in Trump
Election with Nazi-Era Salute," *New York Times*, November 21,
2016, www.nytimes.com/2016/11/21/us/alt-right-salutes-donald-
trump.html.
260. Amelia Tait, "They're turning the frogs gay," *New
Statesman*, March 20, 2017 www.newstatesman.com/science-tech/
internet/2017/03/they-re-turning-frogs-gay-psychology-behind-
internet-conspiracy; Eric Killelea, "Alex Jones' Mis-Infowars: 7
Bat-Sh*t Conspiracy Theories," *Rolling Stone*, February, 17, 2017,
www.rollingstone.com/culture/lists/alex-jones-mis-infowars-7-bat-
sht-conspiracy-theories-w467509/the-government-is-controlling-
the-weather-w467722.
261. Nolan Higdon, "Disinfo Wars: Alex Jones' War on Your

Mind," *Project Censored*, September 26, 2013, www.projectcensored.
org/disinfo-wars-alex-jones-war-mind/; Staff, "Alex Jones: 'I'm
Ready to Die for Trump,'" *Media Matters*, February 6, 2017,
mediamatters.org/video/2017/02/06/alex-jones-i-m-ready-die-
trump/215248; Corky Siemaszko, "InfoWars' Alex Jones Is a
'Performance Artist,' His Lawyer Says in Divorce Hearing," *NBC
News*, April 17, 2017, www.nbcnews.com/news/us-news/not-fake-
news-infowars-alex-jones-performance-artist-n747491.
262. Mollie Reilly, "Fox's Lou Dobbs Lets Trump Take Over
Interview to Rant about Fake News," *Huffington Post*, October 25,
2017, www.huffingtonpost.com/entry/lou-dobbs-trump_interview_
us_59f1209ce4b0438859151b62?iqs.
263. Oliver Darcy, "Sean Hannity said he wouldn't campaign on
stage at Trump's rally. Hours later, he did exactly that," *CNN*,
November 6, 2018 www.cnn.com/2018/11/06/media/trump-rally-
missouri-hannity/index.html.
264. Nancy Isenberg, *White Trash: The 400-Year Untold History of
Class in America* (New York: Viking Press, 2016).
265. Staff, "Hardball's Chris Matthews Identifies the 'Alt-Right'
as 'A Group of White Nationalists—That's What They Are,'
*Media Matters*, November 21, 2016, www.mediamatters.org/
video/2016/11/21/hardballs-chris-matthews-identifies-alt-right-
group-white-nationalists-thats-what-they-are/214595.
266. Ted Hesson and Wesley Morgan, "Trump's troop deployment
to the border comes under fire," *Politico*, October 29, 2018,
www.politico.com/story/2018/10/29/caravan-mexico-border-
troops-89900.
267. Dan Lamothe, "Pentagon drops 'Faithful Patriot'
as name for controversial military border deployment,"
*Washington Post*, November 7, 2018, www.washingtonpost.
com/national-security/2018/11/07/pentagon-drops-faithful-
patriot-name-controversial-military-border-deployment/?utm_
term=.37906bb5795e.
268. Ibid.
269. Louis Jacobson, "Donald Trump's Pants on Fire claim about
'treason,'" *Politico*, February 6, 2018, www.politifact.com/truth-
o-meter/statements/2018/feb/06/donald-trump/donald-trumps-
pants-fire-claim-about-treason/.
270. Ibid.
271. Anna Ringstrom and Jeff Mason, "Sweden Mocks Trump's
'Alternative Facts' on Fictional Refugee Incident," *National Memo*,
February 19, 2017, www.nationalmemo.com/sweden-mocks-trump-

incident/; Justin Carissimo, "Sean Spicer cites fake Atlanta terror attack story," *The Independent*, February 9, 2017, www.independent. co.uk/news/world/americas/sean-spicer-creates-fake-atlanta-terror-attack-story-a7570561.html; Samantha Schmidt and Lindsey Bever, "Kellyanne Conway cites 'Bowling Green massacre' that never happened to defend travel ban," *Washington Post*, February 3, 2017, www.washingtonpost.com/news/morning-mix/wp/2017/02/03/kellyanne-conway-cites-bowling-green-massacre-that-never-happened-to-defend-travel-ban/?utm_term=.b269b8573955.

272. Graves, Greenberg, Jacobson, Kruzel, Sanders, Sherman, Tobias, and Valverde, "Fact-checking Donald Trump's 2018 State of the Union speech," *Politifact*, www.politifact.com/truth-o-meter/article/2018/jan/30/fact-checking-donald-trumps-2018-state-union-speec/.

273. Chuck Todd, "Conway: Press Secretary Gave 'Alternative Facts,'" *NBC News Meet the Press*, January 22, 2017, www.nbcnews.com/meet-the-press/video/conway-press-secretary-gave-alternative-facts-860142147643; Brian Stelter, "White House Press Secretary attacks media for accurately reporting inauguration crowds," *CNN*, January 21, 2017, www.money.cnn.com/2017/01/21/media/sean-spicer-press-secretary-statement/; Jonathon Lemire," Trump Draws Far Smaller Inaugural Crowd Than Obama," *US News & World Report*, January 20, 2017, www.usnews.com/news/politics/articles/2017-01-20/trump-draws-far-smaller-inaugural-crowd-than-obama.

274. Ibid. Todd; ibid. Stelter; ibid. Lemire.

275. Laignee Barron, "Here's What the EPA's Website Looks Like After a Year of Climate Change Censorship," *Time*, March 1, 2018, time.com/5075265/epa-website-climate-change-censorship/.

276. Anthony Zurcher "Does Trump still think climate change is a hoax?" *BBC*, June 2, 2017, www.bbc.com/news/world-us-canada-40128034

277. "Scientists Agree: Global Warming Is Happening and Humans are the Primary Cause," *Union of Concerned Scientists*, www.ucsusa.org/global-warming/science-and-impacts/science/scientists-agree-global-warming-happening-humans-primary-cause#.XA7Oz-J7nb0.

278. Ben Riley-Smith, "Donald Trump says climate change not hoax, but takes aim at 'political agenda' of scientists," *Telegraph*, October 15, 2018, www.telegraph.co.uk/news/2018/10/15/donald-trump-says-climate-change-not-hoax-takes-aim-political/.

279. Foreign Staff, "Earth's temperature to rise 1.5C as early as 2030 amid dire warnings from UN climate panel," *Telegraph*, October 8, 2018, www.telegraph.co.uk/news/2018/10/08/earths-temperature-rise-15c-early-2030-amid-dire-warnings-un/.

280. Ibid.

281. Op. cit. Riley-Smith, "Donald Trump says climate change not hoax, but takes aim at 'political agenda' of scientists."

282. "Scientists Agree: Global Warming Is Happening and Humans Are the Primary Cause," *Union of Concerned Scientists*, www.ucsusa.org/global-warming/science-and-impacts/science/scientists-agree-global-warming-happening-humans-primary-cause#.XA7Oz-J7nb0.

283. "Fact check: Trump's Paris Agreement withdrawal announcement," *Climate Analytics*, climateanalytics.org/briefings/fact-check-trumps-paris-agreement-withdrawal-announcement/; Tom DiChristopher, "Trump says 'the coal industry is back,'" *CNBC*, August 23, 2018, www.cnbc.com/2018/08/23/trump-says-the-coal-industry-is-back-the-data-say-otherwise.html.

284. James Carson, "What is fake news? Its origins and how it grew in 2016," March 16, 2017, www.telegraph.co.uk/technology/0/fake-news-origins-grew-2016/.

285. Katy Steinmetz, "The Dictionary Is Adding an Entry for 'Fake,'" *Time*, Sep 27, 2017, time.com/4959488/donald-trump-fake-news-meaning/; Tim Hains, "Trump: NBC Prints 'A Lot of Fake News Lately,'" *Real Clear Politics*, October 11, 2017, www.realclearpolitics.com/video/2017/10/11/trump_nbc_gives_a_lot_of_fake_news_lately.htm.

286. Ibid. Steinmetz; and Summer Meza, "'Fake News' Named Word of the Year," *Newsweek*, November 2, 2017, www.newsweek.com/fake-news-word-year-collins-dictionary-699740.

287. Chris Cillizza, "Donald Trump just claimed he invented 'fake news,'" *CNN*, October 8, 2017, www.cnn.com/2017/10/08/politics/trump-huckabee-fake/index.htm.

288. "Fake News," April 15, 2012-April 15, 2017, *Google Trends*, www.trends.google.com/trends/explore?geo=US&q=%22fake%20news%22.

289. Amarnath Amarasingam, *The Stewart/Colbert Effect: Essays on the Real Impacts of Fake News* (Jefferson, NC: McFarland, 2011).

290. Kevin Young, *Bunk: The Rise of Hoaxes, Humbug, Plagiarists, Phonies, Post Facts, and Fake News* (Minneapolis, MN: Graywolf Press, 2017).

291. Pamela Engel and Natasha Bertrand, "3 events Brian

Williams is suspected of lying about," *Business Insider*, February 13, 2015, www.businessinsider.com/what-brian-williams-has-lied-about-2015-2.

292. Eric Hananoki, Ben Dimiero and Joe Strupp, "O'Reilly Lied About Suicide of JFK Assassination Figure: Former Colleagues Say," *Media Matters*, February 24, 2015, www.mediamatters. org/blog/2015/02/24/oreilly-lied-about-suicide-of-jfk-assassination/202655; David Corn and Daniel Schulman, "O'Reilly Cameraman Disputes Fox News Host's Falklands 'War Zone' Story," *Mother Jones*, March, 30, 2015, www.m.motherjones.com/politics/2015/03/cameraman-disputes-bill-oreilly-falklands-war-story; Jon Greenberg, "Bill O'Reilly: 'I never said I was on the Falkland Islands,'" *Pundit Fact*, March 3, 2015, www.politifact.com/punditfact/statements/2015/mar/03/bill-oreilly/oreilly-i-never-said-i-was-falkland-islands/; Olivia Marshall, "Another Fabrication: O'Reilly Never Witnessed the Murder of Nuns in El Salvador (Updated)," *MediaMatters*, February 25, 2015, www.mediamatters. org/blog/2015/02/25/another-fabrication-oreilly-never-witnessed-the/202667; Jeremy Holden and Joe Strupp, "As O'Reilly Spins, News Sources Further Undermine His JFK Story," *MediaMatters*, February 26, 2015, www.mediamatters.org/blog/2015/02/26/as-oreilly-spins-new-sources-further-undermine/202691iams.html.

293. Carl Bernstein, "The CIA and the Media: How America's Most Powerful News Media Worked Hand in Glove with the Central Intelligence Agency and Why the Church Committee Covered It Up," *Rolling Stone*, 1977, www.carlbernstein.com/magazine_cia_and_media.php; Nancy E. Bernhard, *U.S. Television News and Cold War Propaganda 1947-1960* (New York: Cambridge University Press, 1999).

294. Ibid. Bernstein. For more on this topic see Brian Covert's work in chapter six of Mickey Huff and Andy Lee Roth, *Censored 2017: Fortieth Anniversary Edition* (New York: Seven Stories Press, 2016), or see *Played By the Mighty Wurlitzer: The Press, the CIA, and the Subversion of Truth* at www.projectcensored.org/played-mighty-wurlitzer-press-cia-subversion-truth.

295. Ibid. Bernstein.

296. Dan Collins, "3rd Columnist on Bush Payroll," *CBS*, January 26, 2005, www.cbsnews.com/news/3rd-columnist-on-bush-payroll/.

297. Jordan Chariton, "Here's the real bombshell revealed in Donna Brazile's book about the Dems," *CNBC*, November 6, 2017 www.cnbc.com/2017/11/06/donna-brazile-book-shows-real-cancer-eating-at-democrats-commentary.html; "Did Sanders

Supporters Throw Chairs at Nevada Democratic Convention?,"
*Snopes*, May 2016, www.snopes.com/fact-check/did-sanders-
supporters-throw-chairs-at-nevada-democratic-convention/.
298. Scott Shane **and** Alan Blinder, "Secret Experiment in
Alabama Senate Race Imitated Russian Tactics," *New York Times*,
December 19, 2018, www.nytimes.com/2018/12/19/us/alabama-
senate-roy-jones-russia.html?module=inline.
299. Ibid.
300. Craig Silverman and Jeremy Singer-Vine, "Most Americans
Who See Fake News Believe It, New Survey Says," *BuzzFeed*,
December 6, 2016, www.buzzfeed.com/craigsilverman/fake-news-
survey?utm_term=.qpBx4YRnD#.roO3p4q7Q.
301. Ibid.
302. Brian Stelter, "Trump calls journalists 'bad people' at rally a
week after newsroom shooting," CNN, July 6, 2018, www.money.
cnn.com/2018/07/06/media/trump-montana-rally-media-attacks/
index.html.
303. Christopher Rosen, "All the times Donald Trump has called
the media 'fake news' on Twitter," *Entertainment Weekly*, July 24,
2017, ew.com/tv/2017/06/27/donald-trump-fake-news-twitter.
304. Rebecca Morin, "Trump administration splits over journalists
as 'enemy of the people,'" *Politico*, August 2, 2018, www.politico.
com/story/2018/08/02/trump-media-enemy-people-ivanka-white-
house-76058.
305. Michael M. Grynbaum and Eileen Sullivan,"Trump Attacks
the Times, in a Week of Unease for the American Press," *New
York Times*, February 20, 2019, www.nytimes.com/2019/02/20/us/
politics/new-york-times-trump.html?module=inline.
306. Ibid.
307. Brian Stelter, "Trump calls journalists 'bad people' at rally a
week after newsroom shooting," *CNN*, July 6, 2018, www.money.
cnn.com/2018/07/06/media/trump-montana-rally-media-attacks/
index.html; for more on the use of the term "mainstream" media,
and why we refer to it normally as corporate or establishment
media, see Peter Phillips, "How Mainstream Media Evolved Into
Corporate Media: A Project Censored History," *Censored Notebook*,
February 7, 2019, www.projectcensored.org/how-mainstream-
media-evolved-into-corporate-media-a-project-censored-history/.
308. Katie Rogers and Maggie Haberman, "For Trump's Aides,
Celebratory Dinners and a Hunger for Revenge," *New York Times*,
March 26, 2019, www.nytimes.com/2019/03/26/us/politics/white-
house-mueller-report.html.

309. Meghan Keneally, "A look back at Trump comments perceived by some as encouraging violence," *ABC News*, October 19, 2018, www.abcnews.go.com/Politics/back-trump-comments-perceived-encouraging-violence/story?id=48415766.

310. Ibid.

311. Erik Wemple, "What can CNN do to stop Trump's abuse?," *Washington Post*, July 27, 2018, www.washingtonpost.com/blogs/erik-wemple/wp/2018/07/27/what-can-cnn-do-to-stop-trumps-abuse/?utm_term=.8bbf03f03534.

312. Op. cit. Keneally, "A look back at Trump comments perceived by some as encouraging violence."

313. M. David and Jackson Marciana, "CBS Reporter Arrested at Trump Rally Told 'Go Back to Iraq' Before Cops Slammed Him to the Ground," *Counter Current News*, March 13, 2016, www.countercurrentnews.com/2016/03/cops-arrested-reporter-at-a-trump-rally/.

314. Daniel Arkin, "Donald Trump Criticized After He Appears to Mock Reporter Serge Kovaleski," *NBC News*, November 26 2015, www.nbcnews.com/politics/2016-election/donald-trump-criticized-after-he-appears-mock-reporter-serge-kovaleski-n470016.

315. Cheryl K. Chumley, "Jim Acosta, CNN: Journalists should march and chant, 'We're not the enemy of the people,'" *Washington Times*, August 3, 2018, www.washingtontimes.com/news/2018/aug/3/jim-acosta-cnn-journalists-should-take-streets-and/.

316. Michael Calderone, "Trump Takes Authoritarian Stance in Portraying Journalists as Anti-American Enemy," *Huffington Post*, August 23, 2017, www.huffingtonpost.com/entry/donald-trump-portrays-journalists-as-anti-american_us_599da653e4b0d8dde99a844c?ecx.

317. Sam Levin and Julia Carrie Wong, "Greg Gianforte sentenced to community service for assaulting Guardian reporter," *The Guardian*, June 12, 2017, www.theguardian.com/us-news/2017/jun/12/republican-greg-gianforte-sentenced-assaulting-guardian-reporter.

318. Lauren Gambino and Julia Carrie Wong "Press groups ask Congress to investigate Greg Gianforte over body-slamming reporter," *The Guardian*, June 2, 2017, www.theguardian.com/us-news/2017/jun/02/greg-gianforte-body-slam-reporter-congress-investigation.

319. Seung Min Kim and Felicia Sonmez, "At Montana rally, Trump praises congressman for assaulting reporter," *Washington Post*, October 19, 2018, www.washingtonpost.com/politics/

at-montana-rally-trump-praises-congressman-for-assaulting-reporter/2018/10/18/1e1d0d1e-d304-11e8-8c22-fa2ef74bd6d6_story.html?utm_term=.87ac1af6bb8.

320. Karl Vick, "The Guardians and the War on Truth, " *Time*, December 2018, time.com/person-of-the-year-2018-the-guardians/.

321. Edward Felsenthal, "The Choice," *Time*, December 2018, www.time.com/person-of-the-year-2018-the-guardians-choice/.

322. Terry Nguyen, "The Alt-Right Movement: An 'Intelligently New' Form of Populist, White Supremacist Thinking," *Study Breaks*, December 5, 2016, www.studybreaks.com/2016/12/05/alt-right-movement-intelligently-new-form-populist-white-supremacist-thinking/; Farron Cousins, "Tomi Lahren Admits She Doesn't Know Why NFL Players Are Protesting, but She Hates Them Anyway," *TroFire*, October 22, 2017, www.trofire.com/2017/10/22/tomi-lahren-admits-doesnt-know-nfl-players-protesting-hates-anyway; Meera Jagannathan and Nicole Bitette, "Comedy Central's 'Roast of Rob Lowe' Writers Reveal the Jokes Ann Coulter Rejected," *NY Daily News*, September 6, 2016, www.nydailynews.com/entertainment/tv/roast-rob-lowe-writers-reveal-jokes-ann-coulter-rejected-article-1.2780089; Caroline Framke, "Trevor Noah Didn't 'Destroy' Tomi Lahren on The Daily Show. What He Did Was Much Better," *Vox*, December 4, 2016, www.vox.com/culture/2016/12/4/13807584/daily-show-tomi-lahren-interview; Michael Darer, "Trevor Noah's Interview with Tomi Lahren Is a Perfect Example of Why the White Liberal 'Discourse' Fetish Is So Damn Absurd," *Huffington Post*, December 3, 2016, updated December 9, 2016, www.huffingtonpost.com/entry/trevor-noahs-interview-with-tomi-lahren-is-a-perfect_us_58425f75e4b0b93e10f8e231; Yesha Callahan, " If You're a 'Pretty' Racist, You Can Get Cupcakes from Trevor Noah," The Grapevine blog, *The Root*, December 7, 2016, www.theroot.com/blog/the-grapevine/if-youre-a-pretty-racist-you-can-get-cupcakes-from-trevor-noah/; Ann Coulter, "Weinstein's Pimps: Revenge of the Ugly Girls," *Town Hall*, October 18, 2017 www.townhall.com/columnists/anncoulter/2017/10/18/weinsteins-pimps-revenge-of-the-ugly-girls-n2397024; Amelia Tait, "They're turning the frogs gay," *New Statesman*, March 20, 2017 www.newstatesman.com/science-tech/internet/2017/03/they-re-turning-frogs-gay-psychology-behind-internet-conspiracy; Eric Killelea, "Alex Jones' Mis-Infowars: 7 Bat-Sh*t Conspiracy Theories," *Rolling Stone*, February, 17, 2017, www.rollingstone.com/culture/lists/

alex-jones-mis-infowars-7-bat-sht-conspiracy-theories-w467509/
the-government-is-controlling-the-weather-w467722; Rebecca
Hersher, "After Comments on Pedophilia, Breitbart Editor Milo
Yiannopoulos Resigns," *National Public Radio*, February 21, 2017,
www.npr.org/sections/thetwo-way/2017/02/21/516473521/after-
comments-on-pedophilia-breitbart-editor-milo-yiannopoulos-
resigns.
323. Brian Stelter, "CNN Hires Corey Lewandowski as Political
Commentator," *CNN*, June 23, 2016, money.cnn.com/2016/06/23/
media/corey-lewandowski-cnn/index.html; Michael Calderone,
"CNN Chief Jeff Zucker Defends Hiring Ex-Trump Campaign
Manager Corey Lewandowski," *Huffington Post*, September 20,
2016, www.huffingtonpost.com/entry/jeff-zucker-donald-trump_
us_57e1855ce4b0e28b2b50b454; ibid. Framke, "Trevor Noah
Didn't 'Destroy' Tomi Lahren"; Abigail Tracy, "Ann Coulter,
High Priestess of Trumpism, Takes a Victory Lap," *Vanity Fair*,
September 20, 2016, www.vanityfair.com/news/2016/09/ann-
coulter-donald-trump.
324. Karen Tumulty, "Who Is Corey Lewandowski? His Rise—and
His Relationship with Donald Trump," *Washington Post*, March 30,
2016, www.washingtonpost.com/politics/trump-and-lewandowski-
an-unlikely-pair-of-kindred-spirits/2016/03/30/d82a58ca-f511-
11e5-8b23-538270a1ca31_story.html?utm_term=.66186a5e3d00.0.
325. Ibid.
326. David Catanese, "The Rise and Fall of Corey
Lewandowski," *US News*, June 20, 2016, www.usnews.com/news/
articles/2016-06-20/the-rise-and-fall-of-corey-lewandowski-shows-
a-trump-campaign-in-perpetual-disorder.
327. Brian Stelter, "CNN Hires Corey Lewandowski as Political
Commentator," *CNN*, June 23, 2016, money.cnn.com/2016/06/23/
media/corey-lewandowski-cnn/index.html; Michael Calderone,
"CNN Chief Jeff Zucker Defends Hiring Ex-Trump Campaign
Manager Corey Lewandowski," *Huffington Post*, September 20,
2016, www.huffingtonpost.com/entry/jeff-zucker-donald-trump_
us_57e1855ce4b0e28b2b50b454; Caroline Framke, "Trevor Noah
Didn't 'Destroy' Tomi Lahren on The Daily Show. What He
Did Was Much Better," *Vox*, December 4, 2016, www.vox.com/
culture/2016/12/4/13807584/daily-show-tomi-lahren-interview;
Abigail Tracy, "Ann Coulter, High Priestess of Trumpism, Takes
a Victory Lap," *Vanity Fair*, September 20, 2016, www.vanityfair.
com/news/2016/09/ann-coulter-donald-trump.
328. Tom Embury-Dennis, "Donald Trump praises CNN

commentator fired for tweeting Nazi salute as 'a source of truth,'"
*Independent*, October 17, 2017, www.independent.co.uk/news/
world/americas/donald-trump-cnn-commentator-nazi-salute-
tweet-fired-jeffrey-lord-praise-truth-a7996881.htm/.

329. Brian Beutler, "Sherrod Critic: She Used 'Lynching' to Gin
Up Democratic Voters," *Talking Points Memo*, July 28, 2010, www.
talkingpointsmemo.com/dc/sherrod-critic-she-used-lynching-to-
gin-up-democratic-voters.

330. Nick Wing, "A Donald Trump Fanboy Tried to Whitesplain
the KKK to Van Jones, and Things Got Heated," *Huffington Post*,
March 2, 2016, www.huffingtonpost.com/entry/jeffrey-lord-van-
jones-cnn_us_56d667cbe4b0871f60ed365a.

331. Josh Delk and Joe Conch, "CNN Cuts Ties with Jeffrey Lord
After 'Sieg Heil' Tweet," *The Hill*, August 10, 2017, thehill.com/
homenews/media/346117-cnn-fires-jeffrey-lord-after-nazi-salute-
to-liberal-activist-on-twitter.

332. Alex Shephard, "Jeff Zucker has turned CNN into a Trump
reality show," *The New Republic*, December 2016, newrepublic.com/
minutes/141847/jeff-zucker-turned-cnn-trump-reality-show.

333. Ryan Grenoble, "GOP Senator Blames 'Paid Protesters' for
Deluge of Phone Calls," *Huffington Post*, February 2, 2017, www.
huffingtonpost.com/entry/cory-gardner-paid-protesters-trump-
calls_us_58937d6ee4b07595d05a5087.

334. Caitlin Yilek, "Sebastian Gorka: Trump won't comment on
Minnesota mosque bombing until 'fake hate crime' ruled out,"
*Washington Post*, August 8, 2017, www.washingtonexaminer.com/
sebastian-gorka-trump-wont-comment-on-minnesota-mosque-
bombing-until-fake-hate-crime-ruled-out/article/2630928; Derek
Hawkins, "Trump Didn't Lie, Jeffrey Lord Says on CNN. He Just
Speaks A Different Language — 'Americanese,'" *Washington Post*,
March 21, 2017, www.washingtonpost.com/news/morning-mix/
wp/2017/03/21/trump-didnt-lie-jeffrey-lord-says-on-cnn-he-
just-speaks-a-different-language-americanese/?tid=sm_fb&utm_
term=.1d7fc6354591.

335. Jenna Johnson and Ashley Parker, "Spicer: Hitler 'didn't
even sink to using chemical weapons,' although he sent Jews to
'the Holocaust center,'" *Washington Post*, April 11, 2017, www.
washingtonpost.com/news/post-politics/wp/2017/04/11/spicer-
hitler-didnt-even-sink-to-using-chemical-weapons-although-he-
sent-jews-to-the-holocaust-center/?utm_term=.92ca17ea1722.

336. Op. cit. Hawkins, "Trump Didn't Lie, Jeffrey Lord Says on
CNN."

337. Ed Pilkington, "'Truth isn't truth': Giuliani trumps 'alternative

facts' with new Orwellian outburst," *The Guardian*, August 19, 2018, www.theguardian.com/us-news/2018/aug/19/truth-isnt-truth-rudy-giuliani-trump-alternative-facts-orwellian.

338. Daniel Kurtzman, "Donald Trump's Craziest Quotes of All Time," *Thought Co.*, September 1, 2017, www.thoughtco.com/donald-trump-quotes-crazy-racist-idiot-2733864; Daniella Diaz, "Trump calls Clinton 'a nasty woman,'" *CNN*, October 20, 2016, www.cnn.com/2016/10/19/politics/donald-trump-hillary-clinton-nasty-woman/index.html.

339. Video/ audio transcript of Trump's lewd remarks: www.youtube.com/watch?v=SPomcb0_IaE.

340. Ibid.

341. Staff, "CNN's Jake Tapper: Trump's 'Nasty Woman' Comment 'Revealed a Level of Hostility and Anger,'" *Media Matters* October 20, 2016, www.mediamatters.org/video/2016/10/20/cnns-jake-tapper-trumps-nasty-woman-comment-reveaed-level-hostility-and-anger/213968; Staff, "On Fox, Bill Bennett Defends Trump Calling Hillary Clinton a 'Nasty Woman,'" *Media Matters* October 20, 2016, www.mediamatters.org/video/2016/10/20/fox-bill-bennett-defends-trump-calling-hillary-clinton-nasty-woman/213966.

342. Staff, "18 revelations from Wikileaks' hacked Clinton emails," *BBC*, October 27, 2016, www.bbc.com/news/world-us-canada-37639370.

343. Eric Bradner, "Trump delivers harsh remarks on Clinton at charity dinner," *CNN*, October 21, 2016, www.cnn.com/2016/10/20/politics/al-smith-dinner-hillary-clinton-donald-tump/index.html.

344. Donald Judd, "Stormy Daniels' attorney accuses Trump legal team of 'thuggish behavior,'" *CNN*, March 22, 2018, www.cnn.com/2018/03/22/politics/stormy-daniels-michael-avenatti-donald-trump-michael-cohen-cnntv/index.html.

345. Mark Halperin and John Heilemann, *Double Down: Game Change 2012* (New York: Penguin 2013).

346. *Get Me Roger Stone*, NetFlix, 2017.

347. Rebecca Shapiro, "Van Jones: A Nazi Assassinatcd an American 'in Broad Daylight': This is not a time to talk about 'both sides,'" *Huffington Post*, August 14, 2017, www.huffingtonpost.com/entry/van-jones-nazi-assassinated-an-american-in-broad-daylight_us_5991258fe4b08a2472755dbb" www.huffingtonpost.com/entry/van-jones-nazi-assassinated-an-american-in-broad-daylight_us_5991258fe4b08a2472755dbb.

348. Marina Fang, "Trump's Unwillingness to Directly Denounce

White Supremacy Grows Conspicuous," *Huffington Post*, August 13, 2017, www.huffingtonpost.com/entry/trump-white-house-response-charlottesville_us_59908c5ce4b090964297cdf5?yyq.
349. Ibid.
350. Matthew Nussbaum, "Trump goes off script, and white supremacists cheer," *Politico*, August 15, 2017, www.politico.com/story/2017/08/15/trump-white-supremacists-charlottesville-241672.
351. Eric Hananoki, "How Donald Trump emboldened Charlottesville white supremacists: Trump's response to Charlottesville is another wink and nod to white supremacists," *Media Matters*, August 12, 2017, www.mediamatters.org/blog/2017/08/12/how-donald-trump-emboldened-charlottesville-white-supremacists/217601.
352. Jessica Schulberg, "Controversial Trump Aide Katharine Gorka Helped End Funding for Group That Fights White Supremacy," *Huffington Post*, August 15, 2017, www.huffingtonpost.com/entry/katharine-gorka-life-after-hate_us_59921356e4b09096429943b6; Louis Jacobson, "Are there white nationalists in the White House?" *Politifact*, August 15th, 2017, www.politifact.com/truth-o-meter/article/2017/aug/15/are-there-white-nationalists-white-house.
353. Evan Osnos, "Donald Trump and the Ku Klux Klan: A History," *The New Yorker*, February 29, 2016, www.newyorker.com/news/news-desk/donald-trump-and-the-ku-klux-klan-a-history.
354. Dana Liebelson, "White Nationalist Calls Trump's Denouncement of Hate Groups 'Kumbaya Nonsense,'" *Huffington Post*, August 14, 2017, www.huffingtonpost.com/entry/white-nationalist-calls-presidents-denouncement-of-hate-groups-kumbaya-nonsense_us_59923778e4b09096429961e8; Hayley Miller, "Ex-KKK Leader David Duke Has Meltdown After Trump Condemns White Supremacists in Charlottesville," *Huffington Post*, August 14, 2017, www.huffingtonpost.com/entry/david-duke-trump-charlottesville_us_5991d6bae4b08a2472764798; Dominique Mosbergen, "Neo-Nazi Site Daily Stormer Praises Trump's Charlottesville Reaction," *Huffington Post*, August 13, 2017, www.huffingtonpost.com/entry/neo-nazi-daily-stormer-trump-charlottesville_us_59905c7ee4b08a2472750701.
355. Ibid.
356. Ibid.
357. Jessica Schulberg, "Controversial Trump Aide Katharine Gorka Helped End Funding for Group That

Fights White Supremacy," *Huffington Post*, August 15, 2017,
www.huffingtonpost.com/entry/katharine-gorka-life-after-
hate_us_59921356e4b09096429943b6; Dana Liebelson,
"White Nationalist Calls Trump's Denouncement of Hate
Groups 'Kumbaya Nonsense,'" *Huffington Post*, August 14,
2017, www.huffingtonpost.com/entry/white-nationalist-calls-
presidents-denouncement-of-hate-groups-kumbaya-nonsense_
us_59923778e4b09096429961e8; Hayley Miller, "Ex-KKK Leader
David Duke Has Meltdown After Trump Condemns White
Supremacists in Charlottesville," *Huffington Post*, August 14, 2017,
www.huffingtonpost.com/entry/david-duke-trump-charlottesville_
us_5991d6bae4b08a2472764798; Dominique Mosbergen,
"Neo-Nazi Site Daily Stormer Praises Trump's Charlottesville
Reaction," *Huffington Post*, August 13, 2017, www.huffingtonpost.
com/entry/neo-nazi-daily-stormer-trump-charlottesville_
us_59905c7ee4b08a2472750701.
358. Staff, "Fox contributor claims that Trump 'immediately
eviscerated' the KKK, just like Reagan," *Media Matters*, August 17,
2017, www.mediamatters.org/video/2017/08/17/fox-contributor-
claims-trump-immediately-eviscerated-kkk-just-reagan/217674.
359. Matt Gertz, "How Sean Hannity's Charlottesville propaganda
works," *Media Matters*, August 15, 2017, www.mediamatters.org/
blog/2017/08/15/how-sean-hannitys-charlottesville-propaganda-
works/217635.
360. Jeremy Diamond, "Trump calls removal of Confederate
monuments 'so foolish,'" *CNN*, August 17, 2017, www.cnn.
com/2017/08/17/politics/trump-tweet-confederate-statues/index.
html.
361. John Kruzel, "Did Confederate symbols gain prominence in
the civil rights era?," *Politifact*, August 15, 2017, www.politifact.
com/punditfact/statements/2017/aug/15/joy-reid/did-confederate-
symbols-gain-prominence-civil-righ/.
362. Staff, "Fox contributor Tomi Lahren: In removing confederate
statues, the left is trying 'to erase history and to erase every
shred of patriotism,'" *Media Matters*, September, 29, 2017, www.
mediamatters.org/video/2017/09/29/fox-contributor-tomi-lahren-
removing-confederate-statues-left-trying-erase-history-and-erase-
every/218085.
363. Neil Munro, "Democrat Activists Urge National Push Against
Confederate Statues," *Breitbart*, August17, 2017, www.breitbart.
com/politics/2017/08/15/democrat-activists-urge-national-push-
confederate-statues.

364. Ibid.

365. Greg Sargent, "Steve Bannon: Post-Charlottesville racial strife is a political winner for Trump," *Washington Post*, August 17, 2018, www.washingtonpost.com/blogs/plum-line/wp/2017/08/17/steve-bannon-post-charlottesville-racial-strife-is-a-political-winner-for-trump/?utm_term=.3907f09d074a.

366. "Steve Bannon's out at the White House, aftermath of white nationalist protests in Charlottesville," *PBS*, August 18, 2017, www.pbs.org/weta/washingtonweek/episode/steve-bannon's-out-white-house-aftermath-white-nationalist-protests-charlottesville.

367. Jeremy Diamond, "White House seeks to explain never released Niger statement," *CNN*, October 19, 2017, www.cnn.com/2017/10/18/politics/president-donald-trump-niger-statement/index.html.

368. Barbara Starr and Zachary Cohen, "What we know and don't know about the deadly Niger attack," *CNN*, October 19, 2017, www.cnn.com/2017/10/18/politics/us-niger-investigation-what-we-know/index.html.

369. Manuela Tobias, "Donald Trump's misleading comments on Obama's calls to fallen soldiers' families," *Politifact*, October 17, 2017, www.politifact.com/truth-o-meter/article/2017/oct/17/donald-trump-obamas-calls-fallen-soldiers-families/.

370. Ibid.

371. Mallory Shelbourne, "Trump disputes Gold Star widow's account of phone call," *The Hill*, October 23, 2017, thehill.com/homenews/administration/356671-trump-disputes-gold-star-widows-account-of-phone-call.

372. Ibid.

373. Allan Smith, "TRUMP: I remember call to Gold Star widow better than she does because I have 'one of the great memories of all-time,'" *Business Insider*, October 25, 2017, www.businessinsider.com/trump-gold-star-great-memory-2017-10.

374. Ibid.

375. Ibid.

376. Sophie Tatum, "Trump again calls congresswoman's account of Gold Star call a 'total lie,'" *CNN*, October 20, 2017 www.cnn.com/2017/10/20/politics/donald-trump-gold-star-phone-call-tweet/index.html.

377. Manuela Tobias, "Donald Trump's misleading comments on Obama's calls to fallen soldiers' families," *Politifact*, October 17th, 2017, www.politifact.com/truth-o-meter/article/2017/oct/17/donald-trump-obamas-calls-fallen-soldiers-families/.

378. Staff, "Fox & Friends: All the bad reports on Trump's interactions with Gold Star families are just spin," *Media Matters*, October 19, 2017, www.mediamatters.org/video/2017/10/19/fox-friends-all-bad-reports-trumps-interactions-gold-star-families-are-just-spin/218257.

379. Staff, "Fox host claims Rep. Frederica Wilson attacked Gold Star families and was 'racist towards General Kelly,'" *Media Matters*, October 20, 2017, www.mediamatters.org/video/2017/10/20/fox-host-claims-rep-frederica-wilson-attacked-gold-star-families-and-was-racist-towards-general/218288.

380. Tom Teodorczuk, "Dan Rather says Trump's conduct over call to Gold Star widow is 'unforgivable,'" *Market Watch*, October 26, 2017, www.marketwatch.com/story/dan-rather-says-trumps-conduct-over-call-to-gold-star-widow-is-unforgivable-2017-10-20.

381. Angie Drobnic Holan, "Fact-checking Benghazi: The rhetoric hasn't matched up with reality," *Politifact*, May 16, 2014, www.politifact.com/truth-o-meter/article/2014/may/16/fact-checking-benghazi-our-most-recent-round-/.

382. David Jackson and Tom Vanden Brook, "Trump says he did not 'specifically' authorize Niger mission that killed four US soldiers," *USA Today*, October 25, 2017, www.usatoday.com/story/news/politics/2017/10/25/trump-says-he-did-not-specifically-authorize-niger-mission-killed-four-u-s-soldiers/799276001/.

383. Carla Herreria, "Rachel Maddow Defends Niger Theory After Experts Call It 'Conspiracymongering,'" *Huffington Post*, October 21, 2017, www.huffingtonpost.com/entry/rachel-maddow-defends-niger-ambush-theory_us_59ebbfa8e4b00f08619f4390.

384. Ibid.

385. Laura Seay, "This Is Not Trump's Benghazi: The deaths of US troops in Niger were a tragedy, but there's no need for conspiracy theories," *Slate*, October, 20 2017, www.slate.com/articles/news_and_politics/foreigners/2017/10/do_not_try_to_turn_niger_into_trump_s_benghazi.html.

386. Office of the Director of National Intelligence, "Intelligence Community Assessment, Assessing Russian Activities and Intentions in Recent US Elections," ICA 2017-01D, January 6, 2017, www.dni.gov/files/documents/ICA_2017_01.pdf.

387. Eugene Kiely, "Timeline of Russia Investigation: Key moments in the FBI probe of Russia's efforts to influence the 2016 presidential election," *Fact Check*, November 20, 2017, www.factcheck.org/2017/06/timeline-russia-investigation/.

388. Ibid.

389. Ibid.

390. Ibid.

391. Ibid.

392. Ibid.

393. Adam Goldman, Michael S. Schmidt, and Nicholas Fandos, "F.B.I. Opened Inquiry Into Whether Trump Was Secretly Working on Behalf of Russia," *New York Times*, www.nytimes.com/2019/01/11/us/politics/fbi-trump-russia-inquiry.html.

394. Ibid.

395. Interview with Anderson Cooper, *360*, CNN, February 20, 2019, www.youtube.com/watch?v=xPfx5DC1m3Y

396. Mark Mazzetti, Maggie Haberman, Nicholas Fandos, and Michael S. Schmidt, "Intimidation, Pressure and Humiliation: Inside Trump's Two-Year War on the Investigations Encircling Him," *New York Times*, February 19, 2019, www.nytimes.com/2019/02/19/us/politics/trump-investigations.html.

397. Ibid.

398. Sean Hannity, "The mainstream media's obsession of the week—Flynn and Mueller's partisan witch-hunt," *Fox News*, December 6, 2018, www.foxnews.com/opinion/sean-hannity-the-mainstream-medias-obsession-of-the-week-flynn-and-muellers-partisan-witch-hunt.

399. Katelyn Polantz and Evan Perez, "Manafort intended for polling data to go to 2 Ukrainian oligarchs who owed him millions," *CNN*, January 09, 2019, www.cnn.com/2019/01/09/politics/manafort-ukrainian-oligarchs/index.html.

400. Kiely, "Timeline of Russia Investigation," *Fact Check*, November 20, 2017, www.factcheck.org/2017/06/timeline-russia-investigation/.

401. Jonathan Chait, "The Republicans Have Developed a Theory of Alt-Collusion to Defend Trump From Mueller," *New York Magazine*, October 26, 2017, nymag.com/daily/intelligencer/2017/10/alt-collusion-the-gop-theory-to-defend-trump-from-mueller.html.

402. Julie Hirschfeld Davis, "Trump, at Putin's Side, Questions U.S. Intelligence on 2016 Election," *New York Times*, July 16, 2018, https://www.nytimes.com/2018/07/16/world/europe/trump-putin-election-intelligence.html.

403. Ibid.

404. Jack Holmes, "Some U.S. Senators Are Increasingly Sounding Like Conspiracy Theorists," *Esquire*, January 24, 2018, www.

esquire.com/news-politics/a15868999/ron-johnson-secret-society-fbi/

405. Ibid.

406. Jack Holmes, "Republicans Are All In On the 'Secret Society' Conspiracy Theory," *Esquire*, January 25, 2018, www.esquire.com/news-politics/a15881201/secret-society-theory/.

407. Chad Day and Eric Tucker, "Mueller recommends no prison for Flynn, citing substantial cooperation," *Chicago Tribune*, December 4, 2018, www.chicagotribune.com/news/nationworld/politics/ct-mueller-nsa-flynn-russia-probe-20181204-story.html.

408. Catherine Lucey and Zeke Miller, "Trump odd man out as presidents assemble for Bush funeral," *Associated Press*, December 6, 2018, www.apnews.com/f10420da35394d30b37d69ec27be6bb6.

409. Edward-Isaac Dovere and Matthew Nussbaum, "Obama warned Trump about Flynn, officials say. The White House, however, continues to blame Obama for not revoking Flynn's security clearance," *Politico*, May 8, 2017, https://www.politico.com/story/2017/05/08/obama-warn-trump-michael-flynn-238116

410. Joel B. Pollack, "Michael Flynn Sentencing Document Shows Collusion — Between Media, Deep State, and Obama Admin," *Breitbart*, December 5, 2018, www.breitbart.com/crime/2018/12/05/pollak-michael-flynn-sentencing-document-shows-collusion-between-media-deep-state-and-obama-admin.

411. Dylan Matthews, "Why Paul Manafort pleaded guilty to 'conspiracy against the United States,'" *Vox*, March 13, 2019, www.vox.com/2018/9/14/17860410/conspiracy-against-the-united-states-paul-manafort-plea.

412. Timothy Johnson, "Paul Manafort's Russian collusion smoking gun of little interest to Fox News," *Media Matters*, January 9, 2019, www.mediamatters.org/people/paul-manafort.

413. Staff, "Sean Hannity calls Manafort guilty verdict 'an unmitigated disaster for Mueller,'" *Media Matters*, August 21, 2018, www.mediamatters.org/video/2018/08/21/sean-hannity-calls-manafort-guilty-verdict-unmitigated-disaster-mueller/221050.

414. Newt Gingrich, "Mueller probe has gone from a witch hunt to an inquisition of Trump and allies," *Fox News*, December 14, 2018, www.foxnews.com/opinion/newt-gingrich-mueller-probe-has-gone-from-a-witch-hunt-to-an-inquisition-of-trump-and-allies

415. As written about and cited by the authors in chapter 2 of Andy Lee Roth and Mickey Huff, eds., *Censored 2018: Press Freedoms in a "Post-Truth" World* (New York: Seven Stories Press), pp. 126–127.

416. Alan Macleod, "Misreporting Manafort: A Case Study in

Journalistic Malpractice," *Fairness and Accuracy in Reporting*, December 3, 2018, www.fair.org/home/misreporting-manafort-a-case-study-in-journalistic-malpractice/.

417. Aaron Blake, "A tale of 3 Trump-Russia 'smoking guns' in 36 hours," *Washington Post*, December 4, 2017, www.washingtonpost. com/news/the-fix/wp/2017/12/04/a-tale-of-3-would-be-trump-russia-smoking-guns/; Chris Cillizza, "This may be the smoking gun in the Russia investigation Analysis," *CNN*, January 18, 2019, www.cnn.com/2019/01/18/politics/buzzfeed-trump-cohen-russia/index.html; Aaron Maté, "The Manafort Revelation Is Not a Smoking Gun," *The Nation*, January 11, 2019, www.thenation.com/article/manafort-no-smoking-gun-collusion/.

418. The authors of this book have written about these issues at length for Project Censored in *Censored 2017*, *Censored 2018*, and *Censored 2019*, all from Seven Stories Press, New York.

419. Rich Noyes, "Study: TV News Is Obsessed with Trump-Russia Probe," *Newsbusters*, June 27, 2017, www.newsbusters.org/blogs/nb/rich-noyes/2017/06/27/study-tv-news-obsessed-trump-russia-probe.

420. Thom Hartmann, "Has 'Cover-Up General' William Barr Struck Again?," *Common Dreams*, March 26, 2019, www.commondreams.org/views/2019/03/26/has-cover-general-william-barr-struck-again; J Pat Brown, "While at the CIA, William Barr drafted letters calling for an end to the Agency's moratorium on destroying records," *Muckrock*, April 16, 2019, www.muckrock.com/news/archives/2019/apr/16/cia-barr-crest/.

421. At the time this book went to press, the House Judiciary Committee voted to hold Barr in contempt of Congress after Mueller noted that Barr lied to Congress and the public about the contents of his report on Trump, Russia, and the 2016 election, prompting what House Speaker Nancy Pelosi called a "constitutional crisis." Mary Clare Jalonick, Lisa Mascaro and Jonathan Lemire, " Pelosi Pledges methodological action on constitutional crisis,'" *Washington Post*, May 9, 2019, www.washingtonpost.com/politics/courts_law/dispute-rises-to-new-level-with-contempt-citation-for-barr/2019/05/09/e320d408-7212-11e9-9331-30bc5836f48e_story.html?utm_term=.1a8e991094bf; Frank Newport, "Top Issues for Voters: Healthcare, Economy, Immigration," *Gallup*, November 2, 2018, www.news.gallup.com/poll/244367/top-issues-voters-healthcare-economy-immigration.aspx.

422. Dan Merica, Gregory Krieg, Eric Bradner, Daniella Diaz,

Jasmine Wright and Donald Judd, "Apathy, anger and relief," *CNN*, March 30, 2019, www.cnn.com/2019/03/30/politics/mueller-ends-voters-react/index.html?utm_source=feedburner&utm_medium=feed&utm_campaign=Feed%3A+rss%2Fcnn_latest+%28RSS%3A+CNN+-+Most+Recent%29; Harry Enten, "Unlike Mueller, health care will likely be a top issue in 2020," *CNN*, March 26, 2019, www.cnn.com/2019/03/26/politics/health-care-2020-campaign-issue/index.html.

423. Aaron Maté, "MSNBC'S Rachel Maddow Sees a 'Russia Connection' Lurking Around Every Corner," April 12 2017, *The Intercept*, www.theintercept.com/2017/04/12/msnbcs-rachel-maddow-sees-a-russia-connection-lurking-around-every-corner/.

424. Ibid.

425. Matt Taibbi, "Putin Derangement Syndrome Arrives," *Rolling Stone*, April 3, 2017, www.rollingstone.com/politics/politics-features/putin-derangement-syndrome-arrives-114557/.

426. A.J. Katz, "Ratings: MSNBC Is a Top 5 Cable Network, and Drawing More Total Viewers Than CNN," *Ad Week*, November 28, 2018, www.adweek.com/tvnewser/november-2018-ratings-msnbc-is-a-top-5-cable-network-and-is-drawing-more-total-viewers-than-cnn/386033.

427. Staff, "Maddow, Other MSNBC Hosts See Ratings Drop, Fox Up," *US News*, March 27, 2019, www.usnews.com/news/business/articles/2019-03-27/maddow-other-msnbc-hosts-see-ratings-drop-fox-up.

428. Philip Bump, "No, the White House didn't intentionally edit a question to Putin out of a video," *Washington Post*, July 25, 2018, www.washingtonpost.com/news/politics/wp/2018/07/25/no-the-white-house-didnt-intentionally-edit-a-question-to-putin-out-of-a-video/?utm_term=.1959785e8d53.

429. Glenn Greenwald, "Yet Another Major Russia Story Falls Apart. Is Skepticism Permissible Yet?," *The Intercept*, September 28 2017, www.theintercept.com/2017/09/28/yet-another-major-russia-story-falls-apart-is-skepticism-permissible-yet/.

430. Scott Shane, "Russia Isn't the Only One Meddling in Elections, We Do It Too," *New York Times*, February 17, 2018, www.nytimes.com/2018/02/17/sunday-review/russia-isnt-the-only-one-meddling-in-elections-we-do-it-too.html.

431. Ibid.

432. Ibid.

433. WikiLeaks, *Vault 7: Projects*, 2017, www.wikileaks.org/vault7/#Marble%20Framework.

434. Russell Berman, "The Trump Scandals That Have Slipped by Congress," *The Atlantic*, March 25, 2019, www.theatlantic.com/politics/archive/2019/03/mueller-non-russia-trump-scandals-congress/585643/.

435. Staff, "Rolling Stone's Matt Taibbi," *Axios*, March 24, 2019, "Russiagate is this generation's WMD," www.axios.com/russiagate-indictments-rolling-stone-matt-taibi-c5be6a1d-60f6-49d8-882c-70ebda2bd890.html.

436. Chris Hedges, "Mueller Report Ends a Shameful Period for the Press," *Truthdig*, March 25, 2019, www.truthdig.com/articles/mueller-report-ends-a-shameful-period-for-the-press/.

437. Ian Schwartz, "Glenn Greenwald vs. David Cay Johnston: Trump Mueller Probe 'Saddest Media Spectacle I've Ever Seen,'" *Real Clear Politics*, March 25, 2019 www.realclearpolitics.com/video/2019/03/25/glenn_greenwald_vs_michael_cay_johnston_on_trump_mueller_probe_saddest_media_spectacle_ive_ever_seen.html.

438. Chris Hedges, "The Day That TV News Died," *Bill Moyers*, March 25, 2013, www.billmoyers.com/2013/03/25/the-day-that-tv-news-died/.

439. Jack Crowe, "Glenn Greenwald Claims MSNBC Banned Him for Breaking with Collusion Narrative," *National Review*, March 26, 2019, www.nationalreview.com/news/glenn-greenwald-claims-msnbc-banned-him-for-breaking-with-collusion-narrative/.

440. T.A. Frank, "The Hard Truths and High Cost of the Russiagate Scandal," *Vanity Fair*, March 25, 2019 8:36 PM www.vanityfair.com/news/2019/03/the-hard-truths-and-high-cost-of-the-russiagate-scandal.

441. Paul Jay, "Democrats' Russiaphobia Hid Trump's Real Crimes," *Real News Network*, March 26, 2019, www.therealnews.com/stories/democrats-russophobia-hid-trumps-real-crimes.

442. Ian Bogost, "The Mueller Industrial Complex Collapses," *The Atlantic*, March 25, 2019, www.theatlantic.com/technology/archive/2019/03/mueller-investigation-ends-along-its-industry/585634/.

443. Brett Samuels, "Cohen: Trump described his campaign as 'the greatest infomercial in political history,'" *The Hill*, February 27, 2019, thehill.com/homenews/house/431802-cohen-trump-described-his-campaign-as-the-greatest-infomercial-in-political.

444. Yochai Benkler, *Wealth of Networks: How Social Production Transforms Markets and Freedom* (New Haven, CT: Yale University Press, 2006), p. 27.

445. Noam Chomsky, *Who Rules the World?* (New York: Penguin Books, 2016).

446. Nolan Higdon, "Effective Critical Media Literacy Pedagogy in Higher Education: Turning Social Justice Theory Into Practice," Ed.D. Dissertation, 2017.

447. Alex Gray, "Formative Content: The troubling charts that show young people losing faith in democracy," *World Economic Forum*, December 1, 2016, www.weforum.org/agenda/2016/12/charts-that-show-young-people-losing-faith-in-democracy/.

448. Jean M. Twenge and Kristin Donnelly, "Generational differences in American students' reasons for going to college, 1971–2014: The rise of extrinsic motives," *Journal of Social Psychology* 156, no. 6 (2016): pp. 620–629.

449. Henry Giroux, *Neoliberalism's War on Higher Education* (Chicago: Haymarket Books, 2014), p. 67; Dan Friedman, "Americans owe $1.2 trillion in student loans, surpassing credit card and auto loan debt totals," *New York Daily News*, May 17, 2014; Daniel Golden, *The Price of Admission: How America's Ruling Class Buys Its Way Into Elite Colleges and Who Gets Left Outside the Gates* (New York: Crown, 2006).

450. Daniel Yankelovich, *Wicked Problems Workable Solutions: Lessons from a Public Life* (New York: Rowman & Littlefield, 2015), p. 6.

451. Mark Engler and Paul Engler, *This Is an Uprising: How Nonviolent Revolt Is Shaping the Twenty-first Century* (New York: Nation Books, 2016); *The Good Citizen*, David Batstone and Eduardo Mendieta, eds. (New York: Routledge 1999); Timothy Snyder, *On Tyranny: 20 Lessons from the 20th Century* (New York: Tim Duggan Books, 2017); Bruce Levine, *Get Up, Stand Up: Uniting Populists, Energizing the Defeated, and Battling the Corporate Elite* (White River Junction, Vermont: Chelsea Green publishing, 2011); J. Pierson, E. Mante-Meijer, and E. Loos, *New Media Technologies and User Empowerment*, Volume 6 (Berlin, Germany: Peter Lang Publishing, 2011), pp. 163–180.

452. Antonio Lopez, *Greening Media Education: Bridging Media Literacy With Green Cultural Citizenship* (New York: Peter Lang, 2014).

453. Henry Giroux, *Neoliberalism's War on Higher Education* (Chicago: Haymarket Books, 2014).

454. Nolan Higdon, "Effective Critical Media Literacy Pedagogy in Higher Education: Turning Social Justice Theory into Practice," San Francisco State University, Ed.D. Dissertation, 2017.

455. Frederick Douglass, "West India Emancipation" speech, at Canandaigua, New York, August 3, 1857.

456. Cornel West, "Introduction: What Does It Mean to Be an American?," *The Good Citizen*, David Batstone and Eduardo Mendieta, eds. (New York: Routledge 1999).

457. George Washington, "Washington's Farewell Address 1796," *Yale*, 1796. avalon.law.yale.edu/18th_century/washing.asp.

458. Linda S. Behar-Horenstein and Lian Niu, "Teaching critical thinking skills in higher education: A review of the literature," *Journal of College Teaching and Learning* 8, no. 2 (2011): p. 25.

459. Lisa Gueldenzoph Snyder and Mark J. Snyder, "Teaching critical thinking and problem solving skills," *Journal of Research in Business Education* 50, no. 2 (2008): p. 90; Donald L. Hatcher, "Which test? Whose scores? Comparing standardized critical thinking tests," *New Directions for Institutional Research* 2011, no. 149 (2011): pp. 29-39; ibid. Behar-Horenstein and Niu, "Teaching critical thinking skills in higher education," p. 25.

460. Inna Popil, "Promotion of critical thinking by using case studies as teaching method," *Nurse education today* 31, no. 2 (2011): pp. 204-207; ibid. Gueldenzoph Snyder and Snyder, "Teaching critical thinking and problem solving skills," p. 90; Stephen D. Brookfield, *Teaching for critical thinking: Tools and techniques to help students question their assumptions* (New York: John Wiley & Sons, 2011); Chee S. Choy and Pou San O, "Reflective Thinking and Teaching Practices: A Precursor for Incorporating Critical Thinking into the Classroom?" *International Journal of Instruction* Vol. 5, no. 1 (2012): 167-182; Jennifer Wilson Mulnix, "Thinking critically about critical thinking," *Educational Philosophy and theory* 44, no. 5 (2012): pp. 464–479; George Hillocks, "'EJ' in Focus: Teaching Argument for Critical Thinking and Writing: An Introduction," *The English Journal* 99, no. 6 (2010): pp. 24–32.

461. Op. cit. Behar-Horenstein and Niu, "Teaching critical thinking skills in higher education," p. 25.

462. Joseph Kahne, Jessica T. Feezell, and Nam-Jin Lee, "Digital Media Literacy Education and Online Civic and Political Participation," *Youth & Participatory Politics* 6 (2012): pp. 1-24; Rebecca W. Black, "Online Fan Fiction and Critical Media Literacy," *Journal of Computing in Teacher Education* 26 (2009): pp. 75-80; Julie Frechette, "Cyber-Democracy or Cyber-Hegemony? Exploring the Political and Economic Structures of the Internet as an Alternative Source of Information," *Trends* 53, no. 4 (2005): p. 555; Jesse S. Gainer, "Critical Media Literacy in Middle School: Exploring the Politics of Representation," *Journal of Adolescent & Adult Literacy* 53, no. 5 (2010): pp. 364-373; Douglas Kellner and Jeff Share, "Critical Media Literacy, Democracy, and the

Reconstruction of Education," in D. Macedo and S.R. Steinberg, eds., *Media Literacy: A Reader* (New York: Peter Lang, 2007) pp.3–23; Myriam Torres and Maria Mercado, "The Need for Critical Media Literacy in Teacher Education Core Curricula," *Educational Studies* 39 no. 3 (2006): pp. 260–282.

463. Clay Shirky, *Here Comes Everybody: The Power of Organizing Without Organizations* (London: Penguin, 2008); Robert W. McChesney, *Blowing the Roof Off the Twenty-First Century: Media, Politics, and the Struggle for Post-Capitalist Democracy* (New York: New York University Press, 2014); Yochai Benkler, *The Wealth of Networks: How Social Production Transforms Markets and Freedom* (New Haven, CT: Yale University Press, 2006); Manuel Castells, *The Power of Identity: The Information Age: Economy, Society, and Culture* Vol. 2 (New York: John Wiley & Sons, 1997, 2011).

464. Matt Mason, *The Pirate's Dilemma: How Youth Culture Is Reinventing Capitalism* (New York: Simon & Schuster, 2009); *Free and Open Source Software and Technology for Sustainable Development*, Sulayman K. Sowe, Govindan Parayil, and Atsushi Sunami, eds. (New York: United Nations University Press, 2012).

465. Katharine E. Scott and James A. Graham, "Service-learning: Implications for empathy and community engagement in elementary school children," *Journal of Experiential Education* 38, no. 4 (2015): pp. 354–372.

466. Helen Demetriou, *Empathy, Emotion and Education* (Cambridge, UK: Springer, 2018).

467. Michael E. Morrell, *Empathy and Democracy: Feeling, Thinking, and Deliberation* (University Park, PA: Penn State Press, 2010).

468. Alice Miller, *For Your Own Good: Hidden cruelty in child-rearing and the roots of violence* (New York: Macmillan, 1990).

469. Os Guinness, *The Case for Civility and Why Our Future Depends On It* (New York, Harper Collins, 2008).

470. Ibid., p. 3.

471. Staff, "What Is Cultural Competency," National Education Association, 2017, www.nea.org/home/39783.htm.

472. John Dewey, *Experience and Education* (New York: Collier Books, 1938).

473. John Dewey, "Democracy and Education," *Educational Theory* 37, no. 2 (1916): pp. 145–152.

474. Amanda Taggart and Gloria Crisp, "Service learning at community colleges: Synthesis, critique, and recommendations for future research," *Journal of College Reading and Learning* 42, no. 1 (2011): pp. 24–44.

475. Laura Horn, Rachael Berger, and C. Dennis Carroll, "College

Persistence on the Rise? Changes in 5-Year Degree Completion and Postsecondary Persistence Rates Between 1994 and 2000: Postsecondary Education Descriptive Analysis Reports, NCES 2005-156," *National Center for Education Statistics* (2004); Mark G. Chupp and Mark L. Joseph, "Getting the Most Out of Service Learning: Maximizing Student, University and Community Impact," *Journal of Community Practice* 18, no. 2-3 (2010): pp. 190–212.

476. "Queering Anarchism: Addressing and Undressing Power and Desire," C. B. Daring, J. Rogue, Deric Shannon, and Abbey Volcano, eds. (Oakland, CA: AK Press, 2012), p. 3

477. Glenn Greenwald, "Full email from William Arkin, leaving NBC and MSNBC," January 3, 2019, www.medium.com/@ggreenwald/full-email-from-william-arkin-leaving-nbc-and-msnbc-1fb0d1dc692b; Glenn Greenwald, "Veteran NBC/MSNBC Journalist Blasts the Network for Being Captive to the National Security State and Reflexively Pro-War to Stop Trump," *The Intercept*, January 3, 2019, theintercept. com/2019/01/03/veteran-nbcmsnbc-journalist-blasts-the-network-for-being-captive-to-the-national-security-state-and-reflexively-pro-war-to-stop-trump/?fbclid=IwAR2IhVewXlPvnurpsLD08cgP7 fvT1mPgVU3TRXZ7AJOiABtPjMIWzDuHIZM.

478. Ibid.

479. Paul Bedard, "DNC Slaps Trump: 8000 'lies, his SOTU is no different,'" *Washington Examiner*, February 5, 2019, www. washingtonexaminer.com/washington-secrets/dnc-slaps-trump-8-000-lies-his-sotu-is-no-different.

480. Staff, "72% of Americans Follow Local News Closely," *Pew*, April 12, 2012, www.journalism.org/2012/04/12/72-americans-follow-local-news-closely/.

481. Natalie Fenton, "Deregulation or democracy? New media, news, neoliberalism and the public interest," *Continuum* 25, no. 1 (2011), pp. 63-72: Don Heider, *White News: Why Local News Programs Don't Cover People of Color* (Abingdon, UK: Routledge, 2014).

482. Alvin Chang, "Sinclair's takeover of local news, in one striking map," *Vox*, April 6, 2018, www.vox.com/2018/4/6/17202824/ sinclair-tribune-map.

483. Ibid.

484. Marlee Baldridge, "Water in a news desert: New Jersey is spending $5 million to fund innovation in local news," *Nieman Reports*, July 18, 2018, www.niemanlab.org/2018/07/water-in-a-

news-desert-new-jersey-is-spending-5-million-to-fund-innovation-in-local-news/; "News Voices," Free Press, www.freepress.net/issues/future-journalism/local-journalism.

485. Robert W. McChesney and John Nichols, "On federal subsidies for journalism," *Washington Post*, October 30, 2009, www.washingtonpost.com/wp-dyn/content/article/2009/10/22/AR2009102203960.html.

486. Kristen Hare, "Knight Foundation putting $300 million toward rebuilding local news," *Poynter*, February 19, 2019, www.poynter.org/business-work/2019/knight-foundation-putting-300-million-toward-rebuilding-local-news/?fbclid=IwAR2GWOqyzo-rcyXWozTP8WlIf_hqdwOOvZd05dtM3QmYYUD5PsjwGmQF N6M.

487. Ibid.

488. NeimanLab and Victor Pickard, "Predictions for 2019: We will finally confront systemic market failure," *NiemanLab*, December 2018, www.niemanlab.org/2018/12/we-will-finally-confront-systemic-market-failure/?fbclid=IwAR3TeMBPJQw1wM b417PnrEo4-u6JH8V1RtItxN0umckIXrTfgX04cnPL5RY.

489. Regina E. Lundgren and Andrea H. McMakin, *Risk Communication: A Handbook for Communicating Environmental, Safety, and Health Risks* (San Francisco: John Wiley & Sons, 2013); Philip Meyer, *The Vanishing Newspaper [2nd Ed]: Saving Journalism in the Information Age* (Columbia, MO: University of Missouri Press, 2009); Timothy Bajkiewicz and Jessica Smith, "When the Inbox Breaks: An Exploratory Analysis of Online Network Breaking News E-Mail Alerts," *Electronic News* 1, no. 4 (2007): pp. 197–210.

490. Ben Wasike, "Preaching to the Choir? An Analysis of Newspaper Readability Vis-à-Vis Public Literacy," *Journalism*, October 22, 2016, journals.sagepub.com/doi/abs/10.1177/1464884916673387.

491. David Cohen, "Study: 67.3 Percent of Facebook Posts Written at Reading Levels of Fifth Grade or Below," *Ad Week*, June 11, 2014, www.adweek.com/digital/study-trackmaven-reading-level/.

492. Bianca Bosker, "The Binge Breaker," *The Atlantic*, November 2016, www.theatlantic.com/magazine/archive/2016/11/the-binge-breaker/501122/.

493. Robinson Meyer, "The Grim Conclusions of the Largest-Ever Study of Fake News," *The Atlantic*, March 8, 2018, www.theatlantic.com/technology/archive/2018/03/largest-study-ever-fake-news-mit-twitter/555104/.

494. Siva Vaidhyanathan, *Anti-Social Media: How Facebook Disconnects Us and Undermines Democracy* (New York: Oxford University Press, 2018).

495. Ibid., p. 180.

496. Jonathan Swift, "Political Lying," from 1710, in Henry Craik, ed., *English Prose, 1916, Vol. III. Seventeenth Century*, online at Bartleby, www.bartleby.com/209/633.html.

497. Allison Jane Smith, "Commentary: Donald Trump speaks like a sixth-grader. All politicians should," *Chicago Tribune*, May 3, 2016, www.chicagotribune.com/news/opinion/commentary/ct-donald-trump-speech-sixth-grade-level-20160503-story.html; Byron Spice, "Most Presidential Candidates Speak at Grade 6-8 Level: Trump Generally Scores Lowest; Lincoln Remains Benchmark," *Carnegie Mellon University*, March 16, 2016, www.cmu.edu/news/stories/archives/2016/march/speechifying.html; Nina Burleigh, "Trump Speaks at Fourth-Grade Level, Lowest of Last 15 US Presidents, New Analysis Finds," *Newsweek*, January 8, 2018, www.newsweek.com/trump-fire-and-fury-smart-genius-obama-774169.

498. Stephen M. Kohn, "The Whistleblowers of 1777," *New York Times*, June 12, 2011, www.nytimes.com/2011/06/13/opinion/13kohn.html.

499. Mark Hertsgaard, *Bravehearts: Whistleblowing in the Age of Snowden* (New York: Hot Books, 2016) p. 3.

500. Ibid.

501. Jack Mirkinson, "Washington Post's Edward Snowden Editorial Draws Incredulous Reaction," *Huffington Post*, July 2, 2013, www.huffingtonpost.com/2013/07/02/washington-post-edward-snowden-editorial_n_3535146.html?icid=hp_front_top_art; Jack Mirkinson, "'60 Minutes' Trashed for NSA Piece," *Huffington Post*, December 16, 2013, www.huffingtonpost.com/2013/12/16/60-minutes-nsa_n_4452568.html.

502. Blogger at Daily Kos, "Frank Rich Eviscerates David Gregory," *Daily Kos*, June 26, 2013, www.dailykos.com/story/2013/06/26/1219287/-Frank-Rich-Eviserates-David-Gregory; Jack Mirkinson, "David Gregory to Glenn Greenwald: 'Why Shouldn't You Be Charged with a Crime?' (Video)," *Huffington Post*, June 23, 2013, www.huffingtonpost.com/2013/06/23/david-gregory-glenn-greenwald-crime_n_3486654.html; Braden Goyette, "Michael Grunwald, Time Magazine Reporter, Sends Out Shocking Tweet About Julian Assange," *Huffington Post*, August 19, 2013, www.huffingtonpost.

com/2013/08/17/michael-grunwald-julian-assange_n_3773981.
html; Editorial Board at *Washington Post*, "Plugging the Leaks in
the Edward Snowden Case," *Washington Post*, July 1, 2013, www.
washingtonpost.com/opinions/how-to-keep-edward-snowden-
from-leaking-more-nsa-secrets/2013/07/01/4e8bbe28-e278-11e2-
a11e-c2ea876a8f30_story.html?hpid=z4.

503. WikiLeaks, www.wikileaks.org, Luke Harding, *Wikileaks: The
Inside Story of Julian Assange and Wikileaks*, (London: Guardian
Books, 2011); Jake Johnson, "In Effort to 'Protect America From
Tyranny,'" *Common Dreams*, June 6, 2017, www.commondreams.
org/news/2017/06/06/effort-protect-america-tyranny-michael-
moore-launches-trumpileaks.

504. New Knowledge, *The Tactics and Tropes of the Internet Research
Agency*, 2018, disinformationreport.blob.core.windows.net/
disinformation-report/NewKnowledge-Disinformation-Report-
Whitepaper.pdf.

505. Renée DiResta, "The Digital Maginot Line," *ribbonfarm*,
November 28, 2018, www.ribbonfarm.com/2018/11/28/the-digital-
maginot-line/.

506. Ibid.

507. Ibid.

508. Bernays, *Propaganda*, pp. 38–39.

509. Howard Zinn. *You Can't Be Neutral on a Moving Train: A
Personal History* (Boston, Massachusetts: Beacon Press, 2018).

DR. NOLAN HIGDON is a lecturer in history and media studies at California State University, East Bay, and University of San Francisco. Higdon is the co-host of the podcast *Along the Line* and author of numerous articles, blog posts, and book chapters. He is a former co-host of *The Project Censored Show*. He sits on the boards of the Media Freedom Foundation; Action Coalition for Media Education; and Northwest Alliance for Alternative Media and Education. He is one of the founding members of the Global Critical Media Literacy Project; a longtime contributing author to Project Censored's annual books and website; a member of the Union for Democratic Communication steering committee; and adviser to the Media Literacy and Digital Culture graduate program at Sacred Heart University in Connecticut. His academic work primarily focuses on news media, propaganda, critical media literacy, and social justice pedagogies. He has been a guest commentator for the *New York Times*, *San Francisco Chronicle*, Univisión, CBS, NBC, ABC, and Fox.

MICKEY HUFF is the current director of Project Censored, founded in 1976, and president of the nonprofit Media Freedom Foundation. To date, he has edited or co-edited ten annual volumes of *Censored* and has contributed numerous chapters to them, dating back to 2008. His most recent book, with longtime co-editor Andy Lee Roth, is *Censored 2019: Fighting the Fake News Invasion*. Additionally, he has co-authored several chapters on media and propaganda for many other scholarly publications. Huff received the Beverly Kees Educator Award as part of the 2019 James Madison Freedom of Information Awards from the Society for Professional Journalists, Northern California. His next book, co-edited with Roth, is *Censored 2020: Through the Looking Glass*, from Seven Stories Press.

He is currently professor of social science and history at Diablo Valley College in the San Francisco Bay Area, where he is co-chair of the history department. He is also a lecturer in communications at California State University, East Bay, and has taught sociology of media at Sonoma State University. Huff is executive producer and co-host of *The Project Censored Show*, a weekly syndicated public affairs program founded in 2010, which originates from the historic studios of KPFA Pacifica Radio in Berkeley, California, and airs on more than fifty community radio stations.

Huff recently sat on the advisory board for the Media Literacy and Digital Culture graduate program at Sacred Heart University in Connecticut, and currently serves on the editorial board for the journal *Secrecy and Society*. For the past several years, Huff has worked with the American Library Association, the National Coalition Against Censorship, and the national outreach committee of Banned Books Week. He is one of the founding members of the Global Critical Media Literacy Project, and he also represents Project Censored in its role as one of the co-sponsoring organizations for the National Whistleblowers Summit held annually in Washington, D.C. He served as a critical media literacy consultant for Tribeworthy.com, now Credder.com, which allows users to rate news articles and sources for trustworthiness using critical media literacy skills. He is also a longtime musician and composer, and resides with his family in Sonoma County, California.